Interactions 1

Grammar

4th Edition

Elaine Kirn

Darcy Jack

With Contributions by Jill Korey O'Sullivan

McGraw-Hill Contemporary

McGraw-Hill/Contemporary

*A Division of The **McGraw-Hill** Companies*

Interactions 1 Grammar, 4th Edition

Published by McGraw-Hill/Contemporary, a business unit of The McGraw-Hill Companies, Inc., 1221 Avenue of the Americas, New York, NY 10020. Copyright © 2002, 1996, 1990, 1985 by The McGraw-Hill Companies, Inc. All rights reserved. No part of this publication may be reproduced or distributed in any form or by any means, or stored in a database or retrieval system, without the prior written consent of The McGraw-Hill Companies, Inc., including, but not limited to, in any network or other electronic storage or transmission, or broadcast for distance learning.

Some ancillaries, including electronic and print components, may not be available to customers outside the United States.

This book is printed on recycled, acid-free paper containing 10% postconsumer waste.

1 2 3 4 5 6 7 8 9 0 QPD/QPD 0 9 8 7 6 5 4 3 2 1

ISBN 0–07–233015–5
ISBN 0–07–118013–3 (ISE)

Editorial director: *Tina B. Carver*
Series editor: *Annie Sullivan*
Developmental editor: *Jennifer Monaghan*
Contributing author: *Jill Korey O'Sullivan*
Director of marketing and sales: *Thomas P. Dare*
Project manager: *Joyce M. Berendes*
Production supervisor: *Kara Kudronowicz*
Coordinator of freelance design: *David W. Hash*
Interior designer: *Michael Warrell, Design Solutions*
Senior photo research coordinator: *Lori Hancock*
Photo researcher: *Pam Carley/Sound Reach*
Supplement coordinator: *Genevieve Kelley*
Compositor: *Interactive Composition Corporation*
Typeface: *10.5/12 Times Roman*
Printer: *Quebecor World Dubuque, IA*

Photo credits: Chapter Opener 1 © Ulrike Welsch/Photo Researchers; Chapter Opener 2 © PhotoLink/ PhotoDisc/Nature, Wildlife, Environment; Chapter Opener 3 © Laima Druskis/Stock Boston; Chapter Opener 4 © Ethel Wolvovitz/The Image Works; Chapter Opener 5 © Tony Freeman/PhotoEdit; Chapter Opener 6 © Vanessa Vick/Photo Researchers; Chapter Opener 7 © Joel Gordon; Chapter Opener 8 © Elizabeth Crews/Stock Boston; Chapter Opener 9 © Doug Menuez/PhotoDisc/Lifestyles Today; Chapter Opener 10 © Myrleen Ferguson Cate/PhotoEdit; Chapter Opener 11 © StockTrek/PhotoDisc/ Spacescapes; Chapter Opener 12 © M. Siluk/The Image Works.

INTERNATIONAL EDITION ISBN 0–07–118013–3
Copyright © 2002. Exclusive rights by The McGraw-Hill Companies, Inc., for manufacture and export. This book cannot be re-exported from the country to which it is sold by McGraw-Hill. The International Edition is not available in North America.

Interactions 1 **Grammar**

Boost your students' academic success!

Interactions Mosaic, 4th edition is the newly revised five-level, four-skill comprehensive ESL/EFL series designed to prepare students for academic content. The themes are integrated across proficiency levels and the levels are articulated across skill strands. The series combines communicative activities with skill-building exercises to boost students' academic success.

Interactions Mosaic, 4th edition features

- updated content
- five videos of authentic news broadcasts
- expansion opportunities through the Website
- new audio programs for the listening/speaking and reading books
- an appealing fresh design
- user-friendly instructor's manuals with placement tests and chapter quizzes

In This Chapter shows students the grammar points that will be covered in the chapter.

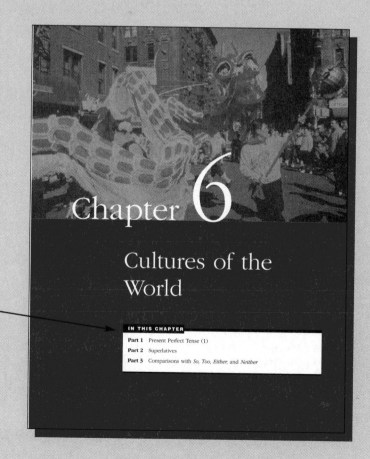

Chapter **6**

Cultures of the World

IN THIS CHAPTER

Part 1 Present Perfect Tense (1)
Part 2 Superlatives
Part 3 Comparisons with *So, Too, Either,* and *Neither*

The Passive Voice with Modal Auxiliaries

Setting the Context

Setting the Context activities introduce key vocabulary and familiarize students with the chapter theme. Introductory activities include model conversations, readings, class discussions, prediction activities, previewing, and pair interviews.

Reading

Medical Technology

Medical technology has developed very quickly over the past few years. New technologies have made it possible to do many things that couldn't be imagined in the past. Many new tests can be given, diseases can be discovered, and operations can be done because of breakthroughs in medical technology. Doctors and scientists predict that in the next few years, many important drugs will be developed, many diseases will be cured, and many operations will be improved. Some amazing choices could also be offered by medical technology in the future. Soon it could be possible to pick the sex, IQ, and eye color of children before they are born. It is even possible that human beings could be cloned (copied exactly) in the future!

But as these amazing technologies develop, some important questions are being asked: Should nature be controlled by technology? Could new technologies make our world less "human"? These questions should be considered carefully as medical technology continues to develop.

Discussion Questions reinforce students' understanding of the topics through comprehension questions and encourage students to express themselves.

Discussion Questions

1. What kinds of things can be done because of breakthroughs in medical
2. What do doctors predict will be done in the next few years?
3. What amazing choices could be offered?
4. What important questions are being asked?
5. What are some examples of modern medical technology?

Pairwork activities encourage students to personalize and practice the target language.

Grammar explanations and charts provide clear, easy to understand, and visually appealing grammar presentations.

5 Take turns asking and answering questions about the food in the pictures on pages 52 and 53. Use *some* or *any* in your questions and answers.

Example: A. Is there any juice in the breakfast picture?
          B. There isn't any juice, but there is some coffee.

6 Describe your favorite ice cream sundae. Your description should include the ice cream flavors and toppings you like. Write sentences using *some* or *any*.

Example: My sundae has some vanilla and chocolate ice cream, but it doesn't have any strawberry ice cream. It has some nuts and whipped cream.

C. A lot of/Many/Much

A lot of, *many*, and *much* are used to express a large quantity of something. *A lot of* may appear before both noncount and plural count nouns. *Many* may appear only before plural count nouns. *Much* may appear only before noncount nouns.

	Examples	Notes
A lot of	She doesn't eat **a lot of** hamburgers. There is **a lot of** salt in this soup. Is there **a lot of** fresh bread at the bakery? Don't you eat **a lot of** apples?	*A lot of* is used in affirmative and negative statements and questions.
Many	**Many** fast-food restaurants serve hamburgers. I don't like **many** kinds of vegetables. Do **many** people have a poor diet? Aren't there **many** eggs in the refrigerator?	*Many* is used in affirmative and negative statements and questions.
Much	They don't eat **much** red meat. We don't drink **much** tea or coffee. Does chicken have **much** cholesterol? Don't they eat **much** fish?	*Much* is used mainly in negative statements and affirmative and negative questions. *Much* usually isn't used in affirmative statements.

Using What You've Learned provides students with opportunities to do less structured, more communicative activities.

Groupwork activities maximize opportunities for discussion.

---

the woman (fixed / was fixing) the lock on her door (while / when) the police
₁₈   ₁₉

(called / were calling). They (told / were telling) her that they found the burglar. When
20   21

she (asked / was asking) how they caught the burglar so fast, she (got / was getting) a
22   23

surprise. The policeman told her "It was easy ma'am. The suspect (ate / was eating)
24

while he (ran / was running) down the street. (While / When) we (stopped / were stop-
25   26   27

ping) him, he (had / was having) big, chocolate stains all over his shirt. We knew then
28

that we had our man."

Using What You've Learned

 8 Play a video of a news segment or a commercial. Watch the video carefully and take notes on what you see and hear. After watching the video, form small groups, then prepare 5–10 past continuous questions about the video. Use your questions to test how much your group members remember about what they saw and heard.

Example questions: 1.   *What color tie was the man wearing?*
                       2.   *Was he looking straight at the camera?*
                       3.   *What was he doing with his hands?*

 9 An alibi is an explanation given by a suspect to prove that he or she was somewhere else at the time of a crime. In this activity, half the class takes the role of detectives who are trying to solve a crime, and the other half takes the role of suspects who must provide alibis.

    As a class, decide the details of the crime (such as the type of crime and the time and place of the crime).

    Then the suspects pair up with a partner to create a detailed alibi to prove that they did not commit the crime. The suspects should use the past tense and the past continuous tense in their alibi.

    Next, one suspect is interviewed by the detectives, while the suspect's partner waits outside. The detectives should ask questions using the past tense and the past continuous tense with *when* or *while*.

Example: *Detective #1:* What were you doing last night at 7:00 when the robbery occured?
          Suspect #1: I was at the Cineplex movie theater watching a movie.
          Detective #2: What movie were you watching?
          Suspect #1: I was watching "Gun Blast 2."
          Detective #3: Who were you with?
          Suspect #1: I was with John Simpson.
          Detective #1: Did anyone see you and John while you were there?

Video news broadcasts immerse students in authentic language, complete with scaffolding and follow-up activities.

Video Activities: Quiz Shows

Before You Watch.

1. Circle the kinds of TV shows you like to watch.

     a. comedies   b. dramas   c. quiz shows   d. soap operas

2. Do you like watching quiz shows on TV? Discuss with a partner.

3. Describe your favorite TV quiz show to your partner.

Watch.   Discuss the following questions with your classmates.

1. On all the game shows you saw in the video, what must contestants do in order to win money?

2. Why do television networks like to make game shows?

3. The contestants on today's game shows are _____

     a. millionaires   b. ordinary people   c. scholars

Watch Again.   Write T if the statements below are true and F if they are false. Then correct all the false statements.

1. In the U.S., you can watch a game show on TV almost every night of the week.

2. Quiz shows are a new idea.

3. The first game show in America was called "Who Wants to be a Millionaire?"

4. If a television show is successful, other networks hurry to copy it.

5. Game shows are cheaper to make than sitcoms.

6. In the short term, American TV networks will stop making game shows.

7. The questions on the new "Twenty-One" show are called "relatable." This means they are about families.

After You Watch.   Complete the following sentences with the correct tense of the verb in parentheses. Then check the video to see if your answers are correct.

1. "Who Wants to be a Millionaire" _____ (start) the current quiz show craze last summer.

2. Other networks quickly _____ (jump) on the bandwagon.

3. Television networks always _____ (clone) shows that are popular, and now they _____ (do) it again.

4. Their motivation _____ (be) greed.

5. In the short term the networks _____ (make) more game shows, more quiz shows.

6. Game shows _____ (be) not a new idea.

7. In the late 1950s, the audience _____ (find out) the show Twenty-One was rigged, and quiz shows _____ (lose) popularity. Now NBC _____ (bring) back Twenty-One.

8. On the new quiz shows, you _____ (have to, not) be a scholar in order to be a millionaire.

9. The sixty-four thousand dollar question is, how long _____ the craze _____ (last)?

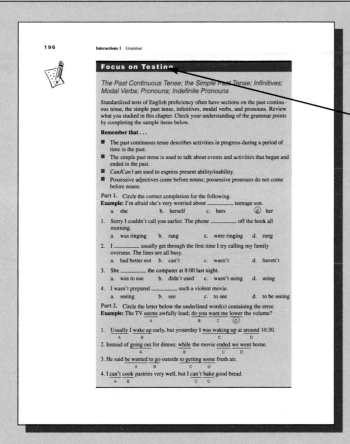

Focus on Testing helps students prepare for academic exams and standardized tests, such as the TOEFL.

Don't forget to check out the new *Interactions Mosaic* Website at www.mhcontemporary.com/interactionsmosaic.

- Traditional practice and interactive activities
- Links to student and teacher resources
- Cultural activities
- Focus on Testing
- Activities from the Website are also provided on CD-ROM

Interactions 1 Grammar

Chapter 1

School Life Around the World

PART 1   # The Verb *Be*

Setting the Context

Conversation

Carlos: Excuse me, is this seat free?
Miguel: Yes, it is.
Carlos: Thanks. (*Carlos sits down.*) I'm Carlos.
Miguel: Hi, Carlos. I'm Miguel. Are you a new student here?
Carlos: Yes, I am. This is my first day at this school. How is this class?
Miguel: It's great! The students are very nice and the professor is a fantastic teacher.
Carlos: Wow! The professor is that good?
Miguel: Yes, he is. Professor Jimenez is one of my favorite teachers.
Carlos: Umm . . . Isn't this professor Allandre's class?
Miguel: No, it isn't.
Carlos: Isn't this room 409?
Miguel: No, it isn't. This is room 406. Room 409 is across the hall.
Carlos: Oops. I'm in the wrong class!

Discussion Questions

1.   Is Miguel a new student?
2.   Is Miguel happy with his class? Why or why not?
3.   Is Carlos's class in room 406?
4.   How does Carlos know he's in the wrong class?
5.   How do you think Carlos feels?

A. Affirmative and Negative Statements; Contractions

The verb *be* has different forms after different subjects.

	Examples	**Notes**
Affirmative	I **am** from Japan. The students **are** late. You **are** twins! The teacher **is** over there.	Use *am* with the pronoun *I*. Use *are* with plural nouns and these pronouns: *we, you, they, these,* or *those*. Use *is* with singular nouns and these singular pronouns: *he, she, it, this,* or *that*.
Negative	I **am not** late. She **is not** in this class.	Use *not* after the verb *be* in negative sentences.

Contractions are short forms. They are used in conversation and informal writing. Full forms are used in more formal writing.

	Full Forms	**Contractions**	
Affirmative	**I am** Mexican. **He is** a new student. **She is** a student. **It is** Tuesday. **We are** cousins. **You are** very smart. **They are** at home.	**I'm** Mexican. **He's** a new student. **She's** a student. **It's** Tuesday. **We're** cousins. **You're** very smart. **They're** at home.	
Negative	**I am not** interested. **He is not** in the office. **She is not** happy. **It is not** here. **We are not** students. **You are not** married. **They are not** friendly.	**I'm not** interested. **He's not** in the office. **She's not** happy. **It's not** here. **We're not** students. **You're not** married. **They're not** friendly.	(no contraction) **He isn't** in the office. **She isn't** happy. **It isn't** here. **We aren't** students. **You aren't** married. **They aren't** friendly.

1 Underline the verb *be* in statements in the conversation between Carlos and Miguel on page 2.

Example: I'<u>m</u> Carlos.

2 Circle the correct words or word parts in each parentheses. The first one is done as an example.

Dave: Hi. I (**'m**/'s) Dave.

Mary: Hello. We ('s/**'re**) Mary and Ellen Johnson.

Dave: Oh, you ('re/n't) twins!

Mary: No, we ('re not/isn't) twins. But we ('m/'re) sisters.

Dave: But you ('s/'re) exactly alike!

Ellen: No, I ('m/'s) nineteen years old, but Mary (isn't/aren't) even eighteen yet.

Dave: I see now. Ellen, you ('re/'s) a little taller, and Mary's eyes (is/are) a little darker. (*Jim enters.*) Hi, Jim. Jim, this (is/are) Mary Johnson and her sister Ellen.

Jim: Hello. Oh! You ('m/'re) twins!

3 Complete the sentences with the correct forms of the verb *be.* Use contractions when possible.

Kami: The instructor __isn't__ (not) here yet. She __is__ late.

Yumiko: No, she __is__ (not). It __is__ early. It __is__ (not) even 9:45. A lot of students __are__ (not) here yet either.

Kami: Well then, let's get a cup of coffee. The snack bar __is__ open.

Yumiko: No, thanks. I __am__ (not) ready for class yet. I have to do the homework.

Kami: The homework __is__ difficult! The exercises __are__ complicated and confusing. Fifteen minutes __is__ (not) enough time to do it.

Yumiko: Ssshhh! You ___*are*___ making me nervous.
₁₁

Kami: I ___*am*___ sorry. But it really ___*not*___ too late to do the homework now.
₁₂   ₁₃

Yumiko: You ___*are*___ probably right.
₁₄

Ex 4   Use the words provided to make present tense statements about the people in the pictures. When an *A* appears in parentheses after the words, make an affirmative statement. When an *N* appears in parentheses, make a negative statement.

Examples: Professor Winters

tall (A)   *Professor Winters is tall.*

an old man (N)   *Professor Winters is not an old man.*

Professor Winters
1. a good teacher (A)
2. a boring speaker (N)
3. very funny (N)
4. in the English department (A)
5. married (A)

Doctor Silbert
6. a scientist (A)
7. bored (N)
8. in the English department (N)
9. friendly (A)
10. busy (A)

These Students
11. in their chairs (A)
12. tired (A)
13. serious students (N)
14. interested in the lesson (N)
15. prepared for the next exam (N)

B. Yes/No Questions and Short Answers

Yes/no questions are questions that may be answered by *yes* or *no*.

	Examples	Notes
Affirmative Questions	**Am I** late? **Are you** from Japan? **Is it** cold?	In a yes/no question, the verb comes before the subject.
Negative Questions	**Aren't you** early? **Isn't that** woman a professor? **Aren't they** twins?	Negative questions are used to express the speaker's belief or expectation.

Questions	Affirmative Answers	Negative Answers	
Am I early?	Yes, you are.	No, you're not.	No, you aren't.
Is he Japanese?	Yes, he is.	No, he's not.	No, he isn't.
Isn't she a scientist?	Yes, she is.	No, she's not.	No, she isn't.
Is it late?	Yes, it is.	No, it's not.	No, it isn't.
Are you students?	Yes, we are.	No, we're not.	No, we aren't.
Aren't those boys twins?	Yes, they are.	No, they're not.	No, they aren't.

Note: Contractions are not used in affirmative short answers. Contractions are usually used in negative short answers.

5   Put two lines under the verb *be* in yes/no questions and short answers in the conversation between Carlos and Miguel on page 2.

Example: Excuse me, <u>is</u> this seat free?

6   Complete these sentences with affirmative or negative forms of the verb *be*. Use contractions when possible.

John: <u>Are</u> you in Professor Jenkins's class?

Estella: Yes, I <u>am</u>.

  1

John: <u>is</u> it a beginning level class?

  2

Estella: No, it <u>isn't</u>. It <u>not</u> an advanced class.

    3   4

John: <u>isn't</u> she a good teacher?

  5

Estella: Yes, she ___is___, but she's very strict.

John: _____ she patient with the students?

Estella: Actually, no, she ___is___.

John: ___are___ the exams difficult?

Estella: Yes, they ___are___!

John: ___are___ the homework overwhelming?

Estella: Yes, it ___is___! ___are___ you interested in the class?

John: Umm. I ___am___ not sure anymore.

7 Write missing questions for the following answers. Many different questions are possible.

Example: A. ___Is Marco a good student?___

   B. Oh, yes. He's the best student in the class.

1. A. ___is Marco in the English Department?___

   B. No, he isn't. He's in the English Department.

2. A. ___is Mary from New York___

   B. No, she isn't. She's from New York.

3. A. _____

   B. Yes, we are.

4. A. ___Is John and Estella are twins?___

   B. Yes, they are.

5. A. ___is you from Maryland?___

   B. No, I'm not.

8 Read the following questions and answers. If there are any mistakes in the under-lined words, rewrite the question or answer correctly. If there are no mistakes, write "correct."

1. A. Is you from Osaka?   ___Are you from Osaka?___

   B. No, I'm not. I'm from Kobe.   ___correct___

2. A. Is your brother a student here also? _____

   B. Yes, he's.   _____

3. A. Are I the only woman in this class? _____

   B. No, you aren't.   _____

4. A. Aren't you in my history class? _____

   B. No, I aren't.   _____

5. A. Is Carlos and Coletta business majors? _____

   B. Yes, they is.   _____

6. A. <u>Is</u> the history department in this building? _____

    B. No, <u>it's</u> isn't.   _____

7. A. <u>Am</u> I early?   _____

    B. Yes, <u>you're</u>.   _____

8. A. <u>Are</u> we in the right place?   _____

    B. Yes, we <u>is</u>.   _____

Using What You've Learned

9 Introduce yourself to a classmate and talk about your classes and your teachers. Use sentences with *be*.

Example: A. Hi, I'm Juan. I'm new here. Are you in this class?

              B. Yes, I am.

              A. Is the professor good?

              B. I'm not sure. She's new here too.

10 Sit in a circle with your class. The first student begins by making two statements about himself or herself using the verb *be* in the present tense. The next student repeats the first student's information and then makes two statements about himself or herself. The third student repeats the first and second students' information, then makes two statements, and so on. If a student forgets any information, group members can help.

Example: A. **I'm** Maria. **I'm** from Barcelona.

              B. **She's** Maria. **She's** from Barcelona. **I'm** Eduardo. **I'm** a business major.

              C. **She's** Maria. **She's** from Barcelona. **He's** Eduardo. **He's** a business major. **I'm** . . .

11 There are many ways to answer yes/no questions without using the words *yes* and *no*. Here are some examples of other affirmative and negative answers.

	Formal	**Informal**
Affirmative	Certainly.	Sure.
	Of course.	Yeah.
	I think so.	Uh-huh.
	Indeed.	Right.
Negative	Certainly not.	Nope.
	Of course not.	No way.
	I don't think so.	Uh-uh.
	I'm afraid not.	Nah.

Play this question-and-answer game quickly. Choose one student to go to the front of the room and answer yes/no questions asked by the other students. This student must answer each question without using the words *yes* or *no*. If the student accidentally answers with *yes* or *no*, another student takes her or his place and continues the game.

Example: A.   Are you a student in this class?

B.   Of course.

C.   Is this your favorite class?

B.   I think so.

D.   Is it cold today?

B.   It is.

A.   Is it raining?

B.   No, it . . . Ooops!
         (*Another student continues.*)

PART 2	# The Simple Present Tense

Setting the Context

Conversation

Alana: Hi, Margo. I'm free for a while before my next class. Are you?

Margo: Yeah, I am.

Alana: Let's get a cup of coffee.

Margo: Great. Get a table, and I'll get the coffee. What do you take in your coffee?

Alana: Cream and sugar. Get a cookie too, please. (*Alana sits at a table, and Margo returns with the coffee.*)

Margo: So, how do you like your classes this semester?

Alana: I like them all, except for math. I don't like the instructor at all!

Margo: Why not?

Alana: Well, he talks too quickly, he rarely explain things clearly, and he isn't very patient. Also, he never takes breaks!

Margo: Does he give exams often?

Alana: Sure he does. He gives quizzes once a week! And he doesn't prepare us for them. I am completely confused in class.

Margo: Maybe you need extra help. Get a tutor.

Alana: That's a good idea. Do you know any math tutors?

Margo: Actually, yes, I do. I know a math teacher and tutor who always explains things slowly and carefully. He's also very patient and kind.

Alana: I like him already. What's his name?

Margo: Mr. Michaels. He's my adviser.

Alana: Mr. Michaels? He's my math teacher!

Discussion Questions

1. Why are Alana and Margo having coffee?
2. How does Alana feel about her math teacher? Why?
3. What is Margo's suggestion?
4. What jobs does Mr. Michaels have?
5. What advice would you give Alana?

A. The Imperative Form: Instructions, Orders, and Suggestions

The imperative form uses the simple form of the verb.

	Examples	**Notes**
Affirmative	Come in.	To give instructions or orders, begin with a verb. The subject *you* is not included as it is understood.
	Sit down, please.	Adding the word *please* makes the instruction more polite.
Negative	Don't talk. Please don't come in.	In negative imperatives, *don't* comes before the verb.

An imperative statement can be formed for the first-person plural subject (*we*) with *let's* + the simple form of a verb.

	Examples	**Notes**
Affirmative **Negative**	Let's have coffee. Let's not wait.	*Let's* = *let us*. *Let's* means "I suggest we . . ."

1 Circle the imperative statements in the conversation between Alana and Margo.

Example: (Let's get a cup of coffee.)

2 Imagine you are a teacher. What instructions would you give your students on the first day of class? Use the following phrases to form affirmative and negative imperative sentences.

Example: be late to class. *Please don't be late to class.*

1. bring your textbooks to class
2. come in quietly

3.   eat in class
4.   drink coffee in class
5.   sleep in class
6.   cheat on tests
7.   speak your native language in class
8.   take notes in class
9.   ask questions in class
10.   talk loudly and clearly

 3 Work with a partner. Take turns making suggestions for each of the following situations, using *let's*.

Example: You are hungry. *Let's get a slice of pizza.*

1.   You are tired.
2.   You need to cash a check.
3.   You need to mail a letter.
4.   You want to get a suntan.
5.   You want to dance.
6.   You want to get some exercise.
7.   You want to do something you've never done before.
8.   You want to do something relaxing.
9.   You want to do something creative.
10.   You want to improve your English.

B. Affirmative and Negative Statements

The simple present tense is used to describe everyday activities and habits, to make general statements of fact, and to express opinions. With some verbs, the simple present shows an existing condition (something that is happening now). The first three notes in the chart below apply to each type of affirmative and negative statement.

	Examples	**Notes**
Everyday Activities and Habits	Andres and Ricardo often **study** math together. I **drink** three cups of tea a day.	An object sometimes follows the verb.
Statements of Fact	Lu **speaks** three languages. Mr. Michaels **teaches** math and **advises** students.	With third-person singular subjects, the verb ends in -*s*.
Opinions	I **don't like** the instructor. He **doesn't teach** math very well.	In negative statements, *do* or *does* comes before *not*. The contractions are *don't* and *doesn't*. The main verb always appears in the simple form.
Existing Conditions	I **hear** music. He **doesn't understand** your question.	Other verbs that describe an existing condition include *like, need, want, seem, know,* and *believe.*

Spelling Rules for -*s* Endings

For the third-person singular verb form, follow these spelling rules:

1. If the simple form of a verb ends in -*y* after a consonant, change the *y* to *i* and add -*es*.

   Examples: carry/carries

             try/tries

2. If the simple form of a verb ends in -*s*, -*z*, -*sh*, -*ch*, -*x*, or -*o* (after a consonant), add -*es*.

   Examples: teach/teaches

             pass/passes

             go/goes

3. There are two irregular verb forms.

             be/is

             have/has

4. In all other cases, add -*s* to the simple form.

   Examples: wear/wears

             work/works

             pay/pays

Pronunciation Note

The -*s* ending is pronounced three ways, depending on the ending of the verb:

1. /*iz*/ after -*ch*, -*sh*, -*s*, -*x*, and -*z* endings

   Examples: teaches, washes, kisses, boxes, buzzes

2. /*s*/ after voiceless endings: *p, t, k,* or *f*

   Examples: stops, hits, looks, laughs

3. /*z*/ after voiced consonant endings

   Examples: calls, listens, plays, sounds, runs

---

4   Underline the simple present tense verbs in statements in the conversation between Alana and Margo on pages 9 and 10.

Example: I <u>like</u> them all, except for math.

5   Use the words provided to make present tense statements about the people in the pictures. When an *A* appears in parentheses after the words, make an affirmative statement. When an *N* appears in parentheses, make a negative statement.

Examples: Mr. Sommers

be 32 years old (A) *Mr. Sommers is 32 years old.*

have a beard (A)   *Mr. Sommers has a beard.*

Mr. Sommers

1. be a teaching assistant (A)
2. be a professor (N)
3. help Mr. Michaels (A)
4. teach three days a week (A)
5. give lectures (N)
6. work with students in small groups (A)
7. wear a suit and a tie (N)
8. like to wear jeans every day (A)
9. carry a briefcase (N)
10. have a board in his classroom (N)

Ms. Wong and Mr. Garcia

11. he be a student advisor (A)
12. she be a college administrator (A)
13. they teach classes (N)
14. they give grades (N)
15. he advise students on their classes (A)
16. she often go to meetings (A)
17. she have an easy job (N)
18. he help students with their problems (A)
19. they have enough time to do all their work (N)
20. they make a lot of money (N)

C. Yes/No Questions and Short Answers

In simple present yes/no questions, a form of the verb *do* comes before the subject with verbs other than *be*. Use *does* with *he, she,* and *it*. Use *do* with *I, you, we,* and *they*. In these questions, the main verb always appears in the simple form. The appropriate form of *do* appears in short answers.

		Possible Answers	
	Examples	**Affirmative**	**Negative**
Affirmative Questions	**Do I look** like my mother?	Yes, you do.	No, you don't.
	Does he do good work?	Yes, he does.	No, he doesn't.
	Does she study a lot?	Yes, she does.	No, she doesn't.
	Does it work?	Yes, it does.	No, it doesn't.
	Do we need our umbrellas?	Yes, you do.	No, you don't.
	Do you have change for a dollar?	Yes, I do.	No, I don't.
	Do they know the address?	Yes, they do.	No, they don't.

		Possible Answers	
	Examples	**Affirmative**	**Negative**
Negative Questions	**Don't I need** a ticket?	Yes, you do.	No, you don't.
	Doesn't he teach English?	Yes, he does.	No, he doesn't.
	Doesn't she play the piano?	Yes, she does.	No, she doesn't.
	Doesn't it bite?	Yes, it does.	No, it doesn't.
	Don't we leave tonight?	Yes, we do.	No, we don't.
	Don't you do the homework?	Yes, I do.	No, I don't.
	Don't they like pizza?	Yes, they do.	No, they don't.

6 Student A asks yes/no questions using the words below. Student B answers the questions with short answers. Student A adds some questions of his or her own.

Example: A. Does this school have a cafeteria?
  B. Yes, it does. (or: No, it doesn't. It only has a snack bar.)
  A. Is the food good?
  B. No, it isn't. It's terrible.

1. this school have a cafeteria
2. the food good
3. the place clean
4. it have comfortable chairs
5. students study there
6. it open late
7. any students work there
8. the place serve hamburgers
9. it have coffee
10. the prices high

7 Change roles. Now Student B asks yes/no questions using the words below. Student A gives short answers. Student B adds some questions of his or her own.

1. your English class difficult
2. you like your English class
3. the classroom big
4. the instructor give many exams
5. you have homework every day
6. you often late to class
7. you sometimes need help with your homework
8. the teacher check your homework
9. you have a textbook
10. you study enough

8 Change partners. Write some yes/no questions about another person, place, or activity at your school (such as the dean of students, the library, or the drama club). Then take turns asking and answering each other's questions.

D. Information Questions and Answers

An information question begins with a question word and cannot be answered by *yes* or *no.* When a form of *do* separates a question word from the subject, the main verb must appear in its simple form.

Question Words	Questions	Possible Answers	Notes
Who	**Who** are your teachers? **Who** is your advisor? **Who** helps you?	My teachers are Mr. Sommers and Ms. Lee. Mr. Michaels is my advisor. Ben and Tom help me.	*Who* refers to people. *Who* can be the subject of a question. *Who* is usually followed by a singular verb.
Whom	**Who** } **Whom** } do you ask?	I ask my tutor.	*Who* (or *Whom*) is also used as an object. *Whom* is used only in formal questions. *Who* is used in informal speech.
What	**What** interests you? **What** is in the bag? **What** do you want? **What** does she teach?	Books and movies interest me. My lunch is in the bag. I want some money. She teaches history.	*What* refers to things. *What* can be the subject of a question. *What* can also used as an object.
Where	**Where** is the snack bar? **Where** are your classes? **Where** does the class meet? **Where** do we go now?	It is in the student center. They are in the new science building. It meets in Moore Hall. We go to English class.	*Where* is used to ask questions about places.
When	**When** is the final exam? **When** are our papers due? **When** does class begin? **When** do you work?	It is next week. They are due on Wednesday. It begins in five minutes. I work on Mondays and Fridays.	*When* is used to ask questions about time.
Why	**Why** is the building closed? **Why** aren't they home? **Why** does he come home so late? **Why** don't you see a doctor?	It's closed because it's a holiday. They're on vacation. He has a job after school. I don't because I'm not that sick.	*Why* is used to ask questions about reasons.
How	**How** is your math class? **How** are you? **How** do you get to school?	Math class is very hard. I'm pretty good. I get there by bus and subway.	*How* can refer to a degree (of something). *How* can refer to a state or condition (for example, health). *How* can refer to a way or a method of doing something.

Note: Contractions for question words + *be* used in informal speech are: *who* + *is* = *who's*; *what* + *is* = *what's*; *where* + *is* = *where's*; *when* + *is* = *when's*; *why* + *is* = *why's*; *how* + *is* = *how's*.

9 Put two lines under the question words in the conversation between Alana and Margo on pages 9 and 10.

Example: So, <u>how</u> do you like your classes this semester?

10   Make information questions for each of the answers given below. Use the simple present tense and the question words *who, what, where, when, why,* or *how.*

Example: _How are you?_

   I'm very well, thanks.

1.   _IS this your Math teacher_ ?
   She's my English teacher.

2.   _____?
   I walk to school.

3.   _What Subject dose he teacher_ ?
   He teaches math.

4.   _When are we taking the test_ ?
   It will be on Friday.

5.   _You can buy this dress_ ?
   I can't because it's too expensive.

6.   _____?
   It is in the refrigerator.

7.   _What color is that_ ?
   It's blue.

8.   _IS that your teacher_ ?
   He is my father.

9.   _When is room 103_ ?
   It's on the first floor.

10.   _____?
   That's horrible!

11   Student A makes information questions using the words below. Student B answers each of Student A's questions. Student A adds some questions of his or her own.

Examples: How . . . your classes this term?
   A.   How are your classes this term?
   B.   They're boring.
        Why . . . you like them?
   A.   Why don't you like them?
   B.   The courses are too easy.

1.   Who . . . your English teacher?
2.   How . . . you like him/her?
3.   Why . . . you like him/her?
4.   Where . . . your teacher from?
5.   When . . . your English class?
6.   Where . . . your English class meet?
7.   What . . . you bring to class?
8.   What textbook . . . you use?
9.   How . . . you like the textbook?
10.   Who . . . you study with?

 **12**   Change roles. Now Student B makes information questions using these words. Student A answers Student B's questions. Student B adds some questions of his or her own.

1. What . . . the first thing you do when you wake up?
2. How . . . you get to school?
3. Who . . . you usually come to school with?
4. When . . . your first class begin?
5. What . . . your first class?
6. When . . . your first class end?
7. Where . . . you go between classes?
8. How . . . you like the food in the cafeteria?
9. What . . . your favorite food in the cafeteria?
10. When . . . you usually go home?

E. Frequency Adverbs

Frequency adverbs modify verbs or adjectives. They describe how regularly or what percentage of time something happens. Here are the meanings of some frequency adverbs in approximate percentages of time:

always = 100%
usually = 90%
often = 70%
sometimes = 50%
occasionally = 20%
rarely = 10%
never = 0%

The charts below give some examples of frequency adverbs in affirmative and negative statements and questions. Notice where the frequency adverbs appear in the statements and questions.

	Examples	**Notes**
Affirmative	Students are **always** busy. He's **often** hungry. She **sometimes** gets sick. Students **occasionally** meet. They're **rarely** together.	In statements, one-word frequency adverbs usually come after the verb *be* but before other verbs.
Negative	I'm not **often** tired. Kim isn't **always** here. Tony is **never** late. She doesn't **often** rest. We don't **ever** want to go there again. They don't **usually** study.	

	Examples	Possible Answers		Notes
		Affirmative	Negative	
Affirmative Questions	Are you **often** homesick? Does the teacher **ever** give quizzes? Do they **always** eat pizza for lunch?	always often	not often	In questions, one-word frequency adverbs usually come after the subject.
Negative Questions	Don't you **ever** get homesick? Doesn't he **often** come to class late? Don't we **always** enjoy the weekend?	yes, sometimes occasionally	no, rarely never	

Note: Use *ever* only in questions, and *never* only in negative statements.

A frequency phrase usually follows the verb phrase.

Examples	Notes
He teaches **three times a week.** We have a test **every month.** Do you relax **now and then?**	Some frequency phrases are: *every day, every other week, every two hours, once a year,* and *now and then.*

13 Put a box around the frequency adverbs and phrases in the conversation between Alana and Margo on pages 9 and 10.

Example: Well, he talks too quickly, he ⬚rarely⬚ explain things clearly, and he isn't very patient.

14 Put the words in parentheses in the correct order to make statements or questions, according to the punctuation given. When you finish, practice the conversation with a partner.

Galina: <u>You often look tired</u>_____, Alek.

(tired / look / you / often)

_____?

1 (get / eight hours of sleep each night / you / usually / don't)

Alek: No. <u>I have eight o'clock classes. 1 or fiver day</u>

2 (I / five days a week / eight o'clock classes / have)   week

Also, _Rearly I get to bed before 2:00am_
3 (rarely / before 2:00 A.M. / get to bed / I)

Galina: Why do you go to bed so late?

Do you go out every night ?
4 (do / go out / every night / you)

Alek: Oh, no. _I never go out during the week_.
5 (never / during the week / I / go out)

My roommeat and I study together every n
6 (my roommate and I / every night / study together)

We don't finish usually, until 1:00 in the Mornin
7 (until 1:00 in the morning / usually / don't / finish / we)

In fact, _____.
8 (rarely / goes to bed / my roommate / before 3:00)

Galina: That's terrible. _Do you always work so hard_
9 (work so hard / always / you / do)

Alek: Yes, because _We're always worried about grades._
10 (always / worried about grades / we're)

Galina: Well, you graduate soon, right? What do you plan to do then?

Alek: Sleep!

 **15**　Take turns using the phrases below to ask and answer present tense questions. Add frequency adverbs to your questions and answers.

Examples:　A.　Do you **often** bring your lunch to school?
　　　　　　　B.　No, not **often**. I **occasionally** bring my lunch to school.
　　　　　　　　　(*Change roles.*)
　　　　　　　B.　Are you **ever** tired in class?
　　　　　　　A.　Yes, I'm **sometimes** tired in class.

1.　stay up all night
2.　cram for a test
3.　get eight hours of sleep
4.　ask questions in class
5.　be worried about school
6.　speak with your advisor

7.　be satisfied with your grades
8.　study with friends
9.　get help from a tutor
10.　ask for advice
11.　not do your homework
12.　be finished with classes by 3:00

Using What You've Learned

 **16**　Play this group game at a fast pace. All students stand up. One student comes to the front of the room to act as the "leader." This leader makes imperative statements beginning with "The leader says," such as "The leader says: touch your toes," and "The leader says: raise your right arm." All students must do what the leader tells them to do if the imperative begins with "The leader says." If the imperative does not begin with "The leader says," then students must not take the action. If a student accidentally follows an imperative that does not begin with "The leader says," that student must sit down. The last student left standing becomes the next leader.

17 Interview three of your classmates. Prepare ten questions to ask the people you interview.

Write some:

- ■ yes/no questions with *do/does* + a verb.
- ■ information questions with question words.
- ■ questions with frequency adverbs.

Examples: STUDENT 1   STUDENT 2   STUDENT 3

1. What's your name?
2. Do you live on campus?
3. Do you ever walk to school?
4. Do you belong to any clubs?

While asking the questions, take notes on your classmates' answers. Keep your notes for Activity 18.

18 Tell the class about one of the classmates you interviewed in Activity 17. Use the notes from your interview to tell your classmates about the person. If possible, make both affirmative and negative statements about the person.

Example: *This is Sam Chen. He doesn't live on campus. He never walks to school. He takes the bus to school. He belongs to the debating club.*

19
1. Cut a piece of paper into six or more pieces.
2. Write one noun, adjective, or adverb on each piece. Turn your pieces of paper over, so no one can see your words.
3. Choose a partner.
4. Your partner turns over one of your pieces of paper and makes a question that can be answered with the word on the paper.
5. Answer your partner's question with a statement.
6. Now you turn over one of your partner's pieces of paper and make a question that can be answered with the word on the paper.
7. Your partner answers your question.
8. Play until there are no more pieces of paper left.

Example: A. (Turns over a piece of paper with the word *black.*)
                  What color is my hair?
               B. It's black.
                  (Turns over a piece of paper with the word *Wednesday.*)
                  When do we have English class?
               A. We have English class on Wednesday.
                  (Turns over a piece of paper with the word *fast.*)
                  How does our teacher speak?
               B. He speaks *fast.*

Personal Pronouns, Possessive Adjectives, and Pronouns

Setting the Context

Conversation

Leon: Hi, Anita. What's up?

Anita: Hi, Leon. I need to buy a dictionary for our ESL class. I can't decide which to buy. What dictionary do you have?

Leon: I don't think you'd like mine. It's very basic. But my roommate, Mario, has a great dictionary. He lets me use it all the time. Actually, I probably use it more than he does.

Anita: Does his dictionary include idioms?

Leon: No, I don't think it does. But Abril's dictionary has idioms.

Anita: I know. I like hers alot, but the bookstore doesn't have it.

Leon: Why don't you ask her what bookstore it's from?

Anita: She says she doesn't remember.

Leon: Hmm. Hey, why don't you get an electronic dictionary?

Anita: Don't you remember? Our teacher won't let us use them.

Leon: Oh, yeah.

Anita: I don't know what to do! All of these dictionaries look the same to me right now.

Leon: I have a suggestion. Go home, relax, and come back to look at them again tomorrow.

Anita: Good idea, Leon.

Discussion Questions

1. How do Leon and Anita know each other?
2. Whose dictionary does Leon use?
3. Why does Anita like Abril's dictionary?
4. Why can't Anita use an electronic dictionary in her ESL class?
5. Describe your own dictionary. Why did you choose it?

A. Personal Pronouns

A pronoun is used in place of a noun. A pronoun can be the subject or object of a sentence. An object pronoun comes after a verb or a preposition. In the following chart the nouns in the examples are underlined. Notice how the pronouns (which appear in bold) are then used in place of the nouns.

Subject Pronoun	Object Pronoun	Examples
I	me	"This is Jack Thomas speaking. **I** am lost. Can you help **me?**"
you	you	"Dave, **you** look different in a suit. I hardly recognize **you.**"
he	him	Carlos is from Mexico. **He** is a new student. I want to talk to **him.**
she	her	Ms. Sanchez is the teacher. **She** teaches Spanish. My brother is in **her** class.
it	it	I just bought a computer. **It** is heavy. I had to carry **it** home.
we	us	"It's Ellen and Betty. **We** are downstairs. Please let **us** in."
you	you	"Yuriko and Hiroshi, **you** look tired. Can I take **you** home?"
they	them	"Ellen and Betty are here. **They** want to come in. Please let **them** in."

1 Underline the subject pronouns and put a double underline under the object pronouns in the conversation between Anita and Leon on page 21.

Example: He lets me use it all the time.

2 Finish the following sentences with the appropriate subject and object pronouns.

Example: I love her but ___she___ doesn't love ___me___.

1. You want to speak to him but __you__ doesn't want to speak to __me__.
2. My sister wants to work with them but __she__ don't want to work with __me__.
3. We visit them but __they__ don't visit __me__.
4. She sends letters to Bill and Kate but __she__ don't send letters to __me__.
5. I am worried about her but __she__ isn't worried about __me__.
6. My mother cooks for my father but __she__ doesn't cook for __me__.

7. He takes photos of us but ___I___ don't take photos of _them_.
8. That woman knows you but ___I___ don't know _her_.
9. The students ask him for advice but _they_ doesn't ask _me_ for advice.
10. We understand them but _they_ don't understand _me_.

B. Possessive Adjectives and Pronouns

Possessive adjectives are followed by a noun. Possessive pronouns are not followed by a noun; they stand alone.

	Forms	Examples
Possessive Adjectives	my	That isn't **my** pen.
	your	These are **your** shoes.
	his	It's **his** problem.
	her	Those are **her** flowers.
	its	**Its** tail is brown.
	our	**Our** seats are here.
	your	I am **your** teacher.
	their	This is **their** car.
Possessive Pronouns	mine	That pen isn't **mine**.
	yours	These shoes are **yours**.
	his	The problem is **his**.
	hers	The flowers are **hers**.
	ours	The seats are **ours**.
	yours	I am **yours**.
	theirs	The car is **theirs**.

3 Circle the possessive adjectives and put a box around the possessive pronouns in the conversation between Anita and Leon on page 21.

Example: *Anita:* Hi, Leon. I need to buy a dictionary for (our) ESL class. I can't decide which to buy. What dictionary do you have?
Leon: I don't think you'd like ⬚mine⬚.

4 Choose the correct word in parentheses.

Example: (I/me/(my)) pencil is broken. Can I borrow (you/your/(yours))?

1. Professor Smith is (me/(my)/mine) biology teacher.
2. (They/(Their)/Theirs) books are here. Where are ((us)/our/ours)?
3. ((She)/Her/Hers) studies with (she/(her)/hers) roommate.
4. ((We)/Us/Our) work on (we/us/(our)) project every Monday.
5. She has (she/(her)/hers) coffee with cream. I have (me/(my)/mine) coffee black.
6. I spend two hours a night on (me/(my)/mine) homework. How long do you spend on (you/(your)/yours)?
7. ((Your)/You/Yours) apartment is closer to school than (I/my/(mine)).

8. (Me/My/Mine) brother is on the debating team with (they/them/their).

9. (He/Him/His) works as a teaching assistant. (He/Him/His) job is very satisfying.

10. The tutor comes to (us/our/ours) house once a week to help (we/us/our) with our schoolwork.

Using What You've Learned

5 Choose one school-related person or place, such as the school library, the cafeteria, an advisor, or a professor. Then write one or two paragraphs about the person or place you chose. Use as many personal pronouns, possessive adjectives, and possessive pronouns as you can. When you have finished, underline and count the number of personal pronouns and possessive adjectives and pronouns you used. The student who used the most should read their paragraphs to the class.

Example: I like our school library. It is in a beautiful building. It has thousands of books. Students can check them out for up to a week, or they can just read them in the library. The librarian is a very nice woman. Her name is Ms. Freed. She is helpful and kind. She tells me how to find information I need. If I don't have a pen, she lets me use hers.

6 Think of a person in your school whom all of your classmates know. This can be a student, a teacher, or an administrator. Without revealing the identity of the person, write ten sentences which give clues about the person's identity. Use personal pronouns, possessive adjectives, and possessive pronouns. Read your clues to the class until someone guesses the identity of your person correctly. That person then reads their clues to the class.

Example: A. She often comes to class late.
               She is a good athlete.
               I am taller than her.
               (pointing to a jacket) That jacket is hers.
               Her name rhymes with "fancy."

           B. Is the person "Nancy"?

           A. Yes! Your turn.

Video Activities: Exchange Students

Before You Watch.   Discuss these questions in a group.

1. Did you have exchange students in your school?
2. What are the advantages and disadvantages of studying in an overseas high school?
3. How do students celebrate graduation from high school?

Watch.   Write answers to these questions.

1. Where does Eda come from?
2. How old do you think she is?
3. Where does she live?
4. What event is Eda going to?
5. At the end of their year in the U.S., how do the visiting students feel about going back to their home countries?

Watch Again.   Read the following statements. Are the statements true or false? Write T for true, F for false.

_____ 1. Brian thinks Turkish people are very different from American people.

_____ 2. Eda is not homesick because she talks to her parents frequently.

_____ 3. About 12 international students are studying in San Diego.

_____ 4. The students are going to return to their countries in five months.

_____ 5. The students are planning to meet again in the future.

After You Watch.   Work with a partner. Student 1 is a high-school senior who is spending a year as an exchange student in the United States. Student 2 is a relative back home. Role-play or write a phone conversation asking and answering questions about Student 1's daily life. Use the simple present tense with frequency adverbs.

Here are some topics to discuss; add any other topics you want.

- Student 1's host family (describe the people)
- Student 1's home, room, and school
- The kind of food Student 1 eats regularly
- The typical weather in Student 1's U.S. home

Chapter 2

Experiencing Nature

PART 1   *There is / There are*

Setting the Context

Conversation

Rafael: (*Looking at a map*) There are about five miles to go until we reach Emerald Lake.

Gil: Five miles?! There are blisters on my feet. I can't walk anymore.

Rafael: There are bandages in my backpack if you need them. Now let's see . . . it looks like there are two different paths we can take. There is one path along the river and there's another through the forest.

Susana: Let's take the forest path! There are beautiful trees and interesting animals in the forest.

Gil: There are also bugs in the forest.

Susana: Oh, Gil! This is a wonderful hike. Why are you so unhappy?

Gil: I guess I'm just hungry and tired.

Susana: Is there a good place for us to stop and have our lunch?

Marta: Why don't we take the path along the river and stop for lunch on the way? There isn't any water in our canteens, so we can fill them up at the river.

Rafael: That sounds like a good plan.

Gil: Look! There's a deer!

Susana: Where?

Gil: Behind that tree! And look—there are two more over there!

Marta: Gil! I don't believe it. Is there a smile on your face?

Gil: Maybe just a small one.

Discussion Questions

1. Where are Rafael, Gil, Susana, and Marta?
2. What decision do they need to make?

3.   Why is Gil unhappy?
4.   What makes Gil smile?
5.   Would you like to be on this hike? Why or why not?

A. There is / There are

Statements and questions can be formed with *there is / there are. There* is used to show that something exists or is in a place. *There is* is used when the noun that follows it is singular; *there are* is used when the noun that follows is plural.

	Examples	**Notes**
Affirmative Statements	**There is** a bee on the flower.	The contraction for *there is* is *there's.*
	There are meadows on the way.	There is no contraction for *there are.*
Negative Statements	**There is no** water in my canteen.	The contraction for *there is no* is *there isn't any.*
	There are no rocks on the trail.	The contraction for *there are no* is *there aren't any.*

		Possible Short Answers	
	Examples	**Affirmative**	**Negative**
Affirmative Questions	**Is there** a river near the trail?	Yes, there is.	No, there isn't. No, there's not.
	Are there any sleeping bags?	Yes, there are.	No, there aren't.
Negative Questions	**Isn't there** a map of the park?	Yes, there is.	No, there isn't. No, there's not.
	Aren't there hills on the hike?	Yes, there are.	No, there aren't.

1   Underline the verb phrases *there is / there are* and the nouns they refer to in the conversation between the hikers on page 28.

Example: There are about five miles to go until we reach Emerald Lake.

2   Form sentences with *there is / there are* and the words below.

Example: (two dogs / in the park) *There are two dogs in the park.*

1.   (many trees / in the park) *There are trees in the park*
2.   (one oak tree / in the park) *There is one oak tree in the Park*
3.   (many birds / in the tree) *There are*
4.   (a bird's nest / in the tree) *There is*
5.   (a couple of baby birds / in the nest) *There are*
6.   (one egg / in the nest) *There is*
7.   (a pond / in the park) *There is*
8.   (some frogs / in the pond) *There are*
9.   (many fish / in the pond) *There is*
10. (a duck / in the pond) *There is*

3 Fill in the blanks with one or more of the following words: *there, there's, is, isn't, are, aren't.*

Harold: Maude, _there's_____ nothing to do in the city. Let's go camping!
₁

Maude: Camping? But _____ any people our age in the mountains.
₂

Harold: Sure _____. And _____ camping equipment in the garage.
₃   ₄

Let's see . . . I think _____ a tent and _____ two sleeping bags.
₅   ₆

Maude: But _____ a camp stove?
₇

Harold: Yes, _____. But _____ no backpacks, and _____ any
₈   ₉   ₁₀

hiking boots.

Maude: That's alright. I don't want to hike anyway. _____ bathrooms and
₁₁

showers at the campground?

Harold: Of course _____.
₁₂

Maude: _____ a hotel nearby? Just in case it rains . . .
₁₃

Harold: I think _____. Come on! Let's go hiking! _____
₁₄   ₁₅

nothing to lose.

4 Describe the picture below. Use sentences beginning with *there is / there are.*

Examples: *There is a deer standing in the meadow.*
There are two people by the river.

Using What You've Learned

5 Student A studies the picture below for one minute and then closes the book. Student B (who continues to look at the picture) then asks Student A questions about the picture, using questions with *is there / are there*. Student A tries to answer Student B's questions from memory.

Example: B. Is there a river?
A. No, there's not. But there's a lake.
B. Is there anything on the lake?
A. Yes. There are two sailboats on the lake.

6 Repeat Activity 5 with a nature picture from a magazine or calendar. This time, Student B answers Student A's questions about the picture.

7 Close your eyes and relax. Think about your favorite park, garden, or other place in nature. Choose a partner. Student A describes the place that he or she has chosen to Student B, with sentences starting with *there is / there are*. As Student B listens, he or she draws a simple picture of the place described. When the drawing is complete, change roles so that Student B describes a place and Student A draws.

PART 2

Questions with *Whose;*
Possessive Nouns

Setting the Context

Conversation

Marta: The sandwiches are all mixed up. This one is mine but whose ham and cheese sandwich is this?

Rafael: That's mine.

Marta: Whose egg sandwich is this?

Rafael: I think it's Gil's.

Marta: No, Gil doesn't like eggs. So it must be Susana's. Did anyone bring fruit?

Rafael: Yeah. Susana brought apples from her grandparents' farm.

Marta: Great. And I brought candy bars from the school's vending machine. So we have plenty of food. But do we have anything to sit down on?

Rafael: I brought my parents' picnic blanket.

Marta: Perfect. Once Gil and Susana get back with the water we can eat.

Rafael: I can't wait. I'm so hungry from the hike, I could eat my backpack!

Discussion Questions

1. Whose picnic blanket did Rafael bring?
2. Where did Marta get the candy?
3. Where are Susana and Gil?
4. Why is Rafael so hungry?
5. Do you enjoy picnic lunches? Why or why not?

A. Questions with Whose

Examples	Possible Answers	Notes
Whose tent is this?	It's Hiroshi's.	*Whose* is used to ask questions about possession.
Whose canteen is that?	It's Carlos's.	
Whose farm is it?	It's Yuri's parents' farm.	
Whose canteens are these?	They're Tomoko's.	
Whose backpacks are those?	They're Ellen's and Julie's.	

Note: Use *this* to refer to an object close to you, and *that* to refer to an object not close to you. Use *these* to refer to objects close to you, and *those* for objects not close to you.

B. Possessive Nouns

		Possessive Forms	Notes
Singular Nouns	Carlos	**Carlos's** or **Carlos'** (car)	If a singular noun ends in -*s*, add '*s* or ' for the possessive form.
	Hiroshi	**Hiroshi's** (boots)	
	tomorrow	**tomorrow's** (weather)	If a singular noun does not end in -*s*, add '*s*.
	the boy	**the boy's** (pencil)	
	the student	**the student's** (book)	
	the lady	**the lady's** (ring)	
	the child	**the child's** (toy)	
	the man	**the man's** (watch)	
Plural Nouns	the boys	**the boys'** (bicycles)	If a plural noun ends in -*s*, add '.
	the students	**the students'** (tent)	If a plural noun does not end in -*s*, add '*s*.
	the ladies	**the ladies'** (coats)	
	the Smiths	**the Smiths'** (house)	
	the men	**the men's** (team)	
	the children	**the children's** (toys)	
	the people	**the people's** (choice)	

1   Circle the possessive nouns in the conversation between Marta and Rafael on page 32.

   Example: I think it's (Gil's).

2 Write questions and answers based on the pictures and the words provided, using *whose* in the questions and possessive nouns in the answers.

1. book / Ellen
    Q: *Whose book is this?*
    A: *It's Ellen's.*

2. clothes / the girls
    Q: Whose clothes is this
    A: It's the girls.

3. sandwich / Francis
    Q: Whose Sandwich is this
    A: It's Francis

4. garbage / other people
    Q: Whose garbage is this
    A: It's the other people

5. sailboat / brother
    Q: Whose Sailboat is this
    A: It's my brother.

6. backpacks / children
    Q: Whose backpacks is this
    A: It's the children.

7. bicycles / those boys

Q: _Whose bicycles is th_'s

A: _It's those boys_ .

8. sleeping bags / my parents

Q: _____?

A: _____.

3 Complete the sentences below. Use the possessive forms of the nouns in parentheses.

1. (Mr. Jones)   That's _Mr. Jones's_ canteen by the tent.

2. (today)   _Today_ weather is going to be hot and sunny.

3. (Sarah parents) _Sarah's parents_ house is on a farm in the country.

4. (women)   The _women's_ showers are over there.

5. (boyfriend)   I don't have a backpack, but you can use my _boyfriend's_.

6. (brothers)   His _brothers'_ names are John and Jeff.

7. (campers)   The _campers'_ tents are falling down in the storm.

8. (wife)   My _wife's_ brother is a forest ranger.

9. (birds)   The _birds'_ nest is high up in the tree.

10. (fishermen)   The _fishermen'_ boat is in the harbor.

Using What You've Learned

4 Each student chooses an object they have with them (such as a watch, a book, a shoe, etc.). They show the object they have selected to the class, then place it in a box or on a desk at the front of the room. After all students have done this, the instructor picks up each object and the class identifies the owner, first by asking a question with *whose,* then by giving an answer using a possessive noun. As each object is identified, it is given back to its owner, until all the objects have been returned.

Example: (*Instructor picks up a ski jacket.*)

A. Whose ski jacket is this?

B. It's Dennis's.

The Present Continuous Tense; Nonaction Verbs

Setting the Context

Conversation

Susana: This is a perfect spot. The birds are singing. The fish are jumping in the lake. It's all so peaceful.

Marta: I know what you mean. I'm so relaxed, I'm not thinking of any of my problems. Unfortunately though, the sky is turning black. We should probably get back to the campground.

Susana: I guess you're right. What are Gil and Rafael doing?

Marta: Gil is taking a nap over by that tree. Listen—he's snoring! And Rafael is collecting rocks.

Susana: Why is he doing that?

Marta: He's taking a geology class. He's learning about different kinds of rocks. I think finding interesting rocks is becoming one of his hobbies.

Susana: Oh! I think it's beginning to rain.

Marta: That's OK. We have raincoats and we're all wearing heavy, waterproof hiking boots.

(Rafael appears) Look, there's Rafael. Hi, Rafael. Perfect timing. Let's get ready to leave.

Susana: What are you looking for, Rafael?

Rafael: My backpack.
Marta: Gil is using it as a pillow.
Rafael: Is he still sleeping? Let's wake him up and head back to the campgrounds.

Discussion Questions

1. What are Susana and Marta doing?
2. What is Gil doing?
3. What is Rafael doing? Why?
4. What would you be doing if you were on this hike? Why?
5. Why are the hikers leaving Emerald Lake?

A. The Present Continuous Tense

The present continuous tense is formed with the present tense of the verb *be* + the *ing* form of a verb. This tense is used to talk about an action happening at the moment of speaking, or an action currently in progress.

Statements		
	Examples	**Notes**
Affirmative	She**'s carrying** a heavy bag. They**'re relaxing** by the lake. We**'re learning** Italian this semester. She**'s majoring** in biology.	In these examples, the action is happening at the moment of speaking. In these examples, the action is currently in progress.
Negative	Hiroshi **isn't wearing** boots. They **aren't** going on the hike. She **isn't keeping** a journal.	Form the negative by placing *not* between the form of *be* and the verb in the *-ing* form.

Yes/No Questions			
	Examples	**Possible Answers**	
		Affirmative	**Negative**
Affirmative	**Is** Carlos **carrying** her backpack? **Are** they **picking** flowers?	Yes, he is. Yes, they are.	No, he isn't. No, they aren't.
Negative	**Isn't** he **walking** on the trail? **Aren't** you **getting** tired?	Yes, he is. Yes, I am.	No, he isn't. No, I'm not.

Information Questions		
	Examples	**Possible Answers**
Affirmative	**When are** we **leaving?** **Why are** you **sneezing?**	We're leaving at noon. I'm getting a cold.
Negative	**Who isn't carrying** a canteen? **Why aren't** they **wearing** shoes?	Anita and Paul aren't. Their feet are hurting them.

Spelling Rules for -ing Verbs

1. If the simple form of the verb ends in a silent -e after a consonant, drop the -e and add -ing.
    Examples: have/having   sneeze/sneezing

2. If the simple form of the verb ends in -ie, change the -ie to y and add -ing.
    Examples: die/dying   untie/untying

3. If the simple form of the verb has one syllable and ends in one consonant following one vowel, double the last consonant and add -ing. **Exception:** If the last consonant is an x or a w, do not double the consonant. **Note:** The letter y at the end of a word is considered a vowel.
    Examples: get/getting   run/running   box/boxing   row/rowing   play/playing

4. If the simple form of the verb ends in an accented (stressed) syllable, follow the rule above for one final consonant after one vowel.
    Example: begín/beginning
    Note: If the last syllable is not accented, just and -ing.
    Example: háppen/happening

5. For all other verbs, add -ing to the simple form.
    Examples: walk/walking   eat/eating   carry/carrying

---

1 Underline the present continuous verb phrases in the conversation between Marta, Susana, and Rafael on pages 36 and 37.

Example: The birds <u>are singing</u>.

2 Fill in the blanks with the present continuous forms of the verbs in parentheses.

Paul: Ah-choo! Ah-choo!

Anita: Paul! Why ____are____ you ____sneezing____?
1 (sneeze)

____because____ you ____getting____ sick?
2 (get)

Paul: Maybe. The water in the river is really cold.

Anita: You ____are____ ____shivering____. Why
3 (shiver)

____are____ you ____not wear____ a shirt and pants?
4 (not wear)

Paul: You're right. I ____am____ ____freezing____.
5 (freeze)

Anita: Where's my book? Oh no! Is that it there in the water? It _____ ____floating____ down the river.
6 (float)

Paul: Ow! (*He hits his back.*)

Anita: What's the matter?

Paul: I think something ____is____ ____biting____ me.
7 (bite)

Anita: Let me see. Oh, Paul! There are ants all over your back!

Paul: Anita, look. The hikers ____are____ ____coming____ back.
<u>8 (come)</u>

Anita: Where? I don't see them.

Paul: They ____are____ ____walking____ down the trail.
<u>9 (walk)</u>

Anita: Oh, yeah. Now I see them. But they ____are____ ____not walking____. They ____are____
<u>10 (not walk)</u>

____running____. I wonder why.
<u>11 (run)</u>

Paul: I don't know.

Anita: There ____i's____ something ____chasing____
<u>12 (chasing)</u>

them. What is that? Is that a deer?

Paul: No, it's a *bear*! They ____are____ ____running____ away from a bear!
<u>13 (run)</u>

3 Describe what is happening in each picture. Write two sentences for each picture using the words provided and the present continuous tense.

1.

- ■ Susana / give / her backpack / to Rafael
- ■ Her back / hurt

Susana is giving her backpack to Rafael.
Her back is hurting.

2.

- ■ Paul / get dressed
- ■ Ants / bite him

Paul is getting dressed
Ants is bite him

3.
- ■ The tents / fall down
- ■ Anita / fix them

The tents is falling down.
Anita is fixing them.

4.
- ■ Susana / make lunch
- ■ The hamburgers / burn

Susana is making lunch.
The hamburgers is burning.

5.
- ■ Marta / sit on a rock
- ■ A snake / come toward her

Marta is sitting on a rock.
A snake is coming toward

6.
- ■ Gil / throw his boots in the river
- ■ They / float away

Gil is throwing his boots in the
They are floating away.

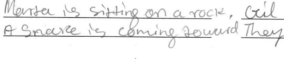

7.
- ■ Rafael / make noise
- ■ The bear / run away

Rafael is making noise.
The bear is running away.

8.
- ■ Marta and Rafael / have lunch
- ■ They eat / apples

Marta and Rafael are having
They are eating apples

4   Look at the pictures with a partner. Student A asks present continuous questions with the cue words provided. Student B answers the questions.

Example: Who / run / with no backpack?

    A.   *Who is running with no backpack?*
    B.   *Susana is running with no backpack.*

1.   the sky / get cloudy?   *The sky is getting cloudy.*
2.   Who / sleep?   *Who is sleeping.*
3.   What / the bear / do?   *What the bear doing.*
4.   What / Paul / wear?   *What is Paul wearing.*
5.   the hikers / have trouble?   *The hikers having trouble.*
6.   What / the deer / do?   *What*
7.   What / happen / to the tents?   *what happening to the tents.*
8.   What / Gil / do?   *what gil doing.*

Change roles. Now Student B asks present continuous questions with the new cue words, and Student A answers.

9. the weather / change?
10. What / the hikers / do?
11. Who / carry / an extra backpack?
12. What / Paul / do?
13. anyone / swim?
14. What / happen / Anita's book?
15. Why / Gil / carry / the boots?
16. What / Anita / do?

B. Nonaction Verbs

Some verbs are not normally used in the continuous tense and usually have only one present tense—the simple present. These verbs include verbs that express feeling and thought, verbs that express possession, and verbs that express sensory perception. There are some very specific cases in which some of these verbs can be used in the continuous form.

Verbs that Express Feeling or Thought			
Verbs			**Examples**
appear	know	recognize	I **know** his telephone number. (NOT: I am knowing his telephone number.)
appreciate	like	remember	
be	love	seem	She **needs** a new jacket. (NOT: She is needing a new jacket.)
believe	mean	suppose	**Do** you **recognize** me? (NOT: Are you recognizing me?)
dislike	need	understand	**What do** you **mean?** (NOT: What are you meaning?)
hate	prefer	want	

Verbs that Express Possession	
Verbs	**Examples**
belong to	Akeno **owns** a house. (NOT: Akeno is owning a house.)
have	**Do** you **have** a car? (NOT: Are you having a car?)
owe	Who **does** this cat **belong** to? (NOT: Who is this cat belonging to?)
own	
possess	

Verbs that Express Sensory Perception	
Verbs	**Examples**
feel see	The pizza **smells** good. (NOT: The pizza is smelling good.)
hear smell	Do you **hear** that noise? (NOT: Are you hearing that noise?)
look taste	They **see** a tree outside their window. (NOT: They are seeing a tree outside their window.)

5   Circle the correct verb or verb phrase in each set of parentheses.

Susana: There are so many stars out! (Are you recognizing / (Do you recognize)) any

constellations?

Marta: Well, I (am thinking/think) that's the Big Dipper.

Susana: Hey, I think I (am seeing/see) a shooting star!

Marta: Oh yes! I (am seeing/see) it too!

Susana: What's that noise?

Marta: I (am not hearing/don't hear) anything.
5

Susana: You (aren't listening/don't listen) closely.
6

Marta: Oh, that noise. That's just Gil (snoring/snore).
7

Susana: No, that's not what I (am meaning/mean). There's another noise. It
8

(is sounding/sounds) like someone speaking.
9

Marta: You're right. I (am thinking/think) Rafael (is talking/talks) in his sleep.
10   11

Susana: I (am wondering/wonder) what he (is dreaming/dreams) about.
12   13

Marta: Probably about being home in his own bed! I'm tired. And we (are having/have)
14

a big day tomorrow. Let's go to sleep.

Susana: OK. Good night!

Using What You've Learned

6   Take turns choosing one item from each list. Pretend you are in that place at that time. Imagine the activities of the people there and use the present continuous tense to describe them to your partner until he or she is able to guess the place and the time.

Example: A.   There are many people here. People are swimming. One man is fishing. Children are playing in the sand.

B.   You're at the beach in summer.

Places	Times
in the mountains	in winter
in the desert	in summer
on a river	in spring
at the beach	in fall
at a lake	
at a park	
in a forest	

7   Take turns choosing one item from each list in Activity 6. This time use nonactive sensory verbs (*see, smell, taste, feel,* and *hear*) to describe the place to your partner, until he or she is able to guess the place.

Example: A.   I hear seagulls. I taste salt air. I feel cold wind.

B.   You're on the beach in the winter.

| **PART 4** | # Modal Verbs: *can, may, might, will* |

Setting the Context

Conversation

Susana: I can't believe it's already time to go home. I'll have great memories of this trip, won't you?
Rafael and *Marta:* Yes!
Susana: What's the first thing you'll do when you get home?
Rafael: I'll take a good, long, hot shower.
Marta: I might take a nap.
Gil: I may order a pizza.
Marta: Don't you want to have a homemade meal?
Gil: Sure, but I can't cook.
Marta: I can. I think I'll make a huge pasta dinner when I get home.
Gil: Sounds delicious. And big. Can you eat it all on your own?
Marta: Probably. But you're welcome to come over and join me if you want.
Gil: I think I may do that!
Rafael: It looks like it might rain again.
Gil: I can't believe it.
Rafael: It'll stop soon.

Susana: Can we do this again next weekend?

Gil: You can. Next weekend I'll be home on my couch, watching TV, and eating junk food!

Discussion Questions

1. What will Rafael do when he gets home?
2. What might Marta do?
3. What might Gil do?
4. Who wants to go hiking next weekend?
5. How do you think each person feels about the hiking trip? Explain your answer.

A. Forms and Patterns

Can, may, might, and *will* are all modal auxiliaries. These are special verb forms. Modals do not change forms; they do not take *-s* or *-ed*. Modals are followed immediately by the simple form of a verb. The following charts show the position of modals in statements and questions.

Statements		
	Examples	**Notes**
Affirmative	I **can** swim. The rain **may** stop soon. The tents **might** fall down. We **will** call you tonight.	In statements, modals come before the simple form of a verb. Don't use *to* before the verb. *Will* is the only one of these modals that can appear as a contraction. The contractions with *will* are: *I will = I'll; he will = he'll; she will = she'll; we will = we'll; you will = you'll; they will = they'll*
Negative	I **cannot** find my watch. We **may not** need the compass. I **might not** come back. He **will not** go with us.	*May not* and *might not* cannot appear as a contraction. The contraction for *cannot* is *can't;* the contraction for *will not* is *won't.*

Yes/No Questions				
	Examples	**Possible Answers**		**Notes**
		Affirmative	**Negative**	
Affirmative	**Can** you go with us? **Might** it rain tonight? **Will** we get there late?	Yes, I **can.** Yes, it **might.** Yes, we **will.**	No, I **can't.** No, it **won't.** No, we **won't.**	In yes/no questions, modals come before the subject.
Negative	**Can't** the children swim? **Won't** it be hot in August?	Yes, they **can.** Yes, it **will.**	No, they **can't.** No, it **won't.**	

Information Questions			
	Examples	**Possible Answers**	**Notes**
Affirmative	What **can** we do?	We **can** run to that tree.	In information questions, modals come after the question word.
	Who **may** visit us?	Carlos **may** visit us.	
	What **might** happen?	You **might** get sick.	
	Where **will** they go?	They**'ll** stay home.	
Negative	What **can't** he eat?	He **can't** eat meat.	
	Who **may not** play?	Hiroshi **may not** play.	
	Who **might not** go?	Ellen and Julie **might not** go.	
	Why **won't** Anita visit?	She **won't** visit because she's too busy.	

B. Meanings

Each modal has more than one meaning or use. The following chart gives examples of the meanings of *can, may, might,* and *will* in this chapter.

Modals	**Meaning**	**Examples**
can	ability	I **can** speak English. (I am able to speak English.)
		He **can't** swim. (He isn't able to swim.)
		Can you dance? (Are you able to dance?)
may **might**	future possibility	It **may** rain. (Maybe it will rain; maybe it won't.)
		I **might** not go. (Maybe I won't go; maybe I will.)
will	future plans predictions	I**'ll** see you tomorrow. (I plan to see you tomorrow.)
		The movie **won't** be crowded. (I predict the movie won't be crowded.)
		Will you buy a tent? (Do you plan to buy a tent?)

1   Underline the modals in the conversation between Susana, Rafael, Marta, and Gil on pages 45 and 46. Identify whether the modals in each sentence or question refer to *ability, future possibility, future plans,* or *prediction.*

Example: I can't believe it's already time to go home. = ability

2   Put the following words into the correct order to form sentences or questions, depending on the punctuation given.

Example: (friend go to a tonight movie with my I may) *I may go to a movie with my friend tonight* .

1.   (you matches a fire can't start without) _____ .
2.   (my mother tomorrow cake favorite bake will my) _____ .

3.   (understand you accent can't my) _____ ?

4.   (study me my you help will for test) _____ ?

5.   (come she us the on hike might with) _____ .

6.   (not me give she her sleeping bag will) _____ .

7.   (you can't awake stay longer) _____ ?

8.   (they won't help us why) _____ ?

9.   (lunch when we can have) _____ ?

10.   (tonight will he where sleep) _____ ?

3   Circle the correct words in each set of parentheses.

There are some clouds, but it (willn't rain / won't rain) today. At least I don't think it
(will rain / will rains). It (can be / will be) a beautiful day. I (might to catch / might catch)
¹   ²   ³   ⁴
some fish. They (can might be / might be) big fish. Uh-oh. There's water coming into
⁵
the boat. There (might be / will to be) a leak. I (not / can't) (see / to see) the bottom of
⁶   ⁷   ⁸
the boat under all the water. Help! Help! What's that noise? It ('ll / might) (is / be) a wa-
⁹   ¹⁰
terfall. Oh, no! It *is* a waterfall! Well, I (mayn't / may not) (will save / save) the boat, but
¹¹   ¹²
I (can / 'll) be able to save my life. I (can / can't) (swim / to swim)!
¹³   ¹⁴   ¹⁵

Using What You've Learned

4 Have a conversation about what you *can* or *can't* do. Start with the following activities, then add other activities to your discussion.

swim	read maps
ride a horse	use a compass
sail a boat	set up a tent

Example: A. I can swim. Can you?

B. Yes, I can. But I can't swim very well. How long can you tread water?

A. I can stay afloat about 15 minutes.

5 Have a conversation about what you *will, may,* and *might* do next weekend. Start with the following activities, then add other activities to your discussion.

go to the park	sleep late
cook	read the paper
study	rent a movie

Example: A. Will you go to the park next weekend?

B. I may.

A. Who might you go with?

B. I may go with my sister. But if it rains, I'll do my laundry instead.

6 Work in small groups. Take turns making statements with modals about each of the following situations. Tell what *may, may not, might, might not, can, can't, will,* or *will not* happen in each situation. Try to come up with as many ideas as possible.

Example: You are driving on an icy mountain road. You go around a curve in the road. A deer suddenly jumps out in front of your car. What might happen?

A. I will hit the deer.

B. I might have an accident.

C. The car might slide on the ice.

D. I will try to stop.

1. You are standing under a big tree. It's raining hard and there is thunder and lightning.
2. You and your friends return to your campground late in the evening after a long hike. There is a bear eating your food.
3. Some campers want to start a fire for dinner. Their matches are wet from the rain last night.
4. Some students are hiking on a new trail. It's almost dark and they're lost.

Video Activities: Winter Storm

Before You Watch.

1. The following places are mentioned in the video. Find them on a map of the United States before you watch: Washington, D.C; New York; Ohio; New England; North Carolina.

2. Work in a group. Make a list of words to describe winter weather in a cold climate.

 Examples: snow   icy   freezing

Watch.

1. This video mainly shows a storm in the _____ part of the U.S.
 a. southern
 b. western
 c. northern
 d. eastern

2. Which of the following words describe the weather conditions you saw in the video?

 snow   fair   storm   rain   icy   freezing   wind   warm   humid

Watch Again.   Match the places on the left with the weather conditions on the right.

Place	Weather conditions
_____ 1. Washington, D.C.	a. 12 inches of snow are expected
_____ 2. New York City	b. drivers of salt trucks and snow plows didn't go to work
_____ 3. New England	c. 5 inches of snow are expected
_____ 4. North Carolina	d. 6 inches of snow fell
_____ 5. Long Island	e. slush

After You Watch.   Play a game called Freeze Frame. One student holds the television remote control. The class begins watching the video again. At one point the student with the remote "freezes" the video on one scene. The class should make sentences describing the scene. Use the present continuous tense to describe actions. Use the simple present tense to describe states.

 Example: The children *are throwing* snowballs. It *looks* cold.

Chapter 3

Living to Eat or Eating to Live?

PART 1

Nouns and Expressions of Quantity

Setting the Context

The Changing American Diet

What are some examples of "typical" American meals? On the weekend, a typical breakfast may consist of two or three eggs, some pancakes with butter and syrup, and a few pieces of bacon. During the week, some people have only toast or a sweet roll and some juice or coffee for breakfast. Or they might eat a bowl of cold cereal with some milk. For lunch, many people eat junk food. For example, they   5 may stop at a fast-food place for a cheeseburger or a hot dog with a little ketchup or mustard and some relish, some french fries, a milkshake or a soft drink, and a few cookies. A typical American dinner consists of meat, a baked potato, and some bread and butter. Dinner often ends with dessert—typically, cake or pie and ice cream.   10

Nutritionists don't believe that the typical American diet is very healthy. Many kinds of American food are high in sugar, salt, fat, caffeine, or cholesterol. These food substances may cause disease. In general, Americans don't eat much whole-grain food, fish, vegetables, and fruit, which contain important vitamins, protein, and fiber.   15

However, some Americans are becoming more interested in good health, and they are changing their eating habits. They are eating more whole-grain bread and cereal, and less white bread and sugared cereal. They are eating more chicken and fish, and less red meat. Many people are eating more fresh vegetables, and fewer frozen or canned vegetables. They are drinking less coffee and   20 soda, and more decaffeinated coffee, herbal tea, and fruit juice.

Discussion Questions

1. What does a "typical" American breakfast consist of?
2. What might an American have for lunch at a fast-food place?
3. Describe a "typical" American dinner.
4. How are some Americans changing their eating habits? What kinds of food are they eating?
5. How does your diet compare with the "typical" American diet?

A. Count and Noncount Nouns

There are two basic types of nouns—count nouns and noncount nouns. Count nouns are things you can count, such as books and pens. Noncount nouns are things you can't count, such as paper and ink.

	Examples		Notes
	Singular	**Plural**	
Count Nouns	a **meal** an **egg** one **waiter** a **chair** one **restaurant**	three **meals** some **eggs** **waiters** some **chairs** **restaurants**	Count nouns have both singular and plural forms. Singular count nouns can have *a/an* before them; most plural count nouns take an *-s/-es* ending.
Noncount Nouns	**butter** some **juice** **electricity** **salt** some **jewelry** **traffic** **freedom** **anger** some **luck**		Noncount nouns are always singular and have no plural form; they do not take *-s* or *-es* endings. Most noncount nouns refer to a whole that is made up of smaller or different parts. Some noncount nouns describe abstract things, such as ideas, feelings, and concepts.

1 Underline the singular count nouns in the reading on pages 52 and 53. Put two lines under the plural nouns. Circle the noncount nouns.

Example: What are some examples of "typical" American meals? On the weekend, a typical breakfast may consist of two or three eggs, some pancakes with (butter) and (syrup), and a few pieces of (bacon).

2 Take turns describing the pictures on pages 52 and 53. Student A describes pictures 1 and 2; Student B describes pictures 3 and 4. Make sentences beginning with *there is / there are* and using noncount nouns and singular and plural count nouns.

Example: *Student A.* There are two plates in the first picture. On one plate, there are two eggs and some bacon.

3 Look around the classroom. For five minutes, write as many sentences as you can about the different count and noncount nouns you see around you.

Example: *There's a clock on the wall. There are books on the shelf. There's some paper on the teacher's desk.*

When you finish, compare your sentences with a classmate. How many similar things did you and your classmate notice? How many different things did you notice?

B. Some *and* Any

Some and *any* refer to an unspecified number or amount. *Some* and *any* may appear before both count and noncount nouns.

	Examples	**Notes**
Some	Please buy **some** napkins. There's **some** milk in that cup. Do you have **some** shopping bags? Would you like **some** spaghetti?	*Some* expresses an indefinite amount. *Some* is used in affirmative statements and questions.
Any	There aren't **any** plates on the table. I don't use **any** salt. Do you have **any** pots in your kitchen? Isn't there **any** fish?	*Any* is used in negative statements and in affirmative and negative questions.

Note: Not any before noncount and plural count nouns means *no*. For example: *There aren't any hot dogs.* = *There are no hot dogs.*

4   Fill in each blank in the following sentences with *some* or *any*. In some cases, either answer may be correct.

1. Mary always eats ___*some*___ fruit for breakfast.
2. I'm going to the supermarket. Do we need ___*any*___ bread?
3. I need to buy ___*some*___ food; I don't have ___*any*___ fruit or vegetables.
4. I want ___*some*___ coffee, but there isn't ___*any*___ decaffeinated coffee left.
5. Are there ___*any*___ supermarkets near your apartment?
6. Taro doesn't have ___*any*___ experience as a cook.
7. I don't have ___*some*___ money to pay the bill.
8. I have ___*some*___ sharp knives in my kitchen.
9. I'd like ___*any*___ onions and ___*some*___ mushrooms on my pizza.
10. John doesn't eat ___*any*___ red meat, but he occasionally eats ___*some*___ fish.
11. There are ___*any*___ great Italian restaurants near here.
12. I don't want ___*some*___ ice cream, but I'd like to try ___*any*___ frozen yogurt.
13. There doesn't seem to be ___*some*___ waiters in the restaurant.
14. I'd like ___*some*___ eggs, but I don't want ___*any*___ bacon.
15. I'm full. I can't eat ___*some*___ more food.

5   Take turns asking and answering questions about the food in the pictures on pages 52 and 53. Use *some* or *any* in your questions and answers.

> **Example:**   A.   Is there any juice in the breakfast picture?
>   B.   There isn't any juice, but there is some coffee.

6   Describe your favorite ice cream sundae. Your description should include the ice cream flavors and toppings you like. Write sentences using *some* or *any*.

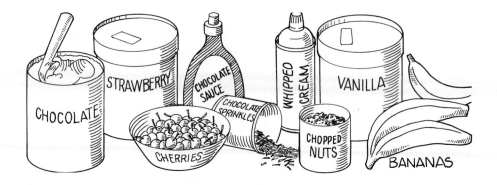

Example: My sundae has some vanilla and chocolate ice cream, but it doesn't have any strawberry ice cream. It has some nuts and some whipped cream.

C. A lot of / Many / Much

A lot of, many, and *much* are used to express a large quantity of something. *A lot of* may appear before both noncount and plural count nouns. *Many* may appear only before plural count nouns. *Much* may appear only before noncount nouns.

	Examples	**Notes**
A lot of	She doesn't eat **a lot of** hamburgers. There is **a lot of** salt in this soup. Is there **a lot of** fresh bread at the bakery? Don't you eat **a lot of** apples?	*A lot of* is used in affirmative and negative statements and questions.
Many	**Many** fast-food restaurants serve hamburgers. I don't like **many** kinds of vegetables. Do **many** people have a poor diet? Aren't there **many** eggs in the refrigerator?	*Many* is used in affirmative and negative statements and questions.
Much	They don't eat **much** red meat. We don't drink **much** tea or coffee. Does chicken have **much** cholesterol? Don't they eat **much** fish?	*Much* is used mainly in negative statements and affirmative and negative questions. *Much* usually isn't used in affirmative statements.

7   Write one question and one answer about each picture, using *a lot of, many,* or *much.*

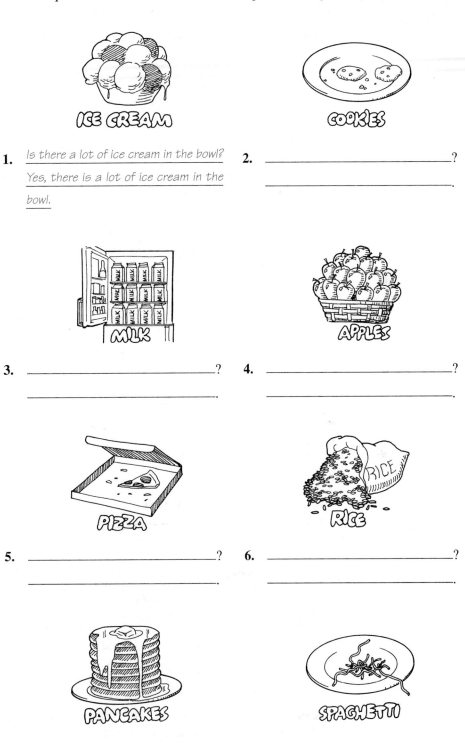

1. _Is there a lot of ice cream in the bowl?_
    Yes, there is a lot of ice cream in the
    bowl.

2. _____?
    _____.

3. _____?
    _____.

4. _____?
    _____.

5. _____?
    _____.

6. _____?
    _____.

7. _____?
    _____.

8. _____?
    _____.

9. _____? 10. _____?

_____. _____.

11. _____? 12. _____?

_____. _____.

D. Common Units of Measure

Units of measure can be used to give specific amounts of either count or noncount nouns. Note that these units make noncount nouns countable. *Of* follows all of the following expressions, except *dozen*.

bag	sugar, potatoes, flour
bar	chocolate, hand soap
bottle	detergent, ketchup, soda
box	cereal, detergent, tissues
bunch	bananas, grapes, flowers
can	soup, beans, soda
carton	eggs, milk
cup, tablespoon, teaspoon	all liquid and dry recipe ingredients
dozen	eggs, bakery products, fruit and vegetables
gallon, quart, pint	all liquids, ice cream
head	cabbage, cauliflower, lettuce
jar	mayonnaise, jam, peanut butter
loaf	bread
package	cookies, potato chips, spaghetti
piece	cake, bread, meat
pound, ounce	meat, fruit and vegetables, cheese
roll	paper towels, toilet paper
stick	butter, gum
tube	toothpaste

8   Identify the quantity of each grocery store item shown below by unit of measure.

1. _____two bottles_____ of soda
2. _____One box_____ of milk
3. _____two boxes_____ of toothpaste
4. _____One bottle_____ of butter
5. _____one ball_____ of lettuce
6. _____one battle_____ of peanut butter
7. _____one battle_____ of jam
8. _____three boxes_____ of hand soap
9. _____One_____ of flour
10. _____ of flowers

9   Make a shopping list of all the items you need to buy the next time you go shopping. Make sure you include a unit of measurement for each item.

Example: *a pound of ham*
               a bottle of olive oil

two bottles of soda
a dozen eggs
two bags of onions

E. Asking Questions with How many *and* How much

How many is used in questions before plural count nouns. *How much* is used in questions before noncount nouns.

	Examples	Possible Answers
How many	*How many* eggs do you want?	two
	How many cakes are you making?	only one
	How many vegetables do you have?	three
How much	*How much* coffee does he drink?	three cups
	How much rice do we need?	ten pounds
	How much pizza can you eat?	two slices

Note: If a unit of measurement is used with a noncount noun, *how many* should be used. For example: *How much coffee does he drink?* can also be expressed as *How many cups of coffee does he drink?*

 **10**   Take turns asking and answering questions about the pictures on pages 57 and 58. Use *how many* or *how much* in your questions.

Example: A.   How much ice cream is in the bowl?
               B.   There's a lot of ice cream. How many cookies are on the plate?
               A.   There are two cookies on the plate. (*or* There aren't many.)

F. A few / A little

A few and *a little* are used to express a small quantity of something. *A few* appears only before plural count nouns. *A little* appears only before noncount nouns.

	Examples	Notes
A few	There are **a few** olives in the jar.	
	Would you like **a few** potatoes?	*A few* and *a little* are used in
	Aren't there **a few** cookies in the box?	affirmative statements and in
A little	I'd like **a little** tomato sauce on my pasta.	affirmative and negative questions.
	Is there **a little** sugar in that bowl?	
	Don't you want **a little** milk in your tea?	

11　Fill in each blank with *a few* or *a little*.

1. I put _____*a little*_____ sugar in my tea.

2. They need _____*a few*_____ pots and pans to cook the dinner.

3. Can you get me _____*a few*_____ apples and _____ orange juice?

4. I'd like _____*a few*_____ napkins, please.

5. Does your brother want _____*a few*_____ pieces of bacon with his eggs?

6. Would you like _____*a little*_____ soup?

7. There are _____*a few*_____ forks, but there aren't any spoons.

8. They're having _____*a few*_____ cups of coffee with their dessert.

9. I like to eat lunch with _____*a few*_____ friends.

10. He needs _____*a few*_____ ice cubes for his soda.

Using What You've Learned

12　The class divides into two groups: group A and group B. Each member of each group writes a unit of measure on one piece of paper and a noun that is used with this unit of measure on another piece of paper. Group A and group B exchange their pieces of paper. Each group works together to match all of the nouns with the appropriate units of measurement. The first group to match up all of the pieces of paper correctly is the winning group.

13　Think of a restaurant or café that you know well. Write a paragraph describing the kinds of food you can order there. (If possible, get a menu from the restaurant or café you have chosen to help give you ideas.) Use count and noncount nouns and expressions of quantity.

Example: *Pongsri is a good Thai restaurant. You can order a lot of delicious Thai food there. They have many chicken, beef, and pork dishes. Many dishes come with rice or noodles. They also serve a lot of fish and other seafood. They have a few salads and some soup.*

When you finish, work with a classmate to read and discuss each other's descriptions. Are the count and noncount nouns used with the right quantity expressions? Would you want to go to your partner's restaurant? Why or why not? Work with your class to make a restaurant guide by collecting, copying, and putting together all the students' paragraphs.

14　Take turns interviewing each other about what you eat in a typical day. The interviewer should ask as may questions with *how many* and *how much* as possible. The person being interviewed should use as many count and noncount nouns and expressions of quantity as possible. Take notes as you interview your partner.

Example: Student A.   *How many meals do you eat a day?*
Student B.   *I usually eat three meals a day. I also usually have a little snack between lunch and dinner. Maybe just a few nuts or a little yogurt.*

When you are finished interviewing each other, use the notes you took while interviewing your partner to tell the class about what your partner eats in a typical day.

PART 2   Comparisons

Setting the Context

Conversation

Dolores: Diane! Hello, there!
Diane: Oh, hello, Dolores.
Dolores: My goodness! You certainly have a lot of things in your cart!
Diane: Yes, well, you know we have five children.
Dolores: Are you buying Pearly White Dishwashing Liquid? There are cheaper brands.

Diane: It's more expensive than other brands, but I think it lasts longer.

Dolores: Why are you buying that huge package of spaghetti? There are smaller sizes . . .

Diane: The larger size is always cheaper. Well, nice seeing you again . . .

Dolores: Those cherries look nicer than the strawberries in my cart! May I taste one? (*She takes a cherry.*) Oh, my. They're much tastier than the cherries last year.

Diane: Dolores, I have to get home as soon as possible.

Dolores: Do you really like brown rice better than white rice? It cooks more slowly.

Diane: Brown rice tastes just as good as white rice, and it's more nutritious.

Dolores: You know, the sign says this market is cheaper, but I think it's just as expensive as the others. It's farther too. What do you think?

Diane: I think one market is as good as any other. Well, I'll let you go now, Dolores. I know you're as busy as I am.

Discussion Questions

1.   What is Dolores asking Diane questions about?
2.   Why does Diane buy Pearly White Dishwashing Liquid?
3.   Why does Diane buy the larger size package of spaghetti?
4.   What does Dolores think about the cherries in Diane's cart?
5.   Why does Diane buy brown rice?
6.   What do Dolores and Diane think about Save-A-Lot Market?
7.   Is Diane enjoying the conversation? How do you know?

A. Comparisons with As . . . as and Less . . . than

Use the phrase *as* + adjective or adverb + *as* to compare two or more people or things in affirmative and negative statements and questions. You can also use the pattern *less* + adjective or adverb + *than* in some negative comparisons.

	Examples	**Notes**
As . . . as **Affirmative Statements and Questions**	This market is **as expensive as** the others. You're **as busy as** I am. Are the cherries **as nice as** the strawberries?	Affirmative sentences compare things that are the same in some way.
As . . . as **Negative Statements and Questions**	White rice **isn't as nutritious** (**as** brown rice). Brown rice **doesn't cook as quickly** (**as** white rice). Aren't the cherries **as good as** (the cherries) last year?	Negative sentences compare things that are different in some way. You can leave out the words in parentheses if they are understood.
Less . . . than **Negative Statements**	White rice is **less nutritious** (**than** brown rice). Brown rice cooks **less quickly** (**than** white rice).	You can use *less* with many adjectives that have two or more syllables; *less* is usually not used with one-syllable adjectives

1   Underline the phrases with *as . . . as* in the conversation between Diane and Dolores on pages 62 and 63.

2   Compare the items below. Write an affirmative or negative sentence using *as . . . as* and the adjectives under each picture. When possible, write a second sentence using *less . . . than.*

1. expensive

Pie is as expensive as cake.

_____

_____

2. cheap

Milk isn't as expensive as cream.

Milk is less expensive than cream.

_____

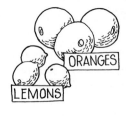

3. delicious

_____

_____

4. sweet

_____

_____

5. nutritious

_____

_____

6. cook quickly

_____

_____

7. healthy

_____

_____

8. fresh

_____

_____

B. Comparisons with . . . -er than and More . . . than

Use the pattern adjective or adverb + *-er than* or *more* + adjective or adverb + *than* to compare two or more people or things that are different.

	Examples	Notes
One-Syllable Adjectives and Adverbs	These cherries are **sweeter than** those. This market is **cheaper than** the others. Brown rice cooks **slower than** white rice. These eggs are **bigger than** those.	Add *-er* to most one-syllable adjectives and adverbs. If a word ends in one vowel and one consonant, double the last consonant and add *-er.*
Two-Syllable Adjectives Ending in -y	This fish is **tastier than** that fish. Thai food is **spicier than** American food. Fruit is **healthier than** ice cream.	If a word ends in *-y*, change the *y* to *i* and add *-er.*
Adjectives and Adverbs with Two or More Syllables	It's **more expensive than** the other brands. It's **more nutritious than** white rice. Fresh vegetables are **more delicious than** frozen ones.	Use *more* with most adjectives and adverbs that have two or more syllables.
Irregular Forms	Cream tastes **better than** milk. Coffee is **worse** for your health **than** tea. The health food store is **farther (or further) than** the supermarket.	The comparative forms of *good, bad,* and *far* are irregular: *good/better* *bad/worse* *far/farther (further)*

3   Circle the comparisons with *-er than* and *more . . . than* and the irregular comparatives in the conversation between Diane and Dolores on pages 62 and 63.

4   Take turns comparing the pairs of food items in each picture. You may want to use words from the following list, as well as words of your own. Make as many sentences as you can for each picture using *as . . . as, less . . . than, -er than,* or *more . . . than.*

expensive	tasty	spicy
healthy	(taste) good	easy (to make)
delicious	(taste) bad	(cook) fast
nutritious	sweet	

Examples: A.   Ice cream isn't as healthy as frozen yogurt.

               B.   Ice cream tastes better than frozen yogurt.

               A.   Ice cream is sweeter than frozen yogurt.

               B.   Ice cream is as expensive as frozen yogurt.

               A.   I don't think that's true. I think frozen yogurt is more expensive.

1.    2.

3.    4.

5.    6.

7.    8.

9.    10.

Compare food from two countries.

C. More Comparisons: as much / as many . . . as and more / less / fewer . . . than

Use *as much / as many . . . as* and *more / less / fewer . . . than* to compare numbers or amounts of count or noncount nouns.

Examples	Notes
Does frozen yogurt have **as many calories as** ice cream?	Use *as many . . . as* with plural count nouns.
Fruit juice doesn't have **as much sugar as** soda.	Use *as much . . . as* with noncount nouns.
I eat **more apples than** oranges. She drinks **more tea than** coffee.	Use *more* before plural count and noncount nouns.
There is **less sugar than** salt in this sauce.	Use *less* only before noncount nouns.
Canned food has **fewer vitamins than** frozen food.	Use *fewer* only before plural count nouns.

5 Compare the food items in the pictures. Use the words under the pictures to make sentences with *as much / as many . . . as* or *more / less / fewer . . . than.*

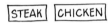

   steak / chicken / market

1. <u>*There's more steak than chicken at the market.*</u>
   <u>*There's less chicken than steak at the market.*</u>

 a chocolate bar / an apple / calories

2. _____

   _____

 peaches / bananas / basket

3. _____

   _____

fish / meat / fat

4. _____

_____

milk / cream / refrigerator

5. _____

_____

fresh carrots / frozen carrots / vitamins

6. _____

_____

6   Read the recipes for brownies from two different cookbooks. Write sentences comparing the ingredients in the two recipes.

Example: _The first recipe uses more chocolate than the second. The first recipe uses as much butter as the second._

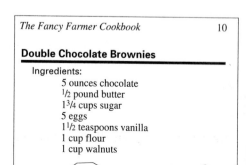

The Fancy Farmer Cookbook	10

Double Chocolate Brownies

Ingredients:
  5 ounces chocolate
  $1/2$ pound butter
  $1^3/4$ cups sugar
  5 eggs
  $1^1/2$ teaspoons vanilla
  1 cup flour
  1 cup walnuts

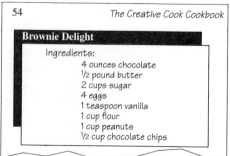

54	The Creative Cook Cookbook

Brownie Delight

Ingredients:
  4 ounces chocolate
  $1/2$ pound butter
  2 cups sugar
  4 eggs
  1 teaspoon vanilla
  1 cup flour
  1 cup peanuts
  $1/2$ cup chocolate chips

Using What You've Learned

7   For ten minutes, write about your eating habits. You can write about what kinds of food you typically eat, where you eat most of your meals, and with whom you eat your meals.

Example: *I eat a lot of beef, chicken, beans, and rice. I like a lot of spices in my food, so I often cook with spices like chili peppers, garlic, onions, and cilantro. Most of the time I eat at home with my roommate. I'm a good cook, so I usually do the cooking. Occasionally I go out to dinner with friends. But I never eat in expensive restaurants.*

When you finish writing, exchange your work with a partner and read about your partner's eating habits. Then, use what you have learned about your partner's eating habits to discuss the similarities and differences between your eating habits. Be sure to use comparative terms in this discussion.

Example: A.   You like spicier foods than I do. I eat foods with fewer hot ingredients.
   B.   But you are as good a cook as I am. You just cook with fewer spices.
   A.   I think you make more exotic dishes than I do.

8   With your partner, choose one of the food dishes from the following list, or another dish that you both know how to make. Separately, make a list of the ingredients from your favorite recipe for that dish.

an omelette	cookies
a fish dish	a kind of soup
pancakes	another kind of dessert
a cake	a meat dish
spaghetti	a vegetable dish

When you finish, compare your lists of ingredients. Make sentences comparing your recipes.

Example recipes:

Alfredo's omelette

1.   *2 eggs*
2.   *1/2 cup grated cheese*
3.   *1 chopped sausage*
4.   *1 small onion, chopped*
5.   *1 clove chopped garlic*
6.   *1 teaspoon chili sauce*

Maria's omelette

1.   *3 eggs*
2.   *3/4 cup grated cheese*
3.   *6 sliced mushrooms*
4.   *1/2 green pepper, chopped*

Example sentences:

Maria: My recipe has more eggs than yours. Your omelette has more ingredients than mine.
Alfredo: My omelette is spicier than yours.

Modal Verbs: Requests, Offers, and Permission

Setting the Context

Conversation

Waiter: Good evening. May I take your order?
Woman: Could we see a menu first?
Waiter: Of course. (*The waiter gives them menus.*)
Man: I'd like the swordfish, please.
Waiter: I'm afraid we're out of the swordfish.
Man: All right. Then I'll have the sea bass.
Waiter: Sorry, we just ran out of that.
Man: The mackerel?
Waiter: None left.
Man: Well, would you tell us what you *do* have?
Waiter: May I suggest the salmon. It's excellent.
Man: (*sigh*) All right.
Waiter: Madame?
Woman: I suppose I'll have the salmon too.
Waiter: Excellent!
Man: I just realized I don't have cash with me. Can we pay with a credit card?
Waiter: No, I'm sorry. You can't. We only accept cash.
Man: Uh-oh. We may have to leave then.
Woman: Before we do, can you tell me where the women's room is?
Waiter: I'm afraid you can't use it. It's out of order.
(*The man and woman get up to leave.*)
Waiter: Come again!

Discussion Questions

1.   Who makes the first request in this conversation? What is the request for?
2.   What does the man try to order? What happens?
3.   Why does the man finally order the salmon?
4.   Why do the man and woman have to leave?
5.   How do you think they feel when they leave? Explain your answer.

A. Modal Verbs: Requests, Offers, and Permission

The modals *may, can, could, will,* or *would* can be used with the simple form of a verb to make requests, offers, and to request permission. In questions, the modal appears before the subject.

Making Requests		
Examples	**Possible Answers**	**Notes**
Could you please **bring** a fork?	Of course.	In these cases, we are asking someone else to do something.
Would you **suggest** a dessert?	I'd be glad to.	*Could* and *would* are used in both informal and formal situations.
Will you **pass** the salt, please?	Certainly.	*Can* and *will* are informal.
Can we **have** a menu, please?	Sure.	

Note: Please makes any request more polite.

Making Offers		
Examples	**Possible Answers**	**Notes**
May I **help** you?	Yes. Can I get a menu?	In these cases, we are offering to do something for someone.
Can I **get** you something to drink?	I'd like an iced tea, please.	*May* is considered formal. *Can* is less formal.

Requesting Permission		
Examples	**Possible Answers**	**Notes**
May we **join** you?	No, you may not.	In these cases, we want something or want to do something and are asking for someone's help or permission.
Could I **borrow** some money?	Yes, you can.	
Can I **use** a credit card?	No, you can't.	*May* is considered formal. *Could* is used in formal and informal requests. *Can* is the least formal.

Note: May is not used in questions in which the subject is *you*.

1   Underline the modal verb phrases in the conversation on page 70. Next to each phrase, put an *R* if it is a request, an *O* if it is an offer, and a *P* if it is a request for permission.

Example: ___May___ I take your order? *O*

2   Imagine yourself in the following situations. Decide on appropriate requests, offers, or requests for permission for each situation.

A. You are having dinner at your good friend's house.

1.   You want to help your friend bring the food to the table. *Can I help you bring the food to the table?*

2.   You want a second helping of rice.

3.   You want the last piece of bread.

4.   You want your friend to give you the recipe.

5.   You want to start clearing the table.

B. You are having tea with a classmate in a cafe. Your teacher walks in.

1.   You want your teacher to join you.

2.   You want the waiter to bring another cup.

3.   You want to pour the tea for your teacher.

4.   You want your friend to pass you the sugar.

5.   You want the waiter to bring the check.

3   Circle the correct words in the parentheses.

Louis: (May / (Would)) you please (pass, to pass) the hot sauce, Jean?
              1   2

Jean: Sure. (Will / (Can)) I have the tartar sauce?
             3

Louis: (Can / Will) I (ask / to ask) you something, Jean? Why do you put tartar sauce
4   5
on your fish? Yuk!

Jean: (*laughing*) (Will / Might) you (be / are) quiet, Louis?
6   7

Louis: Sorry.

Jean: I need more butter. (Can / Are) you call the waiter, Louis?
8

Louis: (*snaps his fingers*) Waiter! (Can / May) you (bring / brings) us more butter,
9   10
please?

Jean: Shh . . . (May / Could) you talk more softly? And (may / would) I (make / to make)
11   12   13
a suggestion? Please don't snap your fingers to get a waiter's attention. It isn't polite.

Louis: Psssst! Waiter!

Jean: (May / Would) I make another request? Please don't hiss at the waiter. That's
14
also rude.

Louis: Oh, I didn't know that. (Will / Can) I wave at him?
15

Jean: Sure, that's fine.

Waiter: Yes, (can / would) I get you something else?
16

Jean: (Could I have / I could have) some more butter, please?
17

Waiter: Sure.

Jean: (Can / Will) we also have the check, please?
18

Waiter: Of course.

Using What You've Learned

4   Write a dialogue for one of the following situations, or make up a situation of your
own. Make sure to use modals for making requests, offers, and requesting permission.
Practice your dialogue and perform it for the class.

1.   A mother and child are in a supermarket. The child wants candy and other sweet
things, but the mother wants to buy healthy food.

Example: A.   Can I have a candy bar?
           B.   How about some fruit? It's much better for you.
           A.   Noooo! I don't want fruit. Will you buy me a cake?

2. Two friends are studying in a room together. One student is cold and the other is warm.

Example: A. May I open the window?
B. I'm actually cold. Will you lend me your sweater?
A. Sure. Then can I turn on the air conditioner?

3. Two roommates are cooking together. One loves spicy food. The other only likes mild foods.

Example: A. Would you chop up that chili pepper?
B. Can you leave the chili pepper out of the sauce?
A. But it will be so bland without it. Can I use garlic and ginger?

Video Activities: Treat Yourself Well Campaign

Before You Watch.   Discuss these questions in a group.

1. What is the difference between "healthy" and "unhealthy" food?
2. Do you think low-fat or nonfat food can be delicious?
3. Do you like American fast food?

Watch.   Write answers to these questions.

1. What kind of food do the Wood brothers like to eat?
2. Describe some of the dishes that the tasters are eating.

Watch Again.   Complete the following statements.

1. The Wood brothers don't eat light dishes because _____.
   a. they're more expensive than fast food
   b. they don't taste as good as "fat" food
   c. they don't care if they get fat
2. "Healthy" food contains _____.
   a. butter
   b. cream
   c. vegetables
   d. lots of salt
3. The pizza does not contain _____.
   a. nonfat cheese
   b. vegetables
   c. nonfat dressing
   d. low-fat sausage

After You Watch.   Play the Supermarket Game. For this game the class should sit in a circle. The teacher begins by saying, "I went to the supermarket, and I bought [*Unit of measure + healthy food*]," for example, "a bag of apples." Next a student repeats what the teacher said and adds another item, for example: "I went to the supermarket, and I bought a bag of apples and a liter of low-fat milk." Each student in the circle then *repeats* the list and *adds* one item. A student who forgets an item on the list is "out." The winner is the last person who can remember the whole list.

Chapter 4

In the Community

PART 1 # Future Verb Forms

Setting the Context

Another Day in Rushville

It's the start of a new day in Rushville. And just like any other day in Rushville, it's going to be busy. It's only 9:00 and already there's a lot of activity in the town square. Do you see the woman who's about to cross the street? That's Ms. Drill, the dentist. She's in a hurry because her office opens in 15 minutes. She's meeting her first patient at 9:15, but she's going to try to get to the bank first. See the   5 man who's going to make a phone call? He's Ms. Drill's patient. He's nervous because he's getting a few teeth pulled. He's probably going to call Ms. Drill's office to cancel the appointment at the last minute.

Look! There's Officer Nabbed. Uh-oh, it looks like he's going to write a ticket. The owner of that car will be surprised when he returns.   10

See the boy on the bicycle who's going to throw the paper? He's the town's newspaper delivery boy. He'll probably break at least one window today. He usually does. If his aim doesn't improve, he's going to lose his job. The woman who's going to get on the bus is Mrs. Tardy, the paper boy's mother. She starts work at 9:00, so she's going to be late for work, as usual. She will have to explain to her   15 boss why she's late again.

See the students behind her? They usually take a later bus but they're taking an exam at 9:30 and don't want to be late for class. They'll probably get there a little early. They will probably come back later for some of the big events happening in town today: the mayor is giving a speech in the square at 11:00, the circus   20
is coming to town this afternoon, and the town council is meeting at 4:00 to discuss local issues. Yes, it's going to be another busy day in Rushville.

Discussion Questions

1. Why is Ms. Drill in a hurry?
2. Who is nervous? Why?
3. What is the paperboy going to do?
4. What time does Ms. Tardy start work? Will she get there on time?
5. Why are the students taking an earlier bus than usual?
6. What is happening in Rushville later today?
7. How is Rushville like your town? How is it different?

A. Be going to

The structure *be + going to +* the simple form of a verb is used to express predictions as well as plans and intentions. It is common in conversation and often sounds like *gonna* in quick, informal speech. Do not use *gonna* in writing.

Statements		
Purpose	**Examples**	
	Affirmative	**Negative**
Predictions	The sky looks grey. It**'s going to rain.** The policeman **is going to give** you a ticket if you park there.	Tomoko **isn't going to arrive** on time for the movie. The cafe **isn't going to be** crowded this early.
Plans and Intentions	We**'re going to eat** at a new restaurant tonight. I**'m going to walk** to school more often.	They **aren't going to go** to the post office today. He **isn't going to run** for mayor again.

Yes/No Questions			
	Examples	**Possible Answers**	
		Affirmative	**Negative**
Affirmative	**Is** the doctor **going to be** in today?	Yes, she is.	No, she isn't.
	Is the post office **going to close** early today?	Yes, it is.	No, it isn't.
	Are we **going to meet** downtown?	Yes, we are.	No, we aren't.
Negative	**Isn't** Raymond **going to come** to the park?	Yes, he is.	No, he isn't.
	Isn't it **going to rain** on Saturday?	Yes, it is.	No, it isn't.
	Aren't they **going to go** to the bank?	Yes, they are.	No, they aren't.

Information Questions		
	Examples	**Possible Answers**
Affirmative	Where **is** she **going to go**?	She is going to go to the supermarket.
	Why **is** Carlos **going to catch** the bus?	He's going to catch the bus because his car isn't working.
	When **are** we **going to meet**?	We are going to meet at five o'clock.
Negative	Why **aren't** you **going to come**?	I have to work.
	Who **isn't going to be** there?	Ellen isn't going to be there.

1   Underline the verb phrases with *going to* in the reading on pages 78 and 79.

Example: And just like any other day in Rushville, it's going to be busy.

2   Look closely at the picture on page 78. Work with a partner to identify and list as many things that are about to happen as you can. Make sure to use the structure *be + going to* + the simple form of a verb.

Example: *A woman is going to cross the street.*

3   For each sentence you created in Activity 2, write one yes/no question and one information question.

Example: *A woman is going to cross the street.*
Is she going to cross the street?
Why is she going to cross the street?

4   The following pictures show people thinking about a change they have decided to make or an action they have decided to take. Write a sentence with *be going to* to express the intention of the person or people in each picture.

1.

2.

The man is going to join a gym

3.

_____

4.

_____

5.

_____

6.

_____

7.

_____

8.

_____

B. The Simple Future Tense

Like *be going to,* the simple future tense expresses intentions. In some cases, *will* and *be going to* are interchangeable. However, *going to* implies that some planning has gone into an intention, while *will* often implies a spontaneous, unplanned intention. Also, unlike *going to, will* is used to express offers, promises, and requests. Only the simple form of the main verb is used with *will*.

Statements		
Purpose	**Examples**	
	Affirmative	**Negative**
Intentions	He**'ll buy** a computer this semester.	She **won't shop** in that store anymore.
Offers and Promises	I**'ll come** to the park with you.	I **won't be** late.
Predictions	It **will be** sunny today.	It **won't rain.**
Requests	**Will** you **drive** me to the video store?	**Won't** you **come** with me?

Yes/No Questions			
	Examples	**Possible Answers**	
		Affirmative	**Negative**
Affirmative	**Will** you **make** an appointment with the doctor?	Yes, I will.	No, I won't.
	Will it **rain** today?	Yes, it will.	No, it won't.
Negative	**Won't** he **go** shopping today?	Yes, he will.	No, he won't.
	Won't they **meet** us at the restaurant?	Yes, they will.	No, they won't.

Information Questions		
	Examples	**Possible Answers**
Affirmative	What **will** you **do** on Saturday?	I'll go shopping.
	When **will** you **go** to the bakery?	I'll go this afternoon.
Negative	Why **won't** you **come** with us?	I don't feel well.
	Why **won't** he **buy** a hot dog from the street vendor?	He's a vegetarian.

5 Double underline the simple future tense verb phrases in the reading on pages 78 and 79.

Example: He'll probably cancel the appointment at the last minute.

6 Shirley is curious about her future and the future of her town. She goes to a fortune teller to ask some questions. Match Shirley's questions with the fortune teller's predictions.

Shirley:

1. How old will I be when I get married?
2. Will I marry someone from this town?
3. Where will I meet my future husband?
4. How many children will I have?
5. Will my children go to school here?
6. Will I open up a business in town?
7. Will I buy a house here in the next few years?
8. What new shops will open in town next year?
9. Will the town's traffic problem improve?
10. Will I be happy in this town?

Fortune teller:

a. Yes, they will.
b. No, you will continue to rent an apartment.
c. Four
d. No, it will get worse.
e. Yes. Very.
f. 29
g. A pet store, a pharmacy, and a few cafes
h. At the supermarket
i. No you won't. You will teach at the high school.
j. Yes, you will marry Bob, the fireman.

7   Rewrite all of the questions in Activity 6 using *going to*.

Example: *How old am I going to be when I get married?*

8   Circle the correct answer in each set of parentheses. In some cases, both answers may be correct.

Chiara: Hi, Angela.

Angela: Chiara!

Chiara: Those shopping bags must be heavy. I ('ll / 'm going to) carry a few for you.
1

Angela: Thanks. What are you doing in town?

Chiara: I ('ll / 'm going to) see if there are any good movies playing at the cinema.
2

Angela: I'm free tonight. I ('ll / 'm going to) go with you if you'd like.
3

Chiara: That would be great.

Angela: I just have to get these groceries home. (Will you / Are you going to) meet me
4

at the movie theatre?

Chiara: Sure. But I don't see your car. How (will you / are you going to) get home?
5

Angela: I ('ll / 'm going to) take the bus.
6

Chiara: Don't be silly. I ('ll / 'm going to) drive you. My car is right here.
7

Angela: That would be great. Oh no, this bag is ripping. The groceries (will / are going
8

to) fall out. I ('ll / am going to) be right back.
9

Chiara: Where are you going?

Angela: I ('ll / 'm going to) get another bag.
10

Chiara: I ('ll / 'm going to) wait for you here.
11

Angela: I ('ll / 'm going to) be back in a minute!
12

C. The Present Continuous and the Simple Present to Express Future Time

In specific situations, the present continuous and the simple present can be used to express future time.

The Present Continuous to Express Future Time	
Examples	**Notes**
We **are moving** to Main Street next week. The town council **isn't meeting** next week.	The present continuous can be used to express future time when the idea of the sentence concerns a planned event or a definite intention.
Where **are** we **meeting** tonight? **Aren't** you **going** downtown this weekend?	Unlike *going to*, the future continuous is used when plans have not only been decided on, but have actually been arranged. Normally a time expression or the context makes it clear that the action or situation is in the future.

The Simple Present to Express Future Time	
Examples	**Notes**
The movie **begins** at 8:00. I **leave** town on Friday. His train **arrives** at 3:00. The museum **opens** at 9:00 tomorrow.	The simple present can be used to express future time in sentences that concern events that are on a definite schedule. Normally a time expression or the context makes it clear that the action or situation is in the future. Only a few verbs are used this way. These verbs include *open, close, begin, end, start, finish, arrive, leave, come,* and *return*.

9 Circle the simple present tense verbs with a future meaning in the reading on pages 78 and 79. Put a box around the present continuous verb phrases used with a future meaning.

Example: She's in a hurry because her office (opens) in 15 minutes. She 's meeting her first patient at 9:15, but she's going to try to get to the bank first.

10 Koto has a busy schedule this weekend. Answer the following questions about his schedule, using the present continuous tense to express future time.

Saturday		Sunday	
8:00 am		8:00 am	
9:00	do Laundry	9:00	sleep
10:00	↓	10:00	↓
11:00	work at café	11:00	work out at gym
12:00 pm		12:00 pm	↓
1:00		1:00	lunch with sister in park
2:00		2:00	↓
3:00		3:00	swim at community pool
4:00		4:00	↓
5:00		5:00	community meeting at Town Hall
6:00	↓	6:00	↓
7:00	dinner with Reiko	7:00	work at café
8:00	↓	8:00	
9:00	movie with Reiko	9:00	
10:00		10:00	↓

1. What is Koto doing first on Saturday morning? *He's doing his laundry first on Saturday morning.*
2. Is he working out at the gym on Sunday morning?
3. When is he working at the café?
4. What is he doing at 7:00 on Saturday night?
5. Who is he seeing a movie with on Saturday night?
6. Is he playing baseball this weekend?

7. Is he sleeping late on Sunday morning?

8. Is he seeing his sister this weekend?

9. Where is he having lunch on Sunday?

10. What is he doing at 5:00 on Sunday?

11 Fill in the blanks with either the simple present form or the present continuous form of the verbs in parentheses.

1. The bus (arrive) ___*arrives*___ at 9:00.

2. She can't come to the park with us this afternoon. She (work) ___*is working*___.

3. (go) ___ you _going_ to the concert tonight?

4. She (leave) _leaves_ in a few minutes. Do you want to go with her?

5. The train (leave) _leaves_ London at 3:00 and (arrive) _arrives_ in Cambridge at 4:00.

6. The museum (open) _opens_ at 9:00.

7. What time (meet) _meeting_ you _at_ your mother tomorrow?

8. What (do) _are_ you _doing_ this weekend?

9. I (take) _takes_ a train to Avignon.

10. What time (begin) _begins_ the film ___?

11. Excuse me. What time (arrive) _arrives_ this train ___ in Barcelona?

12. I (go) _am_ not _going_ out this evening.

Using What You've Learned

12 In a group, brainstorm a list of ways in which you can help your community. Then, choose a way that you personally want to help your community. Make a statement of your intention, then outline the steps you will take to follow through on your intention.

Example: *I'm going to help at the local soup kitchen.*

First, I'll find the number of the soup kitchen in the phone book or from the community center. Then I'll call up the kitchen and find out how to volunteer. I think I'll either sign up to cook food or to serve it. That'll depend on what they need more.

Make an effort to follow through with your plans. Update the class on your progress.

13 Make a calendar for the weekend coming up, like the one on page 85. Write down all of your plans for the coming weekend. You may invent plans if you do not yet have plans. Leave only two spaces blank. Then get together with two other students. Without looking at each other's schedule, try to find one or two times during the weekend when you are all free to get together to study.

Example: A.   What are you doing on Saturday at 11:00?

B.   I'm babysitting for my aunt. What are you doing Saturday at 1:00?

A.   I'm not doing anything then.

C.   But I am! I'm playing softball in the park with some friends.

PART 2

Phrasal Verbs

Setting the Context

Conversation

Mikki: Erika, wake up! Your alarm didn't go off. Get up and get dressed!
Erika: Please go away.
Mikki: You have so much to do today. You can't sleep in. You're giving your speech at the community center tonight.
Erika: Huh?
Mikki: Your speech! To convince the town council not to tear down the old museum to put up a shopping mall.

Erika: Oh, right.
Mikki: A few neighbors are coming here for dinner before the meeting. I'm doing the cooking, but I need you to pick some things up at the supermarket.
Erika: Calm down. There's plenty of time.
Mikki: Not if you want to work out at the gym this afternoon. Also, you need to stop off at the bank to take some cash out. On the way there, you should drop off this overdue video. And you need to fill up the car with gas on your way home.
Erika: Slow down!
Mikki: And remember, you need to come back in time to clean up the house and to go over your notes before the meeting. (Erika pulls the sheet over her head) What are you doing?
Erika: Going back to sleep. Just thinking of all I have to do is making me tired.
Mikki: I give up!
Erika: Mikki?
Mikki: Yes?
Erika: Turn the light off on your way out, would you?

Discussion Questions

1.   Why does Mikki want Erika to get up?

2.   What are some of the things that Erika has to do today?

3.   Why is Erika giving a speech at the community center?

4.   What does Erika do at the end of the conversation?

5.   Do you have trouble waking up in the morning? What helps you wake up?

A. Phrasal Verbs: Forms

A phrasal verb is a verb + a preposition or adverb which together have a special meaning. The preposition or adverb part of the phrasal verb is called a *particle*. Some phrasal verbs are separable, while others are not.

Inseparable Phrasal Verbs		
Phrasal Verbs	**Examples**	**Notes**
ran into	(a) I **ran into** my biology teacher at the library. (b) I **ran into** her at the library.	With phrasal verbs, the direct object goes after the particle. The direct object can be a noun (as in the *a* examples) or a pronoun (as in the *b* examples).
get on	(a) **Get on** the train before it leaves! (b) **Get on** it before it leaves!	
drop by	(a) I'll **drop by** my friend Tom's house. (b) I'll **drop by** his house.	

Separable Phrasal Verbs		
Phrasal Verbs	**Examples**	**Notes**
make up	(a) He may **make up** the time. (b) He may **make** the time **up.** (c) He may **make** it **up.**	With separable phrasal verbs, when the direct object is a noun, it can go after the particle (as in the *a* examples) or between the verb and the particle (as in the *b* examples).
fill out	(a) Please **fill out** this form. (b) Please **fill** this form **out.** (c) Please **fill** it **out.**	When the direct object is a pronoun, it goes between the verb and the particle (as in the *c* examples).
clean off	(a) **Clean off** your shoes. (b) **Clean** your shoes **off.** (c) **Clean** them **off.**	

1   Underline the phrasal verbs in the conversation between Mikki and Erika.

Example: Erika, <u>wake up</u>! Your alarm didn't <u>go off</u>.

2   In each of the following groups of sentences, one of the sentences is incorrect. Put a check by all the correct sentences, and cross out the incorrect sentence.

Example: **drop off** (separable)

    ✓   You need to drop off this video.

    ✓   You need to drop this video off.

    ~~You need to drop off it.~~

    ✓   You need to drop it off.

1. **run into** (inseparable)
   I frequently run into your sister in town.
   I frequently run into her in town.
   I frequently run her into in town.

2. **call up** (separable)
   She calls her father up every week.
   She calls up her father every week.
   She calls up him every week.
   She calls him up every week.

3. **wake up** (separable)
   Don't wake up the children.
   Don't wake up them.
   Don't wake the children up.
   Don't wake them up.

4. **look after** (inseparable)
   Please look after my plants while I'm gone.
   Please look after them while I'm gone.
   Please look them after while I'm gone.

5. **pick up** (separable)
   Will you pick up my mail at the post office?
   Will you pick up it at the post office?
   Will you pick it up at the post office?
   Will you pick my mail up at the post office?

3   Sue is sick and needs her friend John to run many errands for her. Fill in John's part of the dialogue, answering all of Sue's questions with full, affirmative answers. Remember that when the phrasal verb is separable, you can put a pronoun between the verb and the particle. When the phrasal verb is inseparable, a pronoun can only appear (if it is needed at all) after the particle.

1. *Sue:* Will you fill up my juice glass?
   John: Yes, I will fill it up.

2. *Sue:* Will you look after my cat? She shouldn't be any trouble.
   John: Yes, I will look after her.

3. *Sue:* Will you call up the doctor? Her name is in my address book.
   John: Yes, I will call up the doctor

4. *Sue:* Will you take out my roommate's dog? He's making me sneeze.

     John: _Yes, I will take out_____

5. *Sue:* Will you drop off my library books?

     John: _____

6. *Sue:* Will you go to the pharmacy and pick up my prescription?

     John: _____

7. *Sue:* Will you pick up chicken soup for my dinner?

     John: _____

8. *Sue:* Will you call up my mother to let her know I'm sick?

     John: _____

9. *Sue:* Will you drop by later?

     John: _____

10. *Sue:* Will you turn the light off?

     John: _____

B. Phrasal Verbs: Meanings

Inseparable Phrasal Verbs   The following are some examples of inseparable phrasal verbs and their meanings.

Phrasal Verbs	Examples	Meanings
come back	We will **come back** later.	return to a place
drop by	I often **drop by** my aunt's house.	visit informally
get along (with)	They **get along with** their neighbors.	be on good terms with
get off	Driver, I want to **get off** here.	come out or off of a form of transportation
get on	Do you want to **get on** the bus with me?	board a form of transportation
get up	I hate to **get up** early.	arise from bed after sleeping
go away	**Go away!** You're bothering me.	leave
go back	He wants to **go back** to school to get a degree.	return to a place
go off	A gun will **go off** at the beginning of the race.	ring (for an alarm or timer); explode (for a gun)
go over	Let's **go over** the rules of the game one more time.	review
grow up	I want my children to **grow up** in this town.	become an adult
look after	Please **look after** my plants while I'm gone.	take care of
move out (of)	She wants to **move out of** this neighborhood.	leave
move to	She wants to **move to** the city.	relocate to
run into	We always **run into** each other here!	meet accidentally
sleep in	My roommate loves to **sleep in** on the weekends.	sleep late
work out	I'm always tired after I **work out.**	exercise (usually in a gym)

Separable Phrasal Verbs   The following are some examples of separable phrasal verbs and their meanings.

Phrasal Verbs	Examples	Meanings
bring up	She is **bringing up** her kids by herself.	raise children, introduce an idea
call up	I will **call** you **up** tonight.	telephone (verb)
calm down	**Calm down.** You're getting too excited.	relax
clean up	We are going to help **clean up** the park this weekend.	make neat and orderly
drop off	Could you **drop** me **off** downtown?	leave something/someone at a place
fill out	You need to **fill** this form **out** to get your license.	write the information requested on a questionnaire or form
fill up	Don't **fill up** on bread before the meal.	make or become full
get back	He will **get back** by 6:00.	return
give up	I often **give up** my seat on the bus.	surrender, stop trying
help out	We need you to **help out** with the arrangements.	assist
look up	I often **look up** words in the dictionary.	search for information in a reference book
pick up	I have to **pick** my kids **up** in town.	go to get someone/something
put up	They want to **put up** a wall to divide these rooms.	construct, raise
slow down	**Slow down.** Don't drive so fast.	go less quickly
take out	I'm going to **take out** the garbage.	remove, bring outside
tear down	The city is going to **tear down** that building.	pull down, demolish
turn off	The streetlights **turn off** automatically at 6:00 A.M.	stop a machine, light, or faucet
wake up	I **wake up** for work at 7:00.	stop sleeping
work out	The city is trying to **work out** the traffic problem.	find a solution

4   Fill in each of the following blanks with one of the inseparable phrasal verbs from the list on page 90. You may need to change the form of the phrasal verb.

1. The postman is so friendly and easygoing. He ___*gets along with*___ everybody.

2. To get to the football stadium, you need to _____ the bus at Clark Street and _____ at Austin Avenue.

3. My literature professor is always surprised when she _____ students in town.

4. I want to _____ of my apartment. It's too small.

5. I'd like to _____ your neighborhood. It's beautiful!

6. Feel free to _____ any time. I'm always happy to see you.

7. Maria is _____ my cat while I'm out of town.

8. Are you _____ for long? I hope you _____ soon. I miss you already!

9. What time do you usually _____ in the morning?

10.   I don't like to _____ because the morning is my favorite time of day.

11.   The construction workers need to _____ the plans for the house before they start building.

12.   Your son is _____ so quickly. I still think of him as a little boy!

13.   She likes to listen to the radio while she _____.

14.   The race will begin when the gun _____.

15.   I think I left my keys at the post office. I'm going to _____ to check.

5   Fill in each of the following blanks with one of the separable phrasal verbs from the list on page 90. You may need to change the form of the phrasal verb.

1.   He is ___*bringing up*___ his children very well. They are smart, happy, and kind.

2.   Can you please _____ my dress at the dry cleaner's? I can't get this stain out.

3.   My clock is broken. I can't _____ the alarm.

4.   The city is going to _____ those old buildings to make room for a new clinic.

5.   He is _____ the trash. The garbage men are coming tomorrow morning.

6.   _____ your sister. She shouldn't sleep so late on such a beautiful day.

7.   I'll _____ the basket with enough food for a picnic.

8.   She _____ an advertisement for a roommate on the bulletin board in the supermarket.

9.   We should _____ our neighborhood. There's litter everywhere!

10.   He's going to _____ the movie theatre to find out what movies are playing.

11.   _____ your radio. It's disturbing everyone in the park.

12.   Can you please _____ my dress at the dry cleaner's. It should be ready by now.

13.   He _____ forms all day long. He has a very boring job.

14.   She has to _____ her photography class. Her schedule is just too busy.

15.   "What's the plumber's phone number?" "I don't know. You can _____ the number in the phone book."

6   Substitute a phrasal verb for the underlined word(s) in the following sentences.

        Calm down

Example: ~~Relax~~! The policeman isn't giving your car a ticket.

1.   Where can I <u>get</u> a local newspaper?

2.   Would you <u>take care of</u> my dog this weekend while I'm away?

3. I'm going to <u>remove</u> my advertisement from the newspaper.
4. Are you going to <u>return</u> to this school next year?
5. The city is going to <u>construct</u> a new mall in the center of town.
6. Do you want to <u>assist</u> with the preparations for the parade?
7. We can <u>find</u> the phone number of the bank in the phone book.
8. We are going to <u>relocate</u> to an apartment closer to the center of town.
9. Let's go for a walk. We can <u>return</u> later.
10. You can <u>leave</u> your bag at my house before we go to the park.
11. Please <u>enter</u> the bus in the front and <u>exit</u> the bus at the back.
12. Let's <u>review</u> the directions to my house to make sure you understand them.

Using What You've Learned

7   Work with a partner. Write a dialogue for two of the following situations or create two situations of your own. Use as many phrasal verbs as you can for each situation, including the phrasal verbs provided. When you finish, practice your dialogues and perform one of them for the class.

1. You are two roommates studying in a dormitory. One of you wants to listen to the stereo. The other can't study with music playing. Include these phrasal verbs in your dialogue:

    turn on = start (a machine)
    turn off = stop (a machine)
    turn down = lower the volume
    turn up = increase the volume

    Example: A. Please don't turn on the stereo. I'm trying to study.
                  B. Music helps me study.
                  A. Well, I can't study with loud music. Could you turn it down?
                  B. Sure. Is that better?
                  A. No, I can still hear it. Would you turn it off?

2. You are a customer and salesperson in a clothing store. The customer wants to buy a new sweater and is discussing styles and colors with the salesperson. Include these phrasal verbs in your dialogue:

    put on = dress in
    take off = remove
    try on = put on a piece of clothing to check for fit
    pick out = choose

3. You are a student and a librarian. The student wants to find information about a famous writer, artist, or scientist—you choose the person. The student asks the

librarian for help in finding information. Include these phrasal verbs in your dialogue:

find out = discover or learn information about

look up = look for information in a reference book

check out = borrow from the library

fill out = complete a form

Prepositions of Place and Time

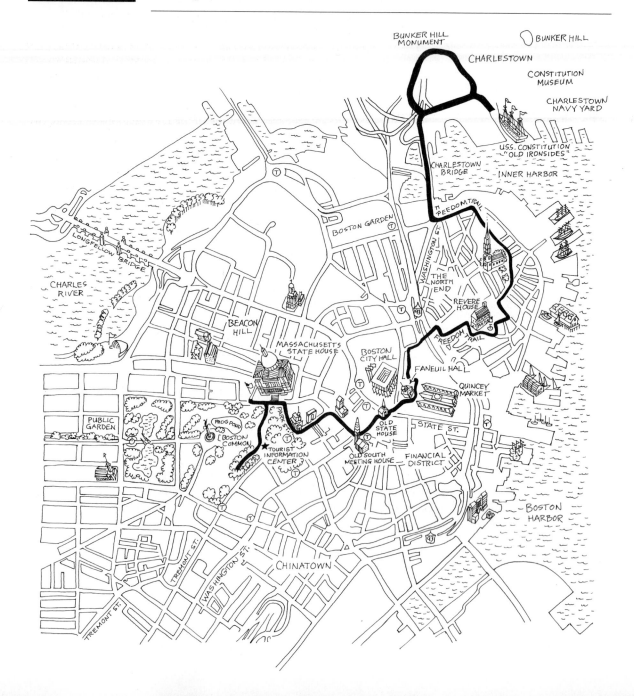

Setting the Context

Boston's Historic Freedom Trail

A great way to see old downtown Boston, Massachusetts, during the day is to walk the Freedom Trail. The trail is three miles long, and it takes you by many famous, historic places from the time of the American Revolution (1775–1783). The trail starts at an information booth in Boston Common, a large park next to Boston's Public Gardens. The booth is on Tremont Street between the Park Street   5
and Tremont Street subway stations. You can get tour information and a trail map at the booth. Here are some of the interesting stops on the trail.

One important stop is the Old State House at Washington and State Streets. Built in 1712, it now has a museum with exhibits about Boston's history. From the Old State House, you can walk through Faneuil Hall and Quincy Market. These   10
old, historic buildings are now a busy center for shopping, dining, and entertainment. Many stores in Quincy Market stay open until 9:00 P.M., making them a perfect place to come back to in the evening, after dinner.

After you leave Quincy Market, you can walk to the North End. This part of Boston has many wonderful Italian shops, cafés, and restaurants. Also in the   15
North End is Revere House, another important stop on the Freedom Trail. It is the home of Paul Revere (1735–1818), patriot of the American Revolution. Built in 1676, it is the oldest standing building in Boston.

The *U.S.S. Constitution,* a famous warship built in 1797, is across the Inner Harbor in the Charlestown Navy Yard. You can walk over the Charlestown Bridge   20
to get there. The *U.S.S. Constitution* is the oldest American warship afloat today. The *U.S.S. Constitution* Museum is near the ship. You can visit the ship for free, but you have to pay to visit the museum.

Near the Charlestown Navy Yard is the Bunker Hill Monument, the last stop on the Freedom Trail. The monument commemorates the Battle of Bunker Hill, an im-   25
portant battle of the American Revolution, fought on June 17, 1775.

After you finish the trail, you will probably be ready for a rest. You may wish to relax in one of Boston's beautiful parks, or get a coffee at one of the many cafés in the North End.

Discussion Questions

1. What kinds of places can you visit along the Freedom Trail?
2. Where is the information booth in Boston Common?
3. How can you get from Quincy Market to the North End?
4. What can you do in the North End?
5. How can you get from the North End to the Charlestown Navy Yard?
6. Would you like to visit Boston? Why or why not?

A. Prepositions of Place and Time

<table>
<tr><th colspan="3">Prepositions of Place</th></tr>
<tr><th></th><th>Examples</th><th>Notes</th></tr>
<tr><td>in</td><td>Eduardo is **in** the library.
Palermo is a city **in** Italy.</td><td>Use *in* before buildings, towns, cities, regions, provinces, countries, and continents.</td></tr>
<tr><td>on</td><td>I live **on** a beautiful street.
The boat is sailing **on** the river.</td><td>Use *on* before streets and bodies of water.</td></tr>
<tr><td>at</td><td>Jen lives **at** 17 Bow Street.
I will meet you **at** the corner of Main Street and Elm Street.</td><td>Use *at* with street addresses and many specific locations.</td></tr>
<tr><td>between</td><td>The video store is **between** the bank and the post office.
The house is **between** two big trees.</td><td>*Between* describes a location between two points.</td></tr>
<tr><td>near</td><td>I hope there is a cash machine **near** the movie theatre.
The professor's office is **near** the chemistry laboratory.</td><td>*Near* describes something close in distance.</td></tr>
<tr><td>far from</td><td>Your house is too **far from** school to walk.
The hospital is **far from** town.</td><td>*Far from* describes something far in distance.</td></tr>
<tr><td>next to</td><td>Her house is **next to** yours.
The restaurant is **next to** the movie theatre.</td><td>*Next to* describes something beside something else.</td></tr>
<tr><td>across from</td><td>The post office is **across from** the police station.
Their house is **across from** a bookstore.</td><td>*Across from* describes something opposite something else.</td></tr>
<tr><td>under</td><td>The boats pass **under** the bridge.
The ball is rolling **under** the car.</td><td>*Under* describes something that is below something else.</td></tr>
<tr><td>over</td><td>The airplane is flying **over** the ocean.
Her office is **over** a café.</td><td>*Over* describes something that is above something else.</td></tr>
<tr><th colspan="3">Prepositions of Time</th></tr>
<tr><th></th><th>Examples</th><th>Notes</th></tr>
<tr><td>in</td><td>The new post office will open **in** January.
Paris is beautiful **in** the springtime.</td><td>Use *in* before years, seasons, months, and parts of the day.</td></tr>
<tr><td>on</td><td>Some stores are closed **on** Sunday.
We'll have a St. Patrick's Day parade **on** March 17th.</td><td>Use *on* before days of the week and dates.</td></tr>
<tr><td>at</td><td>The laundromat opens **at** 9:00.
I love to walk around the city **at** night.</td><td>Use *at* before a specific time of day and with the nouns *noon, night,* and *midnight*.</td></tr>
<tr><td>from . . . to</td><td>The library is open **from** 9:30 A.M. **to** 5:00 P.M.
The parade will last **from** late morning **to** early afternoon.</td><td>Use *from . . . to* with beginning and ending times.</td></tr>
<tr><td>during</td><td>The supermarket is open late **during** the week.
My town is usually covered in snow **during** the winter.</td><td>Use *during* with periods of time.</td></tr>
<tr><td>until</td><td>The coffee shop is open **until** 9:00 P.M.
I am going to live here **until** I graduate.</td><td>Use *until* with ending times.</td></tr>
<tr><td>before</td><td>I want to go to the mountains **before** summer is over.
Run to the store **before** it closes!</td><td>Use *before* to express an earlier event or time.</td></tr>
<tr><td>after</td><td>Let's get a bite **after** the movie.
I like to meet my friends in town **after** class.</td><td>Use *after* to express a later event or time.</td></tr>
</table>

1   Circle the prepositions of place and time in the reading on page 95. Then put a *P* above each preposition of place and a *T* above each preposition of time.

Example: A great way to see old downtown Boston (during) the day is to walk the Freedom Trail.

2   Complete the sentences with prepositions from the list below. You can use each word more than once. In some cases, more than one word may be correct.

at   in   on   from . . . to   until   during   after   near

1.   Boston is _____in_____ Massachusetts, a state _____in_____ the northeastern part of the United States.

2.   The Freedom Trail starts _____at_____ an information booth _____in_____ Tremont Street.

3.   The Old State House is open _____at_____ 9:30 A.M. _____to_____ 5:00 P.M. _____in_____ the summer.

4.   Harvard University, _____is_____ Cambridge, Massachusetts, is the oldest university _____in_____ the United States.

5.   The Bunker Hill Monument is _____near_____ the Charlestown Navy Yard. You can easily walk from the monument to the Navy Yard.

6.   Paul Revere House is located _____ 19 North Street _____ the North End.

7.   The Boston Children's Museum is _____ Congress Street. It is open _____ Friday evenings _____ 9:00 P.M.

8.   Many fine stores _____ Boston are _____ Newbury Street.

9.   Quincy Market is a good place to shop _____ the evening _____ dinner because many shops are open _____until_____ 8:00 P.M. or later.

10.   _____During_____ the summer there are many fireworks displays in Boston. The biggest one is _____ the 4th of July.

3   Use the map and the prepositions of place *in, on, at, between, near, next to, across from, under,* and *over* to answer the questions below. Answer the questions in as many ways as you can, using as many prepositions of place as possible.

Example: Where is the video store? *The video store is above the health food store. It is next to the bank and across from the florist.*

   1.   Where is the movie theatre?
   2.   Where is the dentist's office?
   3.   Where is the ballet school?
   4.   Where is the pet shop?
   5.   Where is the bank?
   6.   Where is the subway?
   7.   Where is the bookstore?
   8.   Where is the café?
   9.   Where is the health food store?
  10.   Where is the movie theatre?
  11.   Where is the florist?
  12.   Where is the gym?

4   The following is a Community Center schedule for the coming week. Answer the questions about the schedule using the prepositions of time: *on, at, from . . . to, during, until, before* and *after*.

	Pool open (10:00-5:00)	Café open (10:00-5:00)	Aerobics class (1:00-2:00)	Computer class (2:00-3:00)	After-school activities (3:00-5:00)	Special events
Monday						7:00 Lecture: Recycling and the Community
Tuesday						
Wednesday						
Thursday						7:30: Poetry reading by local author
Friday						
Saturday						
Sunday	Community Center closed					

1. What time does the café open? *The café opens at 10:00.*
2. What time is the café open until?
3. What hours is the pool open?
4. What Community Center facility is open during the day on Saturday?
5. When is the lecture on recycling?
6. When is the poetry reading?
7. What days is the aerobics class offered?
8. Is the aerobics class offered before or after the computer class?
9. Is the computer class offered in the morning?
10. What day is the Community Center closed?

Using What You've Learned

5 Find a partner who lives in a different neighborhood from yours. Sit back to back with your partner. Take turns describing the main street of your neighborhood, using prepositions of place. As you describe your neighborhood, your partner will draw a map from your description.

Example: A. There is a small bakery between a bank and an Italian restaurant. And there are apartments above all of these businesses.

B. Is there anything next to the bank or the restaurant?

When you finish, turn around to look at each other's drawings. How well did you explain your main street? Now, tell your partner more about the shops and businesses on this street. Make a point of using prepositions of time to tell your partner about the days and times these shops are open.

6 Make a list of things you plan to do this week, without listing the days or times you intend to do these activities, or where you plan to do these activities. When you finish your list, exchange lists with a partner. Then take turns asking questions about the activities on each other's lists. Use prepositions of place and time in your answers.

Example: A. Are you going to the movies on Friday?
        B. No. On Saturday.
        A. What time on Saturday?
        B. At 7:30 in the evening.
        A. Where is the movie playing?
        B. At the Multiplex Cinema on Main Street. When are you going to do the laundry?

PART 4   Articles

Setting the Context

Reading

Read "Boston's Historic Freedom Trail" on page 95 again. Notice the use of the words *a, an, the,* and *some.*

Discussion Questions

1. Where does the trail start?
2. What does the Old State House have?
3. What part of Boston has many Italian restaurants?
4. What is the oldest standing building in Boston?
5. Where is the *U.S.S. Constitution?*
6. What battle was fought on June 17, 1775?

A. Articles

The Indefinite Article   The indefinite article, *a/an,* is used with general nouns and nouns that have not been specified. *A/an* is used with singular count nouns. General, unspecific plural nouns need no article ($\emptyset$).

	Examples	**Notes**
a/an	My town has **an** aquarium. This is **a** beautiful park.	Use *a/an* when you mention something for the first time. Use *a/an* to talk about one of a group of things.
($\emptyset$)	There are **skyscrapers** in the downtown area. How many **subway lines** are there in your city?	Don't use a/an before plural nouns.

Note: Use *a* before words that begin with consonant sounds. Use *an* before words that begin with vowel sounds.

The Definite Article   The definite article, *the,* is used with both count and noncount nouns. It shows that the nouns are specific, special, or unique.

	Examples	Notes
the	My town has **an** aquarium. **The** aquarium is on Baker Street.	*The* is used when an indefinite noun becomes definite as a result of being mentioned a second time.
	The oldest building in my town is **the** library.	*The* is used to talk about something specific, special, or unique.
	Do you want to take **the** subway or **the** bus? We're going to **the** city this weekend.	*The* is used when the speaker and the listener both know the thing or person being spoken of.
(∅)	**Parks** are an important part of any city.	Don't use *the* with plural nouns when you are talking about things in general.

Note: Don't use *the* before names of games (such as *soccer*), or abstract nouns (such as *happiness*).

Using *the* with Names   There are many different rules for the use of *the* with names. Here are a few.

	Examples	Notes
People	the president of the United States the queen of England President Kennedy Queen Elizabeth	Use *the* with titles. Don't use *the* with titles + names of specific people.
Places	Japan Kobe Argentina Buenos Aires	Don't use *the* with names of streets, cities, states, provinces, and most countries. There are some exceptions, for example: *The Hague, the United States, the Netherlands.*
Buildings	the Eiffel Tower the Leaning Tower of Pisa the Taj Mahal	*The* is usually used with names of buildings.
Historical Events	the Storming of the Bastille the French Revolution the fall of the Berlin Wall	*The* is usually used with names of historical events.

1 In the reading on page 95, underline the indefinite articles along with the nouns they correspond to, and double underline the definite articles along with the nouns they correspond to.

Example: A great way to see old downtown Boston during the day is to walk the Freedom Trail.

2 Fill in the blanks with *a, an, the,* or × (for no article). In some cases, more than one answer might be correct.

A.

Where can we stay in <u>*the*</u> city of <u>×</u> Boston? _____ Four Seasons Hotel is
          1   2   3

expensive, but maybe we can find _____*a*_____ smaller hotel in _____*the*_____ part
                                                      4   5

of town further from _____×_____ downtown area.
                                    6

B.

President John F. Kennedy was from _____*a*_____ Massachusetts. There's
                                                              1

_____*a*_____ important building in Boston with his name—_____ JFK
        2   3

Building—on _____ New Sudbury Street.
                              4

C.

I like _____ aquariums. There's _____ interesting aquarium at
              1   2

_____ Boston Harbor. If we go there, we can learn about _____ sea
        3   4

animals and _____ plant life.
                          5

D.

Only a few cities in _____ United States have _____ subway systems.
                              1   2

Boston has _____ subway system and also _____ trolley.
                          3   4

_____ tourists can get on and off _____ trolley at _____
        5   6   7

twelve different places.

E.

Do you like _____ historic ships and _____ monuments? _____
                          1   2   3

U.S.S. Constitution was _____ warship during _____ War of 1812.
                                            4   5

You can learn about _____ Battle of Bunker Hill at _____ Bunker Hill
                                  6   7

Pavilion, which has _____ multimedia program about this famous battle.
                                  8

3 Rewrite the following sentences, correcting any mistakes in the underlined words. If there are no mistakes in a sentence, write *correct* next to the sentence.

Example: Let's play <u>the</u> soccer in <u>a</u> park. *Let's play soccer in the park.*

1. There is <u>a</u> ice cream store on <u>a</u> corner of Main Street and Elm.
2. <u>A</u> baker lives next door to me. <u>A</u> baker sometimes gives me fresh bread.
3. I go to <u>the</u> same café every morning and order <u>a</u> big breakfast.
4. My best friend lives in <u>the</u> Australia.
5. What did you do for <u>a</u> millennium New Year?
6. I work on <u>a</u> second floor of <u>the</u> Romano Building.
7. I have to go to <u>the</u> dentist next week. I have <u>the</u> cavity.
8. "Where can I buy <u>a</u> watch?" "You can buy <u>a</u> watch in town."
9. There is <u>the</u> town council meeting tonight in <u>a</u> library.
10. I'll meet you in <u>a</u> post office in five minutes. I have <u>a</u> letter to mail.

Using What You've Learned

4 What is your favorite place in the city or town you are living in? Write for fifteen minutes on one of the topics below. Be sure to explain why the place is your favorite. Pay special attention to your use of articles.

1. your favorite restaurant or eating place
2. your favorite shopping area or store
3. your favorite cultural place (such as a museum, a concert hall, or a theater)
4. your favorite recreational place (such as an amusement park, a sports arena, or a park)

When you finish writing, exchange papers with another student. Read each other's descriptions. Underline any articles in your partner's description that aren't used correctly and write a question next to any part(s) that you would like to know more about. Return your papers. Read your partner's comments, then discuss any questions you may have about the comments with your partner. Rewrite your description, making any necessary changes.

You may want to make a class book about your city and visit some of your classmates' favorite places.

5 Form groups of three or four. Get a tourist map of your city or town, or another city or town that your group is familiar with. Plan a tour of the city for a tourist who is visiting for three or four days. Agree on at least ten places that the tourist should visit. Each group member takes one day of the trip and writes a plan for that day. Make sure to include details about what the tourist will find in each place and why they should visit the place.

Video Activities: A Homeless Shelter

Before You Watch.   Discuss these questions in a group.

1.   Are there homeless people in your town? Tell what you know about their lives. For example, where do they get food? Where do they sleep?
2.   Who should help homeless people: their families? the community? the government?
3.   Why do some people become homeless?

Watch.   Discuss these questions in a group.

1.   Why does Oceanside need a homeless shelter?
2.   What does the proposed shelter look like?
3.   What is the woman in the hat trying to do?

Watch Again.   Fill in the blanks.

1.   There are _____ homeless people in Oceanside.
2.   However, now there are only _____ shelter beds.
3.   The Oceanside City Council will give _____ dollars for the new shelter.
4.   The new shelter will have _____ beds.
5.   The new shelter will be for single men and women and couples. Families will stay in _____.
6.   The city needs to raise money, and it is also asking people in the community to _____.

After You Watch.   Write about what a recently homeless person is going to do. Use the following terms:

computer class	job interviews	his family
roommate	savings account	business writing classes

Chapter 5

Home

PART 1

The Simple Past Tense (Regular Verbs); *Used to*

Setting the Context

Conversation

Father: Did I ever talk to you kids about the good old days?

Jason: The good old days?

Father: Yes . . . when your mother and I were your age. We worked hard, but we enjoyed life. We didn't need a lot in the 1950s.

Jason: You didn't have many machines then, right? Your family didn't have a computer, or a VCR, or a compact disk player, or . . .

Jessica: What? You mean TV didn't exist?

Father: Oh, television existed, but there was only black and white TV. Anyway, we didn't own a TV. My father decided we didn't need television.

Jessica: What did you do for fun? Did you go to the movies every night?

Father: No, we didn't. We usually stayed home and entertained ourselves.

Jason: How did you live without a TV, and video games, and CDs? Didn't you get bored in the evening?

Father: No, we didn't. The children played games—like checkers and chess. My sister used to play rock and roll records on her record player, and we used to dance. We listened to the radio and discussed current events. My mother and father used to talk a lot.

Mother: Not my family. My parents didn't use to talk much. My father liked to read the paper. My mother knitted and sewed. She also cooked every day. I usually helped in the kitchen.

Jessica: Really? Why did you cook so often? Why didn't you order in pizza?

Mother: Because my father wanted home-cooked meals. Of course, we didn't have a microwave or a food processor or a dishwasher or . . .

Jessica: What? No dishwasher? Who used to wash the dishes?

Mother: I used to wash them, and my sister used to dry them.

Jessica: Didn't your brother do any housework? Didn't your father help?

Mother: No, I'm afraid not. Only the women worked in the house in those days.

Father: Yes, those *were* the good old days.

Mother: Well that's all changed now. Which reminds me—I hope you cleaned the kitchen.
Father: Yes, dear. I did.

Discussion Questions

1. What are the children talking about with their parents?
2. What did the father's family use to do for fun in the evening?
3. How was the mother's family different from the father's family?
4. Who did the housework in the mother's family? Why?
5. Do you think family life is probably better or worse now than it was in the past? Why?

A. Statements with Past Tense Verbs

Use the simple past tense to talk about completed past events and activities.

	Examples	**Notes**
Affirmative	He **helped** her paint her kitchen. I **stayed up** late last night. We **listened** to music after dinner. The children **played** games in the living room.	All regular verbs take an *-ed* ending in the past tense. This form is used for all subjects, both singular and plural.
Negative	Her roommate **didn't like** that restaurant. We **didn't order** a pizza last night. My family **didn't own** a computer until recently. I **didn't live** in a dorm last year.	For negative past tense verbs, use *did not* before the simple form of the main verb. The contraction for *did not* is *didn't*.

Spelling Rules for the Past Tense of Regular Verbs

1. If the simple form of a verb ends in *-y* after a consonant, change the *-y* to *i* and add *-ed*.
    Examples: try/tried   carry/carried   dry/dried
2. If the simple form of a one syllable verb ends in a consonant + a vowel + a consonant, double the final consonant and add *-ed*.
    Examples: plan/planned   stop/stopped   plug/plugged
    Exception: Do not double final *w, x,* or *y*.
    Examples: row/rowed   box/boxed   play/played
3. If the simple form of a two syllable verb ends in a consonant + a vowel + a consonant, double the final consonant only if the last syllable is stressed.
    Examples: permit/permitted   prefer/preferred   occur/occurred
4. If the simple form of a verb ends in *-e*, add only *-d*.
    Examples: tie/tied   change/changed   live/lived
5. Add *-ed* to the simple form of all other regular verbs.
    Examples: want/wanted   ask/asked   belong/belonged

> ### Pronunciation Note
>
> The -ed ending is pronounced three ways, according to the end of the verb:
> - /Id/ after d and t endings
>
>   Examples: existed, needed, wanted, traded
> - /t/ after the voiceless endings s, k, p, f, sh, ch, and x
>
>   Examples: cooked, helped, washed, watched
> - /d/ after the voiced endings b, g, l, m, n, r, v, z, and all vowels
>
>   Examples: robbed, listened, lived, sewed

Expressions of Past Time

Expressions of past time specify the time in the past when an action was completed. Here are some examples of expressions for past time:

yesterday	last year	next
the day before yesterday	in 1998	the next day
yesterday morning	in April 1992	after that
yesterday afternoon	on November 15	at 3:00
yesterday evening	on Tuesday	a few minutes ago
last night	a year ago	a week later
last Monday	a long time ago	then
last week		

1   In the conversation on pages 106 and 107, circle the regular past tense verbs in affirmative statements. Put a box around the negative past tense verbs.

Examples: We (worked) hard, but we (enjoyed) life. We ⊡didn't need⊡ a lot in the 1950s.

2   Fill in the blanks with the correct simple past tense forms of the regular verbs in parentheses.

When I was a child, we ___*didn't stay*___ inside watching TV in hot weather. We
                          1 (not stay)

___*didn't own*___ an air conditioner, so on warm summer evenings, we ___*stayed*___
2 (not own)   3 (stay)

outside on the porch for hours. We children ___*played*___ games or ___*looked*___ at
                                             4 (play)   5 (look)

comic books. My dad _relaxed_ in his chair and _smoked_ his pipe. Some-
6 (relax)   7 (smoke)

times he _tryed_ to do a crossword puzzle in the newspaper. Occasionally
8 (try)

some neighbors _visited_ us on the porch. Then dad _stoped_ reading the
9 (visit)   10 (stop)

newspaper and _discussed_ current events with them. They _argued_ about
11 (discuss)   12 (argue)

politics or the economy.

After my mom _washed_ the dinner dishes, she usually _joined_ us on the
13 (wash)   14 (join)

porch. She and my father _talked_ about the house, the neighborhood, and us
15 (talk)

kids. Sometimes she _peeled_ apples. My dad usually _helped_ my mom.
16 (peel)   17 (help)

When they _finished_ they _hand_ each of us kids an apple. My family
18 (finish)   19 (hand)

always _enjoyed_ those summer evenings on the porch.
20 (enjoy)

3 Think about your childhood. Write an affirmative or negative past tense statement about your childhood using each of the following verb phrases. You can tell about yourself and other family members.

Examples: live in an apartment _We lived in an apartment._
share a bedroom _I shared a bedroom with my sister._

1. live in an apartment
2. share a bedroom
3. work hard
4. clean the house
5. own a computer
6. rent videos
7. usually stay home after dinner

8. watch a lot of TV
9. play games
10. talk on the telephone a lot
11. plant a garden
12. argue
13. visit neighbors or friends
14. help with homework

15.	cook or bake	18.	use a microwave
16.	wash and dry dishes	19.	smoke a pipe
17.	order in food	20.	enjoy being together

B. Yes/No Questions and Short Answers

Simple past tense yes/no questions include *did(n't)* before the subject. Note that the main verb in the question is in the simple form. There is no final *-ed* ending in the question form.

			Possible Answers	
	Examples		**Affirmative**	**Negative**
Affirmative Questions	**Did** your mother **cook** last night?		Yes, she **did.**	No, she **didn't.**
	Did you **move** to a new apartment?		Yes, I **did.**	No, I **didn't.**
	Did the neighbors **visit** last week?		Yes, they **did.**	No, they **didn't.**
Negative Questions	**Didn't** she **rent** a video last night?		Yes, she **did.**	No, she **didn't.**
	Didn't he **call** you at home?		Yes, he **did.**	No, he **didn't.**
	Didn't they **paint** their house a few years ago?		Yes, they **did.**	No, they **didn't.**

4   Underline the yes/no question past tense verb forms in the conversation on pages 106 and 107.

Example: <u>Did</u> I ever <u>talk</u> to you kids about the good old days?

5   What did you do last weekend? First, Student A asks simple past tense questions using the words below, and Student B gives a short answer. Then, Student B asks the questions, and Student A gives short answers. After you give an affirmative short answer to a question, give additional information with a simple past tense sentence.

Examples: A. Did you clean your room last weekend?
  B. No, I didn't.
  A. Did you play any sports last weekend?
  B. Yes, I did. I played tennis on Saturday afternoon.

1.	clean your room?	9.	study at home?
2.	play any sports?	10.	finish your homework?
3.	listen to the radio?	11.	receive any letters or packages?
4.	watch TV?	12.	mail any letters or packages?
5.	cook?	13.	use a computer?
6.	telephone anyone?	14.	surf the Internet?
7.	visit your friends?	15.	stay up late?
8.	wash your clothes?	16.	enjoy yourself?

When you finish, join with another pair of students. Take turns telling the group five things that your partner did (or didn't do) last weekend.

C. Information Questions

Many simple past tense information questions use *did* before the subject; *why* can also have *didn't* before the subject. Note that when *who* or *what* is the subject of the sentence, the main verb is in the simple past tense and *did* is not used before the subject.

Examples	Possible Answers	Notes
Who did you **call?** **What did** you **do** yesterday? **Where did** your relatives **stay?** **When did** your relatives **visit?** **How did** she **find** her apartment? **Why did** you **cook** last night? **Why didn't** you **order** in pizza?	I called my sister. I cleaned my house. They stayed in the upstairs bedroom. They visited last month. She looked in the paper. I wanted to. I wanted a home-cooked meal.	In information questions with *did* and *didn't*, the main verb is in the simple form. There is no *-ed* ending.
What happened last night? **Who argued** a lot?	We rented a video. My sister and I argued a lot.	When *who* or *what* is the subject, the main verb is in the simple past tense and *did* is not used before the subject.

6 Put two lines under the information question forms in the conversation on pages 106 and 107.

Example: What did you do for fun?

7 The following information questions are missing question words. Fill in the blanks with question words from the list below. In some cases, more than one question word will fit. Try to use each question words at least once. Then interview a classmate about his or her childhood, using these questions. The classmate should answer, using the simple past tense. Write your classmate's answers on the lines provided below the questions.

What   Where   When   Who   How   Why

1. _Where_ did you live?
   I like at Riverdale,

2. _Who_ cooked food for your family?
   My sister cooked food for my family.

3. _Who_ shopped for food?
   _____

4. _What_ machines or electronic equipment did your family own?
   _____

5. _Wh_ did you play with?
   _____

6. _What_ games or sports did you play?
   _____

7. _When_ did you start school?

8. _why_ did you like school?

9. _____ did you want to study English?

10. _what_ television programs did you watch?

D. Used to

Used to + the simple form of either a regular or irregular verb expresses a habit or activity that existed in the past but is no longer happening in the present.

	Examples	Notes
Statements	I **used to live** in Brazil. She **used to cook** every day. My parents **didn't use to talk** much.	With *did(n't)* in questions and in negative statements, there is no *-d* ending on *use*.
Questions	Did your parents **use to argue** often? Didn't she **use to live** in New York? Who **used to help** you with your homework?	

8   Put three lines under the verb phrases with *use(d) to* in the conversation on pages 106 and 107.

Example: My sister used to <u>play</u> rock and roll records on her record player, and we used to <u>dance</u>.

9   Joseph is very different now from the way he was ten years ago. Study these pictures of him and the information next to each picture. Then use the cue words below to write a question about Joseph ten years ago, using *use to* for each question. Answer each question with either an affirmative or negative sentence, using *used to* for affirmative statements and *use to* for negative statements.

I'm Joe. I'm a teacher. I live in a small apartment in the city. I'm single. I like poetry, heavy metal music, and spending time alone. I smoke and I like fast food.

Ten years ago

I'm Joseph. I'm a salesperson. I live in a big house in the suburbs with my wife and two kids. I like detective novels, jazz, and spending time with friends. I don't smoke and my wife and I always prepare home-cooked meals.

Now

Examples: (have, long hair) *Did he use to have long hair? Yes, he used to have long hair.*

(wear, tie) *Did he use to wear a tie? No, he didn't use to wear a tie.*

1. (have, beard) _____
2. (wear, glasses) _____
3. (be, single) _____
4. (be, salesperson) _____
5. (be, teacher) _____
6. (smoke) _____
7. (live, apartment) _____
8. (live, suburbs) _____
9. (live, city) _____
10. (have, children) _____
11. (like poetry) _____
12. (read detective novels) _____
13. (listen, jazz) _____
14. (listen, heavy metal) _____
15. (like, spending time alone) _____
16. (like, spending time with friends) _____
17. (prepare, home-cooked meals) _____
18. (eat, fast food) _____
19. (call himself Joe) _____
20. (call himself Joseph) _____

Using What You've Learned

10 Bring to class photographs from books, newspapers, magazines, or other sources that show home and family scenes from the past. Work in small groups. Each group selects one photo and discusses what they see in the photo as well as what the photo shows about home and family life at that time. The group should then make as many past tense sentences as they can about their photo, using regular verbs, or regular and irregular verbs with *use(d) to.* Each group chooses one person to write down the group's sentences, and another person to tell the class about their picture.

11   Use the Internet or reference books to learn more about the "typical" family and home life of a period in the past. You may want to learn more about the period of the photo you examined in Activity 10, or you may wish to choose another time period. Consider focusing on one or more of the following topics:

- the role of each family member
- a typical day in the life of each family member
- the household technology available at the time
- the ways in which families entertained themselves at that time.

When you are ready, give your class an oral report on what you learned, using regular verbs, or regular and irregular verbs with *use(d) to.*

PART 2   The Simple Past Tense (Irregular Verbs); The Past Tense of the Verb *Be*

Setting the Context

Conversation

Antony: Hi Lorenz. What's up?

Lorenz: Hi Antony. I moved into my new apartment last week.

Antony: Why didn't you call me? I told you I was happy to help you move.

Lorenz: It wasn't necessary. My old roommate, Arlo, was there to help.

Antony: Well, how did it go?

Lorenz: It was a disaster. Everything went wrong.

Antony: What happened?

Lorenz: Well, the first problem was that I bought a new couch that didn't fit up the steps.

Antony: What did you do?

Lorenz: I left it with Arlo. He took it back to the old apartment. Anyway, after we brought in all of the furniture, we began to unpack. At one point, I got up on a ladder to hang some pictures, and I lost my balance and fell. I cut my arm on the ladder as I fell.

Antony: What did you do?

Lorenz: Well I really hurt my arm. And the cut bled a lot, so Arlo took me to the hospital to get stitches. That took about two hours. Then, when we finally got back to the apartment, I couldn't find my key.

Antony: Did you lose it?

Lorenz: I thought so, but then Arlo said he saw me take it out at the hospital. So we drove all the way back to the hospital to get it.

Antony: Was it there?

Lorenz: Yes, it was. When we got back to the apartment, we unpacked a little more. Arlo went home at about 10:00, but I kept unpacking. When I finally quit, I was exhausted. I fell asleep as soon as I lay down. I slept through most of the next day.

Antony: Wow. It sounds like you had a really bad move.

Lorenz: Yea, I'm really glad it's over. What's up with you?

Antony: Actually, I came to tell you some news.

Lorenz: What?

Antony: I just got a new apartment. And I . . . um . . . wanted to ask you to help me move in.

Discussion Questions

1. What happened to Lorenz's arm?
2. How did he get to the hospital?
3. What did he forget at the hospital?
4. How did he feel when he quit unpacking?
5. What news did Antony tell Lorenz?
6. Did you ever move or help a friend move into a new home? Did the move go well? Why or why not?

A. Irregular Past Tense Verbs

Many verbs have irregular past tense forms. These verbs do not take an *-ed* ending in the past form.

Examples				
Simple Form	**Past Tense Form**	**Simple Form**	**Past Tense Form**	**Notes**
cost	cost	let	let	The simple and the past forms of some verbs are the same.
cut	cut	put	put	
hit	hit	quit	quit	
hurt	hurt	shut	shut	
bend	bent	send	sent	With some verbs, the simple form ends in *-d* and the past form ends in *-t*.
build	built	spend	spent	
lend	lent			
dream	dreamt	lose	lost	Some verbs have other consonant changes or add a consonant in the past tense.
have	had	make	made	
hear	heard			
begin	began	grow	grew	Many verbs have vowel changes in the past tense.
bleed	bled	know	knew	
come	came	ride	rode	
choose	chose	ring	rang	
drink	drank	run	ran	
drive	drove	sing	sang	
eat	ate	take	took	
fall	fell	tear	tore	
find	found	throw	threw	
get	got	win	won	
give	gave	write	wrote	
be*	was/were	leave	left	Many verbs have consonant and vowel changes in the past tense.
bring	brought	lie	lay	
buy	bought	pay	paid	
catch	caught	say	said	
creep	crept	sell	sold	
do	did	sleep	slept	
fly	flew	teach	taught	
go	went	tell	told	
keep	kept	think	thought	

Note: Verbs that have irregular past tense forms follow the same patterns in affirmative statements, negative statements, yes/no questions, and information questions as regular verbs. See the charts on pages 107, 110, and 111.

*Be is the one exception to the above note. See the following chart for more information on using the past form of the verb *be*.

B. Past of Be

Be is an irregular verb. The simple past tense form of the verb is *was/were*. This irregular verb is used differently than other irregular verbs in statements, yes/no questions and answers, and information questions.

Statements		
	Examples	**Notes**
Affirmative	Mario **was** at home last night. They **were** born in Osaka.	Use *was* with singular nouns and with the pronouns *I, he, she, it, this,* and *that.* Use *were* with plural nouns and with the pronouns *you, we, these,* and *those.*
Negative	I **was not** on the Internet last night. We **were not** hungry for dinner yesterday.	Use *not* after the verb *be* in negative sentences. The contraction for *was not* is *wasn't;* the contraction for *were not* is *weren't.*

Yes/No Questions and Short Answers			
	Examples	**Possible Answers**	
		Affirmative	**Negative**
Affirmative	**Was** your mother born in Columbia? **Were** you asleep at 11:00 last night?	Yes, she **was.** Yes, I **was.**	No, she **wasn't.** No, I **wasn't.**
Negative	**Wasn't** the dog fed this afternoon? **Weren't** those sofas expensive?	Yes, she **was.** Yes, they **were.**	No, she **wasn't.** No, they **weren't.**

Information Questions		
	Examples	**Possible Answers**
Affirmative	**Who was** at your house last week? **Where were** you last week?	My aunt and uncle were there. I was on vacation in Spain.
Negative	**Why wasn't** your sister home for dinner? **Who wasn't** happy with the new apartment?	She was at the library. My mother wasn't happy.

1 Circle the past form of the verb *be* and put a box around the other irregular past tense verbs in the conversation on page 115.

Example: I ☐told☐ you I ⟨was⟩ happy to help you move.

2 Yukata is a Japanese student who has been accepted to Cambridge University in England. In the story below, he tells about leaving his home in Japan and finding a new home in England. Fill in each of the blanks with the past form of the verb in parentheses.

Cambridge University (send) __*sent*__ me the letter of acceptance on May
                                    1

10th. I (let) __*let*__ my father read the letter first. Then he (read) __*read*__ it
              2   3

aloud to the whole family. I know he and my mother (be) __were__ proud. I (be)

__was__ really excited. I (sleep) __slept__ badly that night. The next day I (take)

__took__ my parents downtown.

    We (have) __had__ dinner in a nice restaurant. Two days later, I (go)

__went__ shopping for some new clothes with my mother. The clothes (cost)

__cost__ a lot of money, but my mother proudly (spend) __spent__ the money.

    The day before I (leave) __left__, my friends (throw) __threw__ me a going

away party. It (be) __was__ a great party. The next morning, my alarm clock (ring)

__rang__ but I didn't hear it. We had to hurry. I (get) __got__ ready quickly and my

parents (drive) __drove__ me to the airport. I (catch) __caught__ the plane just in time.

    On the airplane, I (think) __thought__ about my home and my wonderful family

and friends. I (begin) __began__ to get a little homesick.

We (get) __got__ to Heathrow Air-

port in London twelve hours later. After

going through immigration and cus-

toms, I (take) __took__ a train to

Cambridge. Then I (buy) __bought__ a

newspaper and a map of the city at a

shop near my hotel. I (know) __knew__ I only (have) __had__ a week to find an

apartment before school (begin) __began__, so I (read) __red__ the classified

ads.

    I (make) __made__ a lot of telephone calls the first few days, but I didn't have

any luck. Someone (tell) __told__ me to go to an apartment rental agency. I (go)

__went__ to the agency, (pay) __paid__ them a fee, and they (give) __gave__

me a list of available apartments. A week later I (find) __found__ a one-bedroom

apartment in a really nice building. I (meet) _met_ some nice neighbors on my
34

first day in my new apartment.

I still miss home, but I think I (make) _made_ the right decision when I
35

decided to come here.

3   Read the following sentences. If there are any mistakes in the underlined words, correct the mistakes. If there are no mistakes, write "correct" next to the sentence.

Examples: They <u>payd</u> their rent late last month. _paid_
The mail <u>didn't come</u> yesterday.   _correct_

1.   We <u>grow</u> our own herbs last year. _grew_

2.   I <u>losed</u> the key to my house yesterday. _lose_

3.   Why didn't he <u>told</u> me about the new tenant? _tell_

4.   He <u>buyed</u> some plants for his house. _buy_

5.   Who <u>did made</u> the phone call? _make_

6.   <u>Was</u> you with your family last night? _be_

7.   My parents <u>builded</u> a new room onto their house. _build_

8.   She didn't <u>went</u> back home after class yesterday. _go_

9.   When <u>you choose</u> that wallpaper? _chose_

10.   She <u>havd</u> a computer in her old apartment. _h._

11.   They <u>threw</u> me a housewarming party. _throw_

12.   Why <u>she wasn't</u> more excited about her new apartment? _____

13.   She <u>find</u> a roommate last week. _find_

14.   She <u>tired</u> after she cleaned the house. _try_

15.   I <u>was</u> do three loads of laundry last night. _am_

Using What You've Learned

4   Continue the story in Activity 2 on pages 117–119. What do you think happened to Yukata next? Go around the room with each student adding one past tense statement to the story. When possible, use irregular verbs.

Example: A.   Yukata met another Cambridge student in his building.
      B.   The student was a woman.
      C.   Yukata and the woman became friends.
      D.   He asked her out on a date.
      E.   She said yes.
      F.   They went to the movies a week later.

5   Choose a topic from the list below. Prepare a short speech on the topic, using as many irregular past tense verbs as you can.

- My Favorite Childhood Memory
- Life with My Roommate(s)
- My Parents
- (your own topic about your home/family)

   When you are ready, give your speech to the class. After your speech, your classmates will ask you questions about your speech. They will also help you with any mistakes you may have made with irregular past tense verbs.

PART 3	**Connecting Words**

Setting the Context

Conversation

Atsuko: This kitchen is a mess!

Erika: I had to leave without cleaning it last night because I was late for a concert.

Atsuko: You should have cleaned it after you cooked dinner.

Erika: I meant to clean it when I got back. I even thought about it at the concert, because I knew you were going to be mad. When I got home, it was really late and I was exhausted. I fell asleep as soon as I lay down. I meant to wake up early this morning to clean the kitchen, but my alarm didn't go off.

Atsuko: You always have an excuse! You need to start helping out in the apartment or you're going to have to move out. I do almost all of the cleaning and most of the shopping.

Erika: You're right. I don't mean to be so lazy. It's just that I'm busy all day at school and at work, so I'm usually exhausted when I get home. I promise I'll start taking more responsibility. Tell me what you'd like me to do, so I can start right away.

Atsuko: Well, why don't you start doing the mid-week grocery shopping?

Erika: I can't because the shops are closed when I get out of work.

Atsuko: Can't you do it before you go to work?

Erika: No, because I don't have enough time to come home between work and school. Why don't I do it on Saturday or Sunday?

Atsuko: That sounds good, but you need to start being neater in the apartment as well. As soon as I clean a room, you mess it up. Also, you need to help me clean the apartment.

Erika: Let's make a schedule. You clean the apartment the first and third weeks of the month, and I'll clean it the second and fourth weeks. OK? Now I have to leave, or I'll be late for my first class.

Atsuko: Erika?

Erika: Yes?

Atsuko: When are you going to clean the kitchen?

Erika: Oh right! I'll clean it as soon as I get back. Bye!

Discussion Questions

1. Why didn't Erika clean the kitchen last night?
2. Why didn't she clean it this morning?
3. What does Atsuko want Erika to do?
4. Why can't Erika do the shopping during the week?
5. What cleaning schedule does Erika suggest?
6. Do you think it is difficult to live with a roommate? Why or why not?

A. Compound Sentences with And, But, Or, and So

A compound sentence combines two or more independent clauses (complete sentences) with connecting words such as *and, but, or,* and *so.* A comma is used before the connecting word to separate the clauses. A short sentence joined by *and* is sometimes combined without a comma.

	Examples	Notes
and	I do the shopping in my family. + I do the laundry. = I do the shopping **and** the laundry in my family.	*And* adds information and connects similar ideas.
but	I don't really like my neighborhood. + I live there because the rent is cheap. = I don't really like my neighborhood, **but** I live there because the rent is cheap.	*But* shows contrast and connects opposing ideas.
or	Do you live alone? + Do you live with a roommate? = Do you live alone, **or** do you live with a roommate?	*Or* expresses an alternative or a choice.
so	She doesn't like to cook. + She often eats fast food. = She doesn't like to cook, **so** she often eats fast food.	*So* introduces a result.

Note: In the first compound sentence in the chart, *I do the shopping and the laundry in my family,* it is not necessary to repeat the subject *I* after the connecting word *and* because both clauses refer to the same subject.

1 Circle the connecting words in the conversation on page 121.

Example: I had to leave without cleaning it last night (because) I was late for a concert.

2 Combine the following sentences with *and, but, or,* or *so.* In some cases, there might be more than one correct answer.

Example: We stayed home last night. We watched a video. *We stayed home and watched a video last night.*

1. I like the country. I live in the city.
2. He shares an apartment with four other people. It's crowded.
3. We bought a microwave. We bought a coffee maker.
4. I went to bed early last night. I couldn't sleep.
5. Do you want to eat at home tonight? Do you want to go to a restaurant?
6. My husband can make eggs and pasta. He can't make anything more complicated than that.
7. The rent was too expensive. We found another apartment.
8. Our oven broke last week. Our dishwasher broke this week.
9. Are you going to paint this room? Are you going to put up wallpaper?
10. Their apartment is only 700 square feet. It feels much bigger.
11. Do you live in a house? Do you live in an apartment?
12. I looked for my keys. I couldn't find them.

13.   The neighbors were making too much noise. We asked them to be more quiet.

14.   He baked a chocolate cake. He gave everyone a slice.

15.   I cleaned my whole apartment. It will be clean when my mother visits.

B. Complex Sentences with Before, After, As soon as, and When

A complex sentence consists of two or more clauses: an independent clause that is complete by itself, and one or more dependent clauses introduced by a connecting word such as *because, before, after, as soon as,* or *when.* When the dependent clause comes first, a comma is used after it to separate it from the independent clause. No comma is used when a dependent clause comes after an independent clause.

	Examples	**Notes**
because	I felt homesick **because I missed my family.** **Because I missed my family,** I felt homesick.	*Because* shows cause and effect.
before	She lived at home **before she started college.** **Before she started college,** she lived at home.	*Before* shows that something happened earlier in time.
after	I found a roommate **after I agreed to rent the apartment.** **After I agreed to rent the apartment,** I found a roommate.	*After* shows that something happened later in time.
as soon as	We became friends **as soon as he moved in.** **As soon as he moved in,** we became friends.	*As soon as* means "immediately following."
when	Did you have a curfew **when you lived at home?** **When you lived at home,** did you have a curfew?	*When* means "at the time that."

3   Underline the dependent clauses in the conversation on page 121.

Example: I had to leave without cleaning it last night <u>because I was late for a concert.</u>

4   Fill in the blanks with *because, before, after, as soon as,* or *when.* In some cases, more than one word may be possible.

I moved to a new apartment __after__ the neighbors in my old apartment were really inconsiderate. They always had loud parties _____ the weekend came. I don't mind parties that start __befor__ 9:00 or 10:00 o'clock, but most of their parties started __after__ 11:00 or 12:00 o'clock! It often seemed like __when__ I turned off my light and got into bed, the party began. __as soon as__ I called my landlord to complain about the parties, he seemed surprised. He said he was going to call my neighbors __because__ we hung up. __When__ I spoke with the landlord, I felt better. I was relieved __as soon as__ I really thought my neighbors would be more considerate now. But that very night __after__ I turned off my light to go to bed, I heard the music start up again. __After__ a few minutes, people started arriving. I called up a friend and asked if I could sleep at her house __because__ I couldn't stand to have one more sleepless night. I moved out of that apartment the very next day.

5   Use your imagination to add a dependent clause (starting with *because, before, after, as soon as,* or *when*) to each of the following independent clauses.

Example: I get nervous . . . *before I take exams.*

1.   I get nervous . . . __after the speech__

2.   I feel most energetic . . . _____

3.   I feel confident . . . _____

4. I get frustrated . . . _____

5. I study English . . . _____

6. I feel happy . . . _____

7. I get bored . . . _____

8. I learn best . . . _____

9. I feel embarrassed . . . _____

10. I feel tired . . . _____

Using What You've Learned

6 Choose a home-based activity. You can use one of the following activities, or think of one of your own. Write directions explaining how to do your chosen activity. Include the connecting words *and, but, or, so, because, before, after, as soon as,* and *when* in your directions.

- How to cook a food
- How to do a craft (such as knitting, sewing, model making, building a piece of furniture, etc.)
- How to tend a garden
- How to program or work a household appliance (such as a VCR, a coffee machine, or a microwave)

Example: How to Make Scrambled Eggs

You need eggs <u>and</u> butter to make scrambled eggs. You also need a pan <u>or</u> a griddle. First crack open as many eggs as you want <u>and</u> scramble them in a bowl. <u>Before</u> you put the eggs in the pan, melt the butter in the pan. (Do this <u>so</u> the eggs won't stick to the pan.) <u>After</u> all of the butter is melted, pour the eggs into the pan. <u>When</u> the eggs are cooked, remove them from the heat. Don't let them overcook <u>because</u> they will become hard. Serve them <u>as soon as</u> they are ready, <u>so</u> they don't get cold. <u>Before</u> you eat the eggs, you may want to add salt and pepper.

Video Activities: Asthma and Dust Mites

Before You Watch.   Discuss these questions in a group.

1. What do you know about asthma? Tell what you know about the causes and the treatment of this condition.
2. Can you guess what a "dust mite" is?
3. How can people reduce the amount of dust in their house?

Watch.

1. Write words to describe Linda Vine's house.
   Clean
   _____

2. How big do you think dust mites are? _____
3. In Linda Vine's house, you won't find _____.
   a. dust
   b. dust mites
   c. anything made of cloth
4. Write four things Linda Vine does to control dust mites in her house.

   _____

5. What is an easy way to kill dust mites on bedding?

   _____

Watch Again.   Discuss these questions in a group.

1. The announcer says, "Asthma is part genetic and part environment." What does this mean? Can you think of other medical problems like this?
2. Did you know about dust mites before you saw this video?
3. If you had asthma, would it be difficult for you to change your house like Linda Vine did?

After You Watch.   Read the paragraphs below and fill in the blanks with one of the following words: *because, before, after, if, when, and, but, or, so*

Getting Rid of Dust Mites

_____ some children are exposed to dust mites, they get asthma. _____ they already have asthma, dust mites make it worse. Therefore, you should cut down the number of dust mites in the home _____ your child has allergies or asthma. How can you do this?

Dust mites love warm, humid areas filled with dust, _____ pillows, mattresses, carpets, and furniture are great places for them to live. You should wash your sheets and blankets in very hot water every week. If possible, dry them in the sun _____ heat kills dust mites. You should also wash your pillow every week _____ put a plastic cover on it. Vacuuming your carpets every week can help, _____ the best thing to do is to remove all the carpets. Finally, _____ dust mites love warm, humid places, it helps to run your air conditioner and keep the air dry.

Chapter 6

Cultures of the World

PART 1	# Present Perfect Tense (1)

Setting the Context

Conversation

Alex: Is anyone sitting here?

Janet: No. Please have a seat. My name's Janet. I'm from the United States.

Koto: I'm Koto. I'm from Japan.

Alex: Nice to meet you both. I'm Alex. I'm from Brazil.

Asim: And my name's Asim. I'm from Egypt. Alex and I have just arrived in London. Actually, we just met at the airport.

Janet: London is a great city. I think you'll like it.

Asim: What have you done here so far?

Koto: We've gone to the Tower of London, Buckingham Palace, Westminster Abbey, and we've already been to the British Museum twice. That's where Janet and I met.

Alex: (*to Janet*) Does England feel very familiar to you since it's an English-speaking country like the United States?

Janet: Well, there are a lot of similarities between the United States and England, but I've been surprised at how many differences there are, too. I'm always noticing differences in traditions, foods, lifestyle, . . . even language!

Asim: What has surprised you the most?

Janet: Probably how different the people are. All the English people I've met have been very kind. But they've also been much more reserved than I'm used to.

Koto: Actually, I've been to England twice before and I've always felt very comfortable with the people. I think that's because Japanese people are a bit reserved too.

Asim: That's interesting. (*Looking at a menu*) Hmmm. Have you ever heard of Shepherd's Pie?

Janet: Yes. It's a traditional English dish made with layers of meat, potato, and cheese. I've had it once or twice recently. It's not bad. But I think English food is a little bland.

Koto: Not the desserts. Have you tried any traditional English puddings yet? They're delicious!

Alex: I've never had any traditional English foods. I've only had fast food here so far.

Koto: How does English fast food taste?

Alex: A lot like Brazilian fast food! And like the fast food in every country I've ever visited. Fast food is probably the one thing that's the same all around the world!

Discussion Questions

1. What have Koto and Janet done in London so far?
2. How many times have they been to the British Museum?
3. What differences has Janet noticed between English culture and American culture?
4. Why has Koto always felt comfortable in England?
5. What has been the same in every country Alex has visited?
6. Have you ever visited another country? If so, what differences did you notice between that country and your own?

A. Past Participles

The past participle is the verb form used in the present perfect tense.

	Simple Forms	Past Participles	Simple Forms	Past Participles	Notes
Regular Verbs	like	liked	study	studied	For regular verbs, the past participle is the same as the simple past tense (verb + *ed*).
	live	lived	travel	traveled	
	play	played	visit	visited	
Irregular Verbs	be	been	meet	met	For irregular verbs, the past participle often changes spelling and/or pronunciation.
	become	become	pay	paid	
	begin	begun	put	put	
	break	broken	read	read	
	bring	brought	ride	rode	
	buy	bought	ring	rung	
	choose	chosen	run	run	
	come	come	say	said	
	cost	cost	see	seen	
	do	done	send	sent	
	eat	eaten	sit	sat	
	find	found	speak	spoken	
	fly	flown	sleep	slept	
	forget	forgotten	take	taken	
	get	gotten	teach	taught	
	give	given	tell	told	
	go	gone	think	thought	
	have	had	win	won	
	know	known	write	written	

Note: For more irregular verbs, see Appendix 3.

1 Try to complete the missing verb forms without looking at the chart above.

Simple Forms	Past Participles	Simple Forms	Past Participles
1. be	been	11. meet	met
2. begin	begun	12. pay	paid
3. bring	brought	13. read	read
4. buy	bought	14. say	said
5. cost	cost	15. study	studies
6. do	done	16. speak	spoken
7. eat	eaten	17. take	taken
8. live	lived	18. think	thought
9. come	went	19. write	written
10. have	had	20. visit	visten

B. The Present Perfect Tense

The present perfect tense is formed with *have/has* + the past participle form of the verb. The present perfect tense often refers to an event that happened at an unknown or unspecified time in the past. It also refers to repeated past actions. Time expressions often used with this meaning of the present perfect include *already, ever, just, recently, still, yet, so far, up to now, once, twice, three times,* etc. No specific time is given in a past perfect statement or question. (If we use past time expressions such as *yesterday* or *last week,* we use the past tense.)

Statements		
Purpose	**Examples**	
	Affirmative	**Negative**
Actions or Situations at an Unspecified Time in the Past	I**'ve been** to Canada. My parents **have** just **returned** from there.	I **have not been** to India. I **have never seen** the Taj Mahal.
Repeated Actions at Unspecified Times in the Past	I**'ve been** to Canada twice. My parents **have been** there many times.	I **haven't eaten** Indian food more than once or twice. I **haven't traveled** outside my country many times.

Note: The present perfect can be contracted with subject pronouns: *I've, we've, you've, they've, he's, she's,* and *it's.* The negative contractions are *haven't* and *hasn't.*

Yes/No Questions			
	Examples	**Possible Answers**	
		Affirmative	**Negative**
Affirmative	**Have** you ever **been** to New York?	Yes, I have.	No, I haven't.
	Have you ever **seen** the Empire State Building?	Yes, I have.	No, I haven't.
Negative	**Haven't** you ever **been** to New York?	Yes, I have.	No, I haven't.
	Haven't you ever **seen** the Empire State Building?	Yes, I have.	No, I haven't.

Information Questions		
	Examples	**Possible Answers**
Affirmative	Who **has lived** abroad?	Juan has lived abroad.
	Why **have** you **come** here?	I have come to learn about other cultures.
	How many times **have** you **been** here?	I've been here twice.
	How much money **have** you **spent**?	I have spent a lot of money!
Negative	Who **hasn't taken** any pictures?	They haven't.
	Why **haven't** you **brought** a map?	I don't need one.

2   Underline the present perfect phrases in the conversation on pages 128 and 129.

Example: Alex and I <u>have</u> just <u>arrived</u> in London.

3   Fill in the blanks with the correct form of the verbs in parentheses to form the present perfect tense.

Queridos mamãe and papai,

I'm sorry I (not, write) <u>*haven't written*</u> sooner, but I (not, have) <u>have not had</u> a free
                                    1   2
moment! There (be) <u>has being</u> so much to do here in London. I (meet)
                               3
<u>have I met</u> some great people and I am having a wonderful time.
        4

There's so much to tell you, I don't know where to begin. I'll start by telling

you about some of the things that I (do) <u>have met</u> here. I (be) <u>have done</u> to
                                                          5   6

Westminster Abbey, which is the most famous church in England. Also, I (visit)

haven't Visiter Buckingham Palace, which is where the queen lives! I
         7

(ride) _has, read_ double decker buses a few times and I (eat) _have eaten_ tra-
         8   9

ditional English foods like Yorkshire Pudding and Steak and Kidney Pie. (I'm not crazy

about the food, so I (lose) _have lost_ some weight!)
                                  10

   I (speak) _have spoken_ with some English people and they (teach)
                  11

thought me a few things about British culture. I (learn) _have learned_ that
   12   13

pubs are where people go to meet friends and relax. I (go) _have gone_ to pubs a
                                                              14

few times, and I really like them! In the pubs, I (play) _have played_ a few games of
                                                          15

darts, a popular English bar game. I (watch) _have watched_ a few soccer matches on
                                              16

TV at the pubs. I (discover) _have discovered_ that soccer is almost as popular here as it
                              17

is back home in Brazil!

   I (be) _have been_ amazed at how much tea people drink here. I (try) _have_
            18

tried the coffee, but it's usually very weak. I (not, be) _have not been_ able to
   19   20

find really strong coffee like we drink in Brazil.

   Unfortunately, the weather (not, be) _had not been_ very good. It's often rainy and
                                         21

foggy here. I (not see) _have not seen_ sunshine since I left Brazil. With all of this rain, I
                         22

(catch) _had caught_ a little cold.
         23

   I can't wait to tell you more about my trip. I (take) _have taken_ many pho-
                                                          24

tos to show you and I (buy) _have bought_ many souvenirs for everyone at
                            25

home.

   I really like it here, but I think I'd better leave soon—my friends (tell) _has told_
                                                                               26

me that I (begun) _had begin_ to speak with a British accent!
                   27

Besos,

Alex

4   Write present perfect questions for the following answers. Be careful to use the correct question form (yes/no questions *or* information questions) as appropriate.

Example: 1.   Q: *Has he eaten Indian food?*
                      A: Yes, he has eaten Indian food.

              2.   Q: *How many times has he eaten Indian food?*
                      A: He has eaten it only once or twice.

              3.   Q: *Where has he eaten Indian food?*
                      A: He has eaten it in London.

A.

1. Q: *Has she taken picture yet?*
   A: Yes, she has taken a lot of photographs.

2. Q: *How many rolls are there?*
   A: Probably about 6 or 7 rolls.

3. Q: *Where she has taken the picture?*
   A: Mostly of churches and castles.

B.

1. Q: *Have you spent a lot of money on transportation?*
   A: Yes, I've spent a lot of money on transportation.

2. Q: *How much money have you spent?*
   A: About £40.

3. Q: _____?
   A: Double decker buses, the tube, and a few taxi rides.

C.

1. Q: *Have you drunk a lot of tea during your trip?*
   A: Yes, I've drunk a lot of tea during my trip.

2. Q: *How many cups of tea have you taken?*
   A: I've had at least five cups of tea each day.

3. Q: *Have you ever had tea with the queen?*
   A: No, I've never had tea with the queen!

4. Q: *Why she has never invited me?*
   A: Because she's never invited me.

C. Ever, Never, Already, Just, Recently, Still, *and* Yet

These adverbs are frequently used with the present perfect tense.

	Examples	**Notes**
Questions	Have you **ever** been to the British Museum?	*Ever* means "at any time." It comes before the past participle.
	Have you **already** been to the British Museum?	*Already* means "before now." It may come before the past participle or at the end of the question.
	Have you visited the British Museum **already?**	
	Have you visited the British Museum **yet?**	*Yet* means "up to now." It is usually placed at the end of a question.
Affirmative Statements	I've **just** visited that museum.	*Just* refers to the very recent past. *Just* comes before the past participle.
	I've **already** visited that museum.	*Already* and *recently* usually come before the past participle or at the end of the sentence.
	I've visited that museum **already.**	
	I've **recently** visited that museum.	
	I've visited that museum **recently.**	
Negative Statements	I have **never** visited that museum.	*Never* means "not at any time." It must come before the past participle.
	I haven't visited that museum **yet.**	*Yet* usually comes at the end of a negative statement.
	I **still** haven't visited that museum.	*Still* means "up to now." *Still* comes before *has* or *have.*

5 Put a circle around the adverbs *ever, never, already, just, recently, still,* and *yet* in the conversation on pages 128 and 129. Notice the position of these words in the sentences.

Example: We've gone to the Tower of London, Buckingham Palace, Westminster Abbey, and we've (already) been to the British Museum twice.

6 Insert the adverbs in parentheses into the sentences that follows the adverbs. In some cases, there may be more than one possible position for the adverb.

Asim: What should we do today?

Alex: (still) Well, we ~~still~~ haven't been to the British Museum.
    1

Koto: (already) Janet and I have been there twice!
    2

Janet: (recently) I've seen and done so much. I think I'll stay here and do some
    3
laundry. (yet) Also, I haven't had a chance to write any postcards. yet
    4

Alex: Really? (already) I've sent a couple of postcards home.
    5

Koto: I may stay behind too. (never) I've been so tired in my life!
    6

Alex: (still) I can't believe I'm in London! (yet) There's so much I haven't seen.
    7   8

Asim: Why don't we split up so that everyone can do whatever they want to do today?
We can meet up again tonight and do something.

Janet: OK. (yet) Hey, we haven't seen a play in the West End theatre district. Is anyone
    9
interested in doing that tonight?

Koto: That's a great idea. (already) I have information about the shows that are playing.
    10

Asim: I hear Romeo and Juliet is playing. (ever) Have you seen it?
    11

Janet: I love that play. (already) I've seen it twice, but I'd be happy to see it again.
    12

Alex: (never) I've seen it.
    13

Koto: (recently) I read it in school. It would be fun to see it on stage.
    14

Asim: (just) Well then, we've made our plan for the day! We'll meet you back here at
    15
about 6:00.

7 Find the mistakes in each of the following sentences and rewrite the sentences correctly. If there are no mistakes in a sentence, write *correct*. All of the sentences should
be in the present perfect tense.

1. She have been to already the Houses of Parliament.

   She has already been to the Houses of Parliament.

2. I have saw some beautiful English gardens.

   He has seen some beautiful english gardens.

3. Have you yet eat fish and chips?

   Have you not yet eaten fish and chips?

4. Big Ben is the biggest clock I have seen ever.

   Big Ben is the biggest clock I have ~~seen~~ ever seen.

5. I have taken already the London subway three or four times.

   I have already taken the London subway three or four times.

6. Have he watched any of the popular British TV soap operas?

   Have you watched any of the popular British TV soap operas?

7. Many famous tennis players have played at the Wimbledon Tennis Championship in southwest London.

   _____

   _____

8. I has be surprised by how many different English accents there are.

   I have about so much different English accent there are.

9. How much money have you spend on souvenirs?

   Have you hard much money to spend on souvenirs.

10. I had have Yorkshire Pudding twice.

    I have had Yorkshire pudding twice.

11. I not have had the chance to travel to Scotland or Wales.

    I have not had the chance to travel to Scotland

12. We have learn recently a lot about English culture.

    We have recently learn about English culture a lot.

13. We decide to travel to France next.

    Next day we decide to travel to France.

14. You have made yet the reservations?

    Have you made the reservations yet?

Using What You've Learned

8   Play a game of "Find someone who . . .": First make present perfect questions with the cue words in Nos. 1 to 12 below. Each question should begin with "Have you ever . . ." Then when your teacher tells you to begin, quickly go around the classroom, asking your classmates one of the questions until you find someone who says that he or she has done the thing you are asking about. Write down that person's name beside the question, then move on to the next question.

Example: *Student A.*   Have you ever been to another country?

        Student B.   No, I haven't.

        Student A.   Have *you* ever been to another country?

        Student C.   Yes, I have.

        Student A.   Great!

1. be / another country?
2. eat / food from another country?

Paper
Write good Simple, short, complete sentences.
Follow topic   non verb object.

Chapter 6 Cultures of the World   **137**

3. go / to a movie that was made in another country?
4. know / person from another country?
5. write / letter to a person from another country?
6. receive / letter from a person from another country?
7. drink / a popular drink from another country?
8. read / a book by an author from another country?
9. make / a recipe from another country?
10. see / an art exhibit from another country?
11. sing / song from another country?
12. try / learn another language?

The first person who gets names for all of the questions wins the game. The class confirms the winner by checking that the people on the list have done what the winner says they have. The class also asks these people questions to learn more about their experiences.

Example: *Student A.* OK Reiko, who has been to another country?
Reiko (winning student). Tomoko has been to another country.
Student A. Tomoko, *have* you been to another country?
Tomoko. Yes, I have.
Student B. Which country have you been to?
Tomoko. I have been to the United States.

9 Find a classmate, a teacher, a friend, or a family member who has traveled to one or more foreign countries. Interview this person about their experiences in the foreign country or countries. Find out the following:

■ What foreign country or countries has this person been to?
■ What foods has this person eaten in foreign countries?
■ What has this person done in foreign countries?
■ What has this person seen in foreign countries?
■ What has this person bought in foreign countries?

Report back to your class on what you have learned about the person's experiences, using the present perfect tense where appropriate.

10 Technology and the media are making the world a smaller place. As a result, almost all cultures have been influenced by other cultures. Work in small groups to discuss and list the ways in which other cultures have (and have not yet) influenced your own culture. Use the present perfect and the adverbs *never, already, just, recently, still,* and *yet.* Each group shares their completed list with the class.

Examples: Chinese food has become very popular in our country recently.
French fashion has influenced the way we dress.
Western fast food has already had an effect on our diet.
The attitudes of the older generation haven't really been affected yet.

I have already eaten breakfast.

PART 2	# Superlatives

Setting the Context

Reading

Dear Mom and Dad,

My trip is going really well. I met the nicest people in London and we all traveled together by ferry to France. My friend Alex made us laugh throughout the whole trip. Alex is the funniest person of the group. Tomoko is the shyest, Asim is the most thoughtful, and I'm afraid I'm the most talkative!   5

Paris is the most beautiful city I've ever seen. The streets are filled with the most romantic cafes, the people dress in the most fashionable clothes, and everywhere you turn you see the most impressive monuments. The food is really wonderful too. Of course I can't afford to go to the most expensive restaurants, but even the bread is great here! The most common kind of bread is called a   10 baguette. It's a really long, crusty type of roll. In the morning, people often eat that or croissants. French croissants are the flakiest and most delicious bread I've ever had. But the best bread of all is pain au chocolate—a kind of croissant with a chocolate filling. I usually have one of them and a cup of coffee for breakfast. (It's probably the worst thing for my diet!)   15

Today we went to the Louvre, one of the largest art museums in the world. I read that the Louvre has more than eight miles of galleries! It was interesting to see paintings by some of the most important French artists like Monet, Degas, and Renoir. I also got to see the most famous painting in the world—the Mona Lisa.   20

After we left the museum, we wandered down the Champs-Elysees, one of the widest and most glamorous avenues in Paris. I saw the most expensive shops and the most elegant people you can imagine.

There's so much more to tell you, but this is already the longest letter I've ever written you. So I'll end this letter here, but I'll write again soon!   25

Love,
Janet

Discussion Questions

1. How does Janet describe each of her friends? How does she describe herself?
2. How does Janet describe Paris?
3. What does Janet say about the bread in France?
4. What does Janet say about the Louvre museum?
5. What did Janet see on the Champs-Elysees?
6. How do you think a tourist would describe your city?

A. Superlative Forms

Superlatives are used to compare three or more people or things.

	Examples	Notes
One-Syllable Adjectives and Adverbs	Sydney is **the biggest** city in Australia. I think Japanese people work **the hardest.**	Add -est to one-syllable adjectives and adverbs. Use the before the superlative.
Two-Syllable Adjectives	I think the Irish are **the friendliest** people. Finding accommodations is **the most stressful** part of travel.	Two-syllable adjectives ending in er or y usually add -est. The opposite is expressed with the least + adjective. Two-syllable adjectives ending in ful or re usually take most and least.
Other Adjectives and Adverbs	Baseball and football are **the most popular sports** in America. They are **the most frequently watched** sports on TV.	Adjectives of three or more syllables and adverbs of two or more syllables take the most or the least to form the superlative.
Irregulars	The Prado Museum in Spain has some of **the best** paintings in the world. Cairo has **the worst** traffic in Egypt.	The irregular superlative forms are: good/best, well/best, bad/worst, badly/worst, far/farthest, little/least, many/most, and much/most.
Nouns	Who has been to **the most** museums? I have **the fewest** stamps in my passport. I have spent **the least** money.	Use the most or the fewest with count nouns. Use the most or the least with noncount nouns.

Note: A common superlative phrase is: *one of the* + superlative + plural count noun. For example: Greece is *one of the oldest civilizations* in the world.

Spelling Rules for Adjective/Adverb + *est*
1. One-syllable adjectives and adverbs:
For most one-syllable adjectives and adverbs, add -*est*.
Examples: quick/quickest   tall/tallest   long/longest
When the last letter is -*e*, add only -*st*.
Examples: nice/nicest   large/largest   rare/rarest
When the word ends in a single consonant after a single vowel, double the last consonant and add -*est*.
Examples: big/biggest   hot/hottest   thin/thinnest
2. For two-syllable words ending in -*y*, change the -*y* to *i* and add -*est*.
Examples: crazy/craziest   easy/easiest   funny/funniest

1   Underline the superlatives in the reading on pages 138 and 139.

Example: Alex is the <u>funniest</u> person of the group.

2   Give the superlative form of each word.

1. happy *happiest*
2. famous *most famous*
3. lucky *luckiest*
4. good *best*
5. strong *strongest*
6. rich *richest*
7. interesting *most interesting*
8. pretty *prettiest*
9. brave *bravest*
10. beautiful *most beautiful*
11. foolish *most foolish*
12. far *farest*
13. quick *quickest*
14. dangerous *most dangeras*

3   Use your opinions and ideas to fill in the blanks. When you are finished, share your ideas with the class.

Example: *Rio de Janeiro* is the most exciting city in the world.

1. *Paris* is the most beautiful city in the world.
2. *French* is the most beautiful language.
3. *French food* food is the most delicious food in the world.
4. *Tokoyo* is the most expensive city in the world.
5. *Mona lisa* is the most famous city in the world.
6. *galleries* culture is the most interesting culture.
7. *Mona lisa* has the friendliest people in the world.
8. *Paris* is the most fashionable city in the world.
9. _____ is the most historic city in the world.

10. _New York_ is the city with the most traffic.

11. _Maryland_ is the city with the least crime.

12. _U.S.A_ is the country that has the largest cultural influence on the world.

4 Fill in the blanks with the superlative form of the words in parentheses.

Ten Interesting Facts about France:

1. France is (big) _biggest_ country in Western Europe.

2. (high) _highest_ mountain in France is Mont Blanc. It is 4,807 meters high.

3. Some of (important) _most famous_ painting styles started in France. French Impressionists like Renoir and Cubists like Braque are known all over the world.

4. Some of (respect) _most respected_ literature in the world comes from France. Moliere, Racine, Hugo, Saint-Exupery, and Rimbaud are translated into almost every language.

5. The French Revolution occurred in 1789, making France one of (old) _oldest_ democracies in the world.

6. Many people consider French cuisine to be (good) _best_ cuisine in the world.

7. The Eiffel Tower is (popular) _populated_ attraction in France. More than five million people visit the Tower each year.

8. The Tour de France is a three week bicycle race which covers more than 2,000 miles. It is (big) _biggest_ annual sporting event in the world.

9. France produces some of (fine) _finest_ perfumes in the world.

10. France is the second (large) _longest_ producer of wine in the world.

5 Compare these three famous national symbols using the information provided, the cue words, and the superlative form.

The Eiffel Tower
- Height: 300 meters
- Weight: 7,000 tons
- Built between 1887 and 1889
- Number of steps: 1,652
- Average number of visitors (per year): 5.5 million

The Statue of Liberty
- Height: 93 meters
- Weight: 225 tons
- Built between 1875 and 1884
- Number of steps: 354
- Average number of visitors (per year): 4.2 million

The Leaning Tower of Pisa
- Height: 56 meters
- Weight: 16,204 tons
- Built between 1173 and 1350
- Number of steps: 294
- Currently closed for construction

1.   The Leaning Tower of Pisa is (the heaviest / the least heavy).
2.   The Statue of Liberty is (the heaviest / the least heavy).
3.   The Eiffel Tower is (the lowest / the highest).
4.   The Leaning Tower of Pisa is (the lowest / the highest).
5.   The Leaning Tower of Pisa is (the oldest / the most modern).
6.   The Eiffel Tower is (the oldest / the most modern).
7.   The Leaning Tower of Pisa took (the most / the least) time to build.
8.   The Eiffel Tower took (the most / the least) time to build.
9.   The Eiffel Tower has (the most / the fewest) steps.
10.   The Leaning Tower of Pisa has (the most / the fewest) steps.
11.   The Leaning Tower of Pisa has (the most / the fewest) annual visitors.
12.   The Eiffel Tower has (the most / the fewest) annual visitors.

6   Alex, Asim, Koto, and Janet are telling each other some interesting facts about their countries. First fill in the blanks with the superlative forms of the words in parentheses. Then try to identify which facts belong to which speaker. Then match the number of each fact to the correct speaker in the picture below.

1. My country has some of (impressive) _the most impressive_ ancient ruins in the world, such as the Pyramids of Giza.

2. My country has (large) _the longest_ remaining tropical rain forest in the world.

3. Sumo wrestling is one of (popular) _the most popular_ traditional sports in my country.

4. (exciting) _the most exc_ holiday in my country is the fourth of July.

5. Rice is (important) _the most impo_ crop in my country.

6. In my country, we usually eat one of (big) _the biggest_ meals of the year on Thanksgiving Day.

7. Haiku is one of (beautiful) _the most beaut_ styles of poetry. This poetry began in my country.

8. (holy) _the most famous_ holiday in my country is Ramadan.

9. Cairo is (crowded) _the highest crowded_ city in my country.

10. The city with (great) _the most greatest_ number of people in my country is São Paulo.

11. Samba music is one of (famous) _the most famous_ styles of music from my country.

12. The Nile River runs through my country. It is (long) _the longest_ river in the world.

13. The Amazon River runs through my country. It is the second (long) _It is the longest_ river in the world.

14. My native language is one of (difficult) _the most_ languages in the world.

15. Camels are one of (common) _the most_ forms of transportation in the desert areas of my country.

16. Alaska is one of (cold) _the coldest_ states in my country.

17. One of (traditional) _most_ kind of clothing of my country is called the kimono.

18. Baseball started in my country, and it is still one of (popular) _pop famous_ sports there.

19. My country has won the World Cup in soccer (many) _the_ times.

20. My country has one of (diverse) _most_ populations in the world.

Using What You've Learned

7 Work in a small group. Together, write ten trivia questions about other cultures and countries, using superlatives. (You must know the answers to the questions you ask.) Test the other groups on their cultural knowledge by asking them these questions. The group that answers the most questions correctly is the winning group.

Example: What is the most famous museum in Russia? (the Hermitage)
What is the largest country is Central America? (Nicaragua)
What is the most important holiday in Japan? (New Year)

8   Choose a culture that you would like to learn more about. Use the Internet or resource books in the library to find out about this culture. Some of the aspects of the culture you may wish to research are:

- the most famous author(s), artist(s), and musician(s)
- the most popular sport(s)
- the most common food(s)
- the most important holiday(s) and/or festival(s)

When you have finished your research, give an oral report on what you have learned.

PART 3   # Comparisons with *So, Too, Either,* and *Neither; But*

Setting the Context

Conversation

Koto: I wish this wasn't our last day in Venice.
Janet: I do too. I'm excited to go on to Spain tomorrow, but I'll miss Italy.
Asim: I haven't seen half the things I wanted to see here.
Alex: Neither have I.
Janet: Which was your favorite city in Italy?
Alex: I think Rome was my favorite city. All the monuments were fascinating, and so were the churches and palaces.

Koto: Florence was my favorite city. Rome was a bit loud and busy, but Florence wasn't. The central square in Florence was so beautiful, and so were the museums.

Asim: Venice is my favorite city. I've never seen a city without a single car! The narrow streets are magical, and so are the canals.

Janet: I think what I like best about Italy is the pace. Life here seems so relaxed and laid back.

Asim: So is life in Egypt. I think you'd really like it. Egyptians are never too busy to have a cup of tea with a friend.

Alex: Neither are Brazilians. We think that enjoying where you are is more important than being in a hurry to get somewhere else.

Janet: Really? In the United States people always seem to be in a rush. The small towns aren't so bad, but the big cities are. New York can be a crazy place.

Koto: So can Tokyo.

Asim: I've always wanted to see Japan and the United States.

Alex: So have I.

Janet: We should plan to visit each other! We have a spare room in our house.

Koto: We do too!

Asim: After this gondola ride, let's get another caffe latte in San Marco square and talk about it.

Janet: We don't have time! We have to catch the 2:00 train. The 3:00 train doesn't have any seats left, but the 2:00 train does. And if we miss the 2:00 train, we'll get into Spain too late to find a hostel!

Asim: Janet?

Janet: What?

Asim: Relax. Remember? You're not in New York now!

Discussion Questions

1. How do Koto, Janet, Asim, and Alex feel about leaving Italy? Why?
2. Which was Alex's favorite city? Why?
3. Which was Koto's favorite city? Why?
4. Which is Asim's favorite city? Why?
5. What does Janet like most about Italy? How does she compare it to the United States?
6. Do you prefer the lifestyle in Japan and America, or in Egypt and Brazil? Why?

A. Expressing Similarities with So, Too, Either, and Neither

If two sentences that show similarity have different subjects but the same verb, the second sentence can be shortened by using *be* or an auxiliary verb + *too, so, either,* or *neither.* This shortened sentence can either be added to the first sentence as a clause with the conjunction *and,* or it can appear as a separate sentence in response to the first. *So* and *too* are used for affirmative statements; *either* and *neither* are used for negative statements.

So and Too			
	Examples		**Notes**
	Full Form	**Additions with so and too**	**Responses with so and too**	
With be	I love salsa music. Erik loves salsa music.	I love salsa music, **and Erik does, too.** I love salsa music, **and so does** Erik.	A. I love salsa music B. Erik **does, too.** A. I love salsa music. B. **So does** Erik.	*Too* follows the auxiliary verb or *be* in an added clause or a response sentence.
With Auxiliary Verbs	I'm Australian. Erik is Australian.	I'm Australian, **and Erik is, too.** I'm Australian, **and so is** Erik.	A. I'm Australian. B. Erik **is, too.** A. I'm Australian. B. **So is** Erik.	The auxiliary verb or *be* follows *so* in an added clause or a response sentence.

Either and Neither			
	Examples		**Notes**
	Full Form	**Additions with either and neither**	**Responses with either and neither**	
With be	I don't like salsa music. Erik doesn't like salsa music.	I don't like salsa music, **and Erik doesn't either.** I don't like salsa music, **and neither does Erik.**	A. I don't like salsa music. B. **Neither does** Erik. A. I don't like salsa music. B. Erik **doesn't either.**	*Either* follows the auxiliary verb or *be* in an added clause or a response sentence.
With Auxiliary Verbs	I'm not Australian. Erik isn't Australian.	I'm not Australian, **and Erik isn't either.** I'm not Australian, **and neither is Erik.**	A. I'm not Australian. B. Erik **isn't either.** A. I'm not Australian. B. **Neither is** Erik.	The auxiliary verb or *be* follows *neither* in an added clause or a response sentence.

1 Underline the additions and responses with *so, too, either,* and *neither* in the conversation on pages 144 and 145.

Example: *Koto:* I wish this wasn't our last day in Venice.
  Janet: I <u>do too.</u>

2 In each of the following short dialogues, change the sentence in parentheses to a short response, using *so, too, either,* or *neither.* For each sentence, two answers will be possible. Write both possible answers on the lines provided.

Example: *Koto:* Tokyo is a very crowded city.
  Asim: (Cairo is a very crowded city.) <u>*So is Cairo.*</u> OR <u>*Cairo is too.*</u>

1. *Koto:* Most Japanese people live in cities.
   Alex: (Most Brazilian people live in cities.) <u>So is Cairo</u> OR _____
2. *Alex:* Brazil doesn't have a royal family.
   Janet: (The United States doesn't have a royal family.) <u>neither</u> OR
   <u>either</u>

3. *Janet:* New York has a very diverse population.
   Alex: (Sao Paulo has a very diverse population.) _so does_ OR _____

4. *Alex:* Baseball isn't very popular in Brazil.
   Asim: (Baseball isn't very popular in Egypt.) _either_ OR _neither_

5. *Alex:* Brazilians aren't usually shy.
   Janet: (Americans aren't usually shy.) _either_ OR _does neither_

6. *Janet:* Americans celebrate Labor Day.
   Alex: (Brazilians celebrate Labor Day.) _so, too_ OR _Brazil do too_

7. *Koto:* Janet bought a map yesterday.
   Janet: (Alex bought a map yesterday.) _so, too_ OR _Alex so too_

8. *Asim:* I will call home today.
   Koto: (I will call home today.) _so will_ OR _will too_

B. Expressing Contrasts with But

Use *but* to join statements of contrast.

	Examples		Notes
	Full Form	**Additions with *but***	
With *be*	Spanish food is spicy. Irish food isn't spicy.	Spanish food is spicy, **but** Irish food **isn't**.	*But* appears between the two contrasting ideas, and follows a comma.
With Auxiliary Verbs	Columbians speak Spanish. Brazilians don't speak Spanish.	Columbians speak Spanish, **but** Brazilians don't.	

3   Circle the additions with *but* in the conversation on pages 144 and 145.

Example: Rome was a bit loud and busy, (but Florence wasn't).

4   Finish each sentence with the correct auxiliary verb or form of *be*.

Example: Asim has a map, but Koto _doesn't_.

1. The United States is a multicultural nation, but Japan _doesn't_

2. The United States isn't an ancient civilization, but Egypt _does_.

3. Japanese people remove their shoes when they enter a house, but Egyptians _doesn't_

4. The Brazilian flag isn't red, white, and blue, but the American flag _does not_

5. European workers get at least three weeks of vacation time each year, but American and Japanese workers _doesn't_

6. Alex went to the tourist office, but I _wasn't_

7. I have read a few books by Italian authors, but Asim _hasn't_

8. My food wasn't spicy, but his _was_.

9. This hostel is very nice, but the last one _wasn not_

10. Koto and Janet are traveling to Spain tomorrow, but Alex and Asim _aunt_.

5 Use the information in the following pictures to complete the sentences below the drawings. Add clauses of similarity or contrast with *so, too, neither, either,* and *but.*

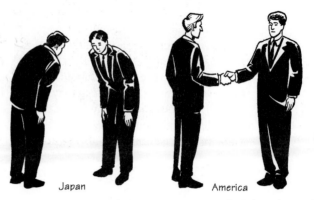

Japan   America

1. Japanese people traditionally bow when they meet, _but Americans don't._

America   Japan

2. Americans like baseball, _Japan do too_

Japan   America

3. Japanese people eat with chopsticks, _but American don't_

4. Men and women don't usually show affection in public in Egypt, _Neithe do_ _Japan_ .

5. Egyptian women sometimes wear veils when they leave their house, _but_ _American don't_

6. Brazilians often greet their friends by kissing them on each cheek, _so do_ _American_.

Brazil   America

7. Brazilians celebrate carnival, so do American.

Japan   America

8. Japanese brides often change into three or four different dresses during their wed-
    ding ceremony and celebration, but America don't

6   Use the information in the chart below to complete each of the following sentences.
      Add clauses of similarity or contrast with *so, too, either, neither,* or *but.*

	Koto	**Janet**
Age	20	20
Height	5' (5 feet)	5'9" (5 feet, 9 inches)
Weight	110 lbs.	130 lbs.
Color hair	black	brown
Color eyes	brown	brown
Brothers/Sisters	none	none
Lives with	mother, father, grandparents	mother (parents are divorced)
Hobbies	shopping, surfing the Internet	shopping, surfing the Internet
Favorite food	sushi	pizza
Favorite sport	baseball	baseball
Favorite holiday	New Year	4th of July

1. Koto is 20, *and so is Janet* .
2. Koto is 5', *but Janet isn't.*
3. Koto weighs 110 pounds, *but so Janet is 130 lbs*
4. Koto has brown hair, *and so Janet too*
5. Koto has brown eyes, *so does Janet.*
6. Koto doesn't have brothers or sisters, and *doesn't either.*
7. Koto lives with her father, *but Janet doesn't live with her*
8. Koto likes shopping and surfing the Internet, *and so is Janet.*
9. Koto's favorite food is sushi, *but Janet isn't.*
10. Koto's favorite sport is baseball, *and so is Janet*
11. Koto's favorite holiday is New Year, *but Janet isn't.*

Using What You've Learned

7 Brainstorm what you know about the food, arts, entertainment, and lifestyle of one or two cultures (you may choose to include cultures you have learned about in this chapter). Then, with your group, compare each of these cultures to your own culture. Discuss and list both the similarities and the differences, using *so, too, either, neither,* and *but.* When each group is finished, each group shares their list with the class.

8 Choose two cultures that you would like to learn more about. Use reference books or the Internet to find out about the lifestyle of the people of these cultures. Compare one or more of the following aspects of the cultures:

- the importance of family
- the pace of life
- the attitudes toward work
- the attitudes toward vacations and leisure time
- the most popular sports, foods, and leisure activities
- the style of dress

When you are finished, give an oral report comparing the cultures you have learned about, using *so, too, either, neither,* and *but* when appropriate.

Video Activities: Chinese New Year

Before You Watch. Discuss these questions in a group.

1. Have you ever seen a Chinese New Year celebration? Describe this experience.
2. Talk about your New Year celebration last year. Where were you? Who was with you? How did you celebrate? Was it a happy time for you?

Watch. Write answers to these questions.

1. In which season is the Chinese New Year? _____
2. Who is the blond woman? _____
3. Which Chinese customs did you see in the video? _____
_____

Watch Again.

1. How is the man going to celebrate the Chinese New Year? Place a check next to the things he says.

   _____ Eat

   _____ Drink alcohol

   _____ Buy gifts for his children

   _____ See dancing

   _____ Light firecrackers

2. Complete this sentence: "Some men are doing the Red Lion Dance. They

   dance for _____. If the _____ likes the dance, he gives them

   _____ envelopes with lucky _____ inside."

3. Why do people light firecrackers on the New Year?

4. The New Year celebrations will continue for _____ days.

After You Watch. Read the list of New Year customs in different cultures. With a partner, ask and answer questions about them with "Have you ever. . . .?"

Example: light a firecracker

A: Have you ever lit a firecracker?
B: Yes, I have / No, I haven't.

a. stay awake until midnight to "greet" the New Year (U.S.)
b. drink champagne (U.S.)
c. light a firecracker (China, U.S.)
d. go to a New Year parade (China)
e. jump over a small burning fire (Iran)
f. take a long hot bath before the New Year (Japan)
g. fly a kite on New Year's Day (Japan)
h. eat apples with honey (Jewish)
i. throw water on your friends to celebrate your joy (Thailand)
j. give or receive money in a red envelope (China, Vietnam)

Chapter 7

Health

PART 1	# Verb + Object + Infinitive; Modal Verbs: *Should, Had better, Have to,* and *Must*

Setting the Context

Conversation

Husband: How was your day, honey?

Wife: Well, I woke up with a bad headache this morning, so I thought I should see Dr. Krank. She advised me to take some pills. She also told me to drink a lot of water with the pills.

Husband: Should I get you some water for your pills?

Wife: No, thanks. I didn't want to take all those drugs, so I decided to go to a nutritionist.

Husband: A nutritionist?

Wife: Yes. He said I'd better change my eating habits, and he persuaded me to buy a lot of health food.

Husband: Oh. That's good.

Wife: Not really. I tried to eat some, but the foods tasted terrible. So then I went to a psychologist.

Husband: Oh? And what did the psychologist want you to do?

Wife: He gave me a lot of books to read. He advised me to read every one of them. He also said that I must learn to relax. So I went to a yoga class. The instructor taught me to stand on my head. She said I have to learn how to breathe correctly.

Husband: Well, how are you feeling now?

Wife: After all that advice, my headache is worse!

Discussion Questions

1. Why did the wife go to a doctor, a nutritionist, a psychologist, and a yoga class?
2. What did each expert advise her to do?
3. Which of these experts do you think she should listen to?
4. What do you do when you don't feel well?

A. Verb + Object + Infinitive

A common sentence pattern is verb + object + infinitive. Only certain verbs can appear before an object + infinitive. A partial list of these verbs appears in the following chart.

Verbs			Examples
advise	expect	remind	The doctor **wants her patient to have** a healthier lifestyle.
allow	force	teach	What did she **ask the patient to do**?
ask	instruct	tell	She **advised the patient to lose** weight.
convince	invite	train	She didn**'t tell her to exercise.**
enable	order	want	She **ordered her not to smoke.**
encourage	persuade	warn	She **encouraged her not to eat** junk food.

Note: The word *not* can come before the main verb or before the infinitive, depending on the meaning of the sentence.

1 Underline the verb + object + infinitive patterns in the conversation on page 154.

Example: She <u>advised me to take</u> some pills.

2 Unscramble the following sentences. The verb + object + infinitive pattern should appear in each sentence.

1. want / sweets and junk food / to buy / kids often / them / their parents
   Kids often want their parents to buy them sweets and junk food.

2. encourage / fruit and vegetables / their children / most parents / to eat
   Most parents encourge their children to eat

3. foods with lots of sugar / kids / tell / not to eat / teachers and dentists
   Teacher and den tell kids not to eat food with a lot of sugar

4. themselves / have to / foods low in sugar / many adults / force / to eat
   Many adults have to force themselves to eat

5. their patients / many doctors / advise / eating foods high in fat / to avoid
   Many doctor advise their patients to avoid eating high in fat foods

6. to exercise / fitness experts / us / at least three times a week / remind
   Fitness expert remind us to exercise least three time a week

7. many people / to prescribe / to help them lose weight / diet pills / their doctors / ask

   Many people ask their doctors to prescribe diet pills to help them ___

8. often / to fix / people / all of their problems / pills / expect

   People often ___

9. tell / diet pills because they can be addictive / their patients / not to take / many doctors

   Many doctors tell their patient not to take diet pills because they can be ___

10. is helping / the media / people / to make healthier lifestyle choices / to convince

   ___

3   Use the cue words under the pictures to write two sentences about each picture. Use the pattern verb + object + infinitive with the present continuous.

1.

- not allow / park for free
- ask / pay $5 for parking

The parking attendant is not allowing the woman to park for free.

He asks her to pay five dollers for parking.

2.

- order / not, park by the fire hydrant
- convince / not, give her a ticket

The Police officer order her not to park by the fire hydrant. The Woman convince the police officer not to give her a ticket.

3.

- invite / take a seat and wait
- remind / not smoke

The receptionist invite the Woman to take a seat and. The receptionist the remind her not to smoke.

4.

- encourage / lose some weight
- advise / start exercising

___

5.

- ask / say "ahh"
- tell / breathe deeply

_____

_____

_____

_____

6.

- instruct / take some medicine
- advise / drink a lot of water with the medicine

_____

_____

_____

_____

B. Modal Verbs: Should, Had better, Have to, and Must

Several modal verbs are used to give advice and express obligation.

	Examples	**Notes**
should	You **should** see a doctor. You **shouldn't** eat so much. What **should** I do?	In affirmative and negative statements and questions, _should_ expresses advice. _Should_ forms a contraction with _not: shouldn't._
had better	That woman **had better** get some help right away. I'**d better** call an ambulance. You'**d better not** wait. Hadn't we **better** leave?	In affirmative and negative statements and help questions, _had better_ expresses strong advice or a warning. _Had_ forms contractions with subject pronouns: _I'd better, you'd better, he'd better, she'd better, we'd better, they'd better_ Questions are usually in the negative form.
have to	I **have to** pick my grandmother up at the hospital today. Did you **have to** wear a cast when you broke your leg?	In affirmative statements and questions, _have to_ expresses personal obligation. Use _have to_ with _I, you, we,_ and _they._ Use _has to_ with _he, she,_ and _it._ Note: The negative form (_does/doesn't have to_) has a different meaning. _Does/ doesn't have to = it is not necessary._
must	You **must** bring your passport to the airport. You **mustn't** drink and drive. **Must** I take a test to get a driver's license?	In affirmative and negative statements and questions, _must_ expresses necessity and great urgency. _Must_ is often used to speak of legal obligations. _Must_ forms a contraction with _not: mustn't._

4   Circle the modals in the conversation on page 154.

Example: Well, I woke up with a bad headache this morning, so I thought I ⟨should⟩ see Dr. Krank.

5   The following directions explain how to take care of a person who has just gotten burned. Replace the underlined portions of each sentence with *you should, you shouldn't, you must,* or *you mustn't.*

1.   *You must*
   ~~It is extremely important to~~ treat the burn as soon as possible to prevent infection.
2.   It is a good idea to make the victim as comfortable as possible.
3.   It is recommended that you pour water on the injury for ten minutes.
4.   It is helpful to remove any clothing or jewelry from the area of the burn.
5.   It is harmful to apply lotions, ointments, or fat to the burn.
6.   Do not remove anything sticking to the burn.
7.   It is necessary to cover the burn with a sterile dressing or a clean piece of material.
8.   It is not a good idea to panic.
9.   It is helpful to reassure the victim.
10.   It is advisable to record details of the victim's injuries.
11.   It is dangerous to delay taking the victim to the hospital.
12.   If no vehicle is available, it is suggested that you call an ambulance.

6   Fill in each of the blanks with either *should (not), must (not), have to,* or *had better (not).* Although in many cases more than one answer may be possible, try to find the most appropriate modal(s) for each sentence.

A.   I have a headache.

1.   You _____*should*_____ lie down.
2.   You _____*must*_____ go out tonight.
3.   You _*had better*_ take more than two aspirins at once, or you'll get sick.

B.   I want to visit my friend in the hospital.

1.   You _have to_ visit between the official visiting hours of 10:00 A.M. and 9:00 P.M.

2.   I think you _must_ register at the reception desk before you go to your friend's room.

3.   You _have to_ bring you friend some flowers.

C.   My child swallowed some of my medication.

1.   You _must_ take her to the hospital immediately!

2.   She will probably _have to_ stay in the hospital overnight.

3.   You _had better_ put your medication away more safely, or it could happen again.

Using What You've Learned

7   Work in groups of four. Each student takes the role of one of the experts shown in the picture on page 154 and gives advice for each of the three situations below, using *should, have to, had better,* and *must.*

Example: *Nutritionist:* The businessman should drink herbal tea to help him relax. *Doctor:* I disagree. I advise him to get a complete physical exam.

1.   A successful middle-aged businessman is under a lot of stress. He is having trouble sleeping.

2.   A teenage girl doesn't want to eat. She is very thin, but she thinks she is still too fat.

3.   A college student is tired all the time. He never exercises. He eats a lot of junk food and drinks a lot of coffee.

What advice did each person give for each situation? Each group tells the class, using the pattern verb + object + infinitive.

Example: Keiko was the nutritionist. She told the businessman to drink herbal tea instead of coffee.

8   Work in small groups. Each student describes a health problem (real or imaginary). The group discusses the problem and agrees on a solution. When you finish, one member from each group reports the problems and solutions to the class.

9   Use the Internet or first aid manuals to learn how to help someone experiencing a medical emergency such as one of the following:

- ■   choking
- ■   heart attack
- ■   severe bleeding
- ■   drug overdose
- ■   electric shock

Write a leaflet explaining the steps the helper *must (not), should (not), had better (not),* and *has to* take in order to help the victim. Illustrate your manual with drawings or with photos cut out of magazines or downloaded from the Internet. Your class may wish to collect all of the completed leaflets to create a class first aid guide.

PART 2 Reflexive Pronouns; Tag Questions

Setting the Context

Conversation

Nadia: You look tired. This isn't your first time at a gym, is it, Ahmed?

Ahmed: Yes it is.

Nadia: Really? Well, you should be proud of yourself for finally coming. It's great, isn't it?

Ahmed: Actually, I'm not sure. Some of the people here are annoying. Look at those people admiring themselves in the mirror. That man is practically kissing himself. And that woman over there keeps weighing herself. She doesn't really think she's going to lose weight after each exercise, does she? These people are all in love with themselves, aren't they?

Nadia: Yea, they are. At least some of them, anyway. But we can just keep to ourselves. (Ahmed stops cycling.)

Nadia: You're not stopping already, are you?

Ahmed: Yes, I am.

Nadia: Aren't you enjoying yourself?

Ahmed: Actually, no, I'm not. I'm afraid I'm going to hurt myself if I do too much on my first day.

Nadia: You aren't going home yet, are you?

Ahmed: Yes, I am.

Nadia: But you want to lose weight and improve your health, don't you?

Ahmed: Yes, I do. But not as much as I want a cheeseburger. Yup, I'm going to make myself a nice, juicy double cheeseburger for lunch, and then I may treat myself to an ice cream sundae for dessert. You aren't interested in joining me, are you?

Nadia: Thanks, but no, I'm not. My body won't get in shape by itself! Also, after I finish exercising, I'm going to town to buy myself some new exercise clothes.

Ahmed: See you later, Nadia.

Nadia: Take care of yourself, Ahmed.

Discussion Questions

1. Why does Nadia tell Ahmed that he should be proud of himself?
2. Why does Ahmed think some of the people in the gym are annoying?
3. Why does Ahmed stop exercising?
4. What is Ahmed going to do?
5. Why doesn't Nadia join him?
6. Do you think physical fitness is important? Why or why not?

A. Reflexive Pronouns

If the subject and the object of a sentence are the same, a reflexive pronoun is used as the object.

Reflexive Pronouns	Examples	Notes
myself	I don't want to exhaust **myself**.	Singular reflexive pronouns end in -*self*.
yourself	Help **yourself** to as much fruit as you want.	
himself	He doesn't like to exercise by **himself**.	
herself	She weighs **herself** every week.	
itself	The problem will take care of **itself**.	
ourselves	Let's buy **ourselves** a yogurt shake.	Plural reflexive pronouns end in -*selves*
yourselves	Don't hurt **yourselves** with those weights.	
themselves	They bought **themselves** new gym clothes.	

Note: By + reflexive pronoun means "alone" or "without any help."

1 Underline and draw an arrow between the reflexive pronouns and the personal pronouns they refer to in the conversation on page 160.

Example: Well, you should be proud of yourself for finally coming.

2 Fill in the blanks with reflexive pronouns: *myself, yourself, herself, himself, itself, ourselves, yourselves,* or *themselves,*

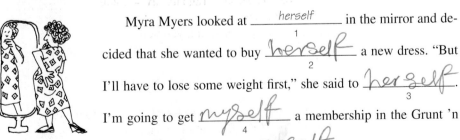

Myra Myers looked at _____*herself*_____ in the mirror and de-
₁

cided that she wanted to buy ___herself___ a new dress. "But
₂

I'll have to lose some weight first," she said to ___herself___.
₃

I'm going to get ___myself___ a membership in the Grunt 'n
₄

Groan Health Club. "We all have to take care of ___ourself___."
₅

The next morning Myra found ___herself___ in a big room with weights and
₆

other exercise equipment. A big sign said, "Do something special for ___itself___
₇

today." One muscular man was measuring ___himself___ with a tape measure. Two

8

other handsome men were looking at ___himself___ in the mirror. "I think I'm

9

going to enjoy ___itself___ here," thought Myra.

10

3   Write a sentence describing each of the following pictures. Use a reflexive pronoun
and one of the verbs listed below for each picture.

introduce   encourage   hurt   weigh
promise   enjoy   buy   look at

1.

Come on, you can do it!!

The woman is encouraging herself.

2.

One carrot juice, please.

JUICE BAR

The woman buying
herself.

3.

The man look at the
mirror.

4.

Hi, I'm Mona.   Hi, I'm Kurt.

The woman and the man
introduce theirself.

5.

The woman and the man
enjoy theirself.

6.

The man weigh him-
self.

7.

The man hurt himself.

8.

I swear, I will never work out again!

GYM

The man promise himself.

B. Tag Questions

A tag question is a statement with a short question attached at the end. People usually use tag questions to ask for clarification or to confirm information they think is true. The subject of a tag is always a pronoun. Tag questions use the same auxiliary verbs as yes/no questions.

	Examples	Expected Answer	Notes
Affirmative	You're a member of this gym, **aren't you?**	Yes, I am.	Affirmative statements usually have negative tags.
	He's exercising, **isn't he?**	Yes, he is.	With affirmative statements and negative tags, the speaker expects an affirmative answer.
	I have a fever, **don't I?**	Yes, you do.	
	She lifts weights, **doesn't she?**	Yes, she does.	
	You saw a doctor, **didn't you?**	Yes, I did.	
	You'll take the medicine, **won't you?**	Yes, I will.	
Negative	You're not getting sick, **are you?**	No, I'm not.	Negative statements have affirmative tags.
	She isn't here now, **is she?**	No, she isn't.	With negative statements and affirmative tags, the speaker expects a negative answer.
	They don't like carrot juice, **do they?**	No, they don't.	
	She doesn't smoke, **does she?**	No, she doesn't.	
	You didn't bring an extra towel, **did you?**	No, I didn't.	
	They can't lift weights, **can they?**	No, they can't.	

4 Circle each tag question in the conversation on page 160.

Example: This isn't your first time at a gym, (is it), Ahmed?

5 Answer each tag question with the answer the speaker expects to hear.

Example: This health club is great, isn't it? _Yes, it is._

1. You don't have any aspirin, do you? _NO I didn't_.
2. This yoga class is getting really crowded, isn't it? _Yes, it is_.
3. Those runners are incredibly fast, aren't they? _Yes they are_
4. Your father smokes two packs of cigarettes a day, doesn't he? _Yes he does._

5. We're not too late for the aerobics class, are we? _Yes, we_ .
6. You were out sick for over a week, weren't you? _No I'm not_ .
7. We met you at a softball game last summer, didn't we? _Yes we did_ .
8. You really like all that healthy food, don't you? _Yes I do_
9. She'll join us later, won't she? _Yes I will_
10. Your roommate plays soccer, doesn't he? _Yes he does_

6   Write the missing pronouns in the blanks.

It's a beautiful day, isn't _he_ ? We

couldn't ask for a better day, could _we_ ?

This is great exercise, isn't _she_ ? Look at

that man! He's running fast, isn't _no_ ? All

the people here are in great shape, aren't

you ? You don't talk much when you run, do _you_ ?

7   Write the missing auxiliary verbs in the blanks. Remember to make the tag affirmative or negative, as appropriate.

You ran in this race last year, _did_ you? The

weather was great then too, _____ it? You finished

that race, _do_ you? But you didn't win,

did you? We're going to do well this year,

_do_ we? You're not getting tired, _did_ you?

I'm not boring you, _don't_ I?

8   Write the missing tag questions in the blanks.

You were in better shape last year,

are ? You also tried harder last

year, _didn't_ ? But you'll finish this

year too, _____ ? We should run

faster, _____ ? We only have a few

more kilometers to run, _____? You can run faster, _____?

5   6

You're not talking much, _____? You're out of breath, _____?

7   8

I'm not annoying you _____? This race is fun, _____?

9   10

Using What You've Learned

9 Write five negative tag questions you expect your partner to answer positively, and five positive tag questions you expect your partner to answer negatively. If possible, these questions should be about health-related activities and habits.

Example: **Negative tag questions:**
You get enough sleep, don't you?
You're a vegetarian, aren't you?

Positive tag questions:
You don't smoke, do you?
You can't run five miles, can you?

After you have prepared your questions, interview your partner with the questions. Take notes on your partner's answers. How many questions did your partner answer as you expected? How many did your partner not answer as you expected? Tell the class what you learned about your partner.

PART 3 # Relative Clauses

Setting the Context

Reading

Dear Grandmother,

Thanks for the book you sent me. The boy who shares my room read it last year. He said it's one of his favorite books. The card you sent with the book was really nice too.

This hospital isn't so bad. All the people who work here are friendly. I especially like the nurse who brings our lunch trays every day. But the food that she brings us is terrible!   5

I'm feeling pretty good. My head feels better and the ribs I broke are healing well. The doctor who examined me said I can go home soon. (The stethoscope that he used was cold!) I'm really looking forward to having the special roast chicken that you cook whenever I come over. Can you make those mashed potatoes that I love too?

Love,   10
Timmy

Discussion Questions

1. What does Timmy thank his grandmother for?
2. What does Timmy think of the people who work in the hospital?
3. What does he think of the food at the hospital?
4. Who told Timmy that he can go home soon?
5. What is Timmy looking forward to?
6. Have you ever been in the hospital? If so, tell about the experience.

A. Who, That, *and* Which *as Subjects of Relative Clauses*

Relative clauses describe, identify, or give more information about the nouns they follow. They have a subject and a verb. *Who, that,* or *which* can be the subject of a relative clause. *Who* is used for people; *which* is used for things; *that* is used for people or things.

You can use a relative clause to combine two simple sentences into one complex sentence.

Example: I like the nurse. + **She** brings the food.

↓

= I like the nurse **who** brings the food.

Examples	Notes
I like the nurse **who (that) brings the food.**	*who/that* = the nurse
The bed **which (that) I sleep in** is comfortable.	*which/that* = the bed

1   Underline the relative clauses with *who, that,* or *which* as subjects in the letter above.

Example: The boy <u>who shares my room</u> read it last year.

2 Combine each of the following pairs of sentences using a relative clause with *who, that,* or *which.*

Example: The nurse takes blood. She is nice.
The nurse who takes blood is nice.

1. The man is sharing my room. He has a lot of visitors.
The man who has a lot of visitors is sharing my room.

2. The flowers are on the table next to my bed. They are very beautiful.
The flowers which are very beautiful on the table

3. The doctor examined me. He told me I was getting better.
The doctor who told me I was getting better examined

4. The patient is allergic to flowers. She has a bunch of flowers in her room.
The patient who has a bunch of flowers in her room is allergic to flowers.

5. The book is on the desk. It's very boring.
The book which is very boring is on the desk.

6. The boy hurt his head. He is in serious condition.
The boy who is in serious condition hurt his head

7. The man broke his legs. He is sitting in a wheelchair.
The man who is sitting in a wheelchair broke his legs

8. The children are painting the man's casts. They are having fun.
The children who are having fun are painting the man casts

9. The television is in my room. It's broken.
The television which is broken in my room

10. The janitor cleans the rooms. He is going to college part time.
The janitor who is going to college part time cleans the rooms.

B. Reduction of Relative Clauses to Relative Phrases

A relative phrase also modifies a noun. However, unlike a relative clause, it does not contain a subject and a verb. You can reduce (shorten) some relative clauses with *who, that,* or *which* to relative phrases.

	Examples	Notes
Relative Clause	The man **who is sharing** my room hates the food.	To make a relative phrase from a relative clause with a *be* form of a verb, leave out the subject pronoun (*who, that,* or *which*) and the *be* form of the verb.
Relative Phrase	The man **sharing my room** hates the food.	
Relative Clause	The flowers **that are on the table** are beautiful.	
Relative Phrase	The flowers **on the table** are beautiful.	
Relative Clause	All the people **who work here** are friendly.	If there is no *be* form of a verb in the relative clause, sometimes you can leave out the subject pronoun and change the verb to its *-ing* form.
Relative Phrase	All the people **working here** are friendly.	

3   Combine each of the following pairs of sentences. Use relative phrases.

Example: The children are staying in this hospital. They are funny.
The children staying in this hospital are funny.

1.   The man is in room 202. He is having an operation tomorrow.
The man is having an operation tomorrow is in room 202.

2.   The nurse wears a small hat. She takes blood from the patients.
The nurse taking blood from the patients wears a small hat.

3.   The magazines are on the table. They belong to the hospital.
The magazines belonging to the hospital are on the table.

4.   The doctor is responsible for all the patients on this floor. He likes to tell jokes.
The doctor telling jokes is responsible

5.   The mountains surround the hospital. They're beautiful.
The mountains beautiful surround the hospital

6.   The nurse is giving the man a shot. She is talking on the phone.
The nurse talking on the phone is giving the man a shot.

7.   The man is waiting for the nurse to get off the phone. He is angry.
The man angry is waiting for the nurse to get

8.   The receptionist is on duty. She speaks Japanese and English.
The receptionist speaks Japanese and English is on duty

9.   The doctor takes care of me. He is from Cambodia.
The doctor from Cambodia takes care of me

10.   The man is in the bed next to mine. He is snoring.
The man snoring who is is in the bed next to mine

4   Study the pictures at the beginning of Part 3 on page 165. Then complete these sentences about the pictures with relative clauses or phrases. There are many possible answers.

1.   The boy who is writing a letter has a bandage on his head.

2.   The boy who is having a visitor is eating a hamburger.

3.   The doctor who is telling jokes is looking at the chart.

4.   The patient who is having operation has casts on his legs.

5.   The woman who is laughing has flowers in her room.

6.   The nurse who is explaining is taking blood from a child.

7.   The man who is sitting on chair is getting an injection from the nurse.

8.   The doctor who is talking on phone is explaining the results to a patient.

C. Who(m), That, *and* Which *as Objects of Relative Clauses*

Who(m), that, or *which* may also be the object of a relative clause. You can use these relative clause pronouns as objects to combine two simple sentences into a complex sentence.

Examples: The nurse is Ms. Alvarez. + He likes **her.**

= The nurse **whom** he likes is Ms. Alvarez.

The food was terrible. + We ate **it** in the hospital.

= The food **that** we ate in the hospital was terrible.

Examples	Notes
The cough **that I had** was annoying.	*That* refers to *the cough. I* is the subject of the relative clause.
The people **who/whom we met** in the hospital were nice.	*Who* is used more often than *whom,* especially in speaking. *Whom* is used only in very formal English.
The injection **which the doctor gave me** was painful. The injection **the doctor gave me** was painful.	The object pronouns *who(m), that,* and *which* are often left out of relative clauses.

5   Combine each of the following pairs of sentences. Use relative clauses with *who(m), that,* or ~~which~~ as objects.

Example: The doctors were running to the emergency room. I saw them.
   The doctors who(m) I saw were running to the emergency room.

1.   The noises at night were scary. I heard them.
     The noises which I heard at night were scary.

2.   The work was very hard and tiring. The nurses did the work.
     The work which the nurses, was very hard and tiring.

3.   The ambulance was shiny and white. The paramedics drove the ambulance.
     The ambulance whom the paramedics drove was shiny.

4.   The patients were in a lot of pain. The nurses checked on them frequently.
     The patients who the nurses checked were in a lot of pain.

5.   The food is terrible. The patients in the hospital have to eat the food.
     The food which the patient eat is terrible.

6. The flowers were very expensive. The patient's friends sent the flowers.

The flowers which the patient's friends sent were very expensive.

7. The movie on TV was boring. I watched it.

The movie that I watched was boring.

8. The pills made me tired. I had to take them.

The pills which I had to take made tired.

Using What You've Learned

6 Write one sentence each about ten people in your class using relative clauses or phrases to describe, identify, or give information about each person. When you finish, share your ideas with the class.

Examples: The woman *who is sitting in front of me* is also in my economics class. The man *on her right* is always kidding around with the teacher. The woman *closest to the door* is a new student.

7 Work in small groups to select a picture from a magazine or a newspaper that shows only one person. Work with your group to form as many relative clauses and phrases as possible to describe the person in the photo. When you have written as many relative clauses and phrases as you can think of, give your photo to your teacher. Your teacher will tape the photos up at the front of the class, so that all students can view them. Then, each group takes a turn reading their sentences out loud to the rest of the class. Based on these sentences, students from other groups should guess which photo these sentences refer to.

Examples: First member of Group A: The woman that is wearing a polka dot dress is beautiful.

Second member of Group A: The woman who has long hair looks angry.

Third member of Group A: The woman sitting in the chair is speaking on the phone.

Member of Group B: (*Pointing to a picture at the front of the room*) That's your picture!

Video Activities: Marathon Man

Before You Watch.   Discuss these questions in a group.

1.   What is a marathon?
2.   Do you think you could run in a marathon?
3.   Why do some people run or jog? Make a list of reasons.
4.   Do you enjoy running? Why or why not?

Watch.   Write answers to these questions.

1.   What is Jerry's personal reason for running? _____
2.   Does he enjoy it? _____
3.   What does Jerry want to challenge Americans to do? _____

Watch Again.   Fill in the missing numbers.

1.   How many miles is a marathon? _____
2.   How many marathons did Jerry run in 1993? _____
3.   How many marathons does Jerry hope to run in 2000? _____
4.   How many marathons has he run so far? _____
5.   How fast does Jerry run a marathon? _____

After You Watch.   With a partner, write a conversation about the following situation. Then role-play your dialogue for the class.

Situation: Student A has decided to start training for a marathon. He/she goes to Student B, who is an experienced marathon runner, to ask for advice.

Use verbs and modals of advice in your dialogue.

> **Example:**   I **advise** you to start jogging every day.
> You **must** quit smoking immediately.

Ex: The nurse (who gave me (reduce) a shot is from canada.
Ex: The work (which) the nurse did was hard and tiring.
Ex: The work the nurse did was hard and tiring
Ex: The nurse from canada gave me a shot.
Ex: The movie I watched was boring.
Ex: The flower the patient's friend sent were very expensive.
Ex: The pills I had to take made tired.

Focus on Testing

Testing is a major feature of academic life. Two basic types of tests exist: subjective and objective. Subjective questions can have a variety of answers, but objective questions have only one correct answer. In this book you will have short practice exams to help prepare you for tests such as the TOEFL. Use these practice exams to help you learn which structures or ideas you don't understand well and need to study more.

Verb + Object + Infinitive; Modal Verbs: *Should, Had better, Have to,* **and** *Must;* **Reflexive Pronouns; Tag Questions; Relative Clauses**

Remember that. . .

- A common sentence pattern is verb + object + infinitive.
- Certain verbs can appear before objects and infinitives.
- Affirmative statements usually have negative tags; negative statements have affirmative tags.

Part 1. Circle the correct completion for the following sentences.
Example: Nora seems _____ happy with her new job in the hospital.

      a. be   b. being   (c.) to be   d. been

1. My mother always treats _____ to only the finest things in life.
    a. myself   (b.) herself   c. ourselves   d. themselves

2. The beach community wasn't very well prepared for the tornado, _____?
    a. was they   b. wasn't they   c. was it   d. wasn't it

3. The doctor wants her patient _____ a healthier lifestyle.
    (a.) to have   b. have   c. has   d. had

4. Let's buy _____ a fruit juice.
    a. themselves   b. yourself   (c.) ourselves   d. ourself

Part 2. Circle the letter below the underlined word(s) containing the error.
Example: I should knowing better than to approach a strange dog.
         A   (B)   C   D

1. The men whose I saw running from the convenience store were all wearing
          A   (B)   C   D
    ski masks.

2. I was surprised to hear that his friends persuaded him to buying a dog.
           A   B   C   (D)

3. You had better not to wait to make an appointment with your doctor.
             A   (B)   C   D

4. This isn't your first time playing soccer, isn't it?
      A   B   (C)   D

Chapter 8

Entertainment and the Media

The Past Continuous Tense; The Simple Past Tense Versus the Past Continuous Tense

Setting the Context

Reading

Good evening and welcome to the Channel 12 6:00 news. In our top story tonight, there was an attempted robbery at the Bartle Bank in Bakerstown at 3:20 this afternoon. The bank was   5
closing for the day when the three robbers burst in. According to eyewitnesses, all three were wearing masks, and two were carrying guns. When they demanded money, a quick-thinking   10
bank teller pushed a silent alarm that signals the local police. The police arrived just as they were making their getaway. The suspects were racing down Barker St. when the police caught up with them and arrested them.

In other news, a fire burned down a private home in Clayton Corner last night.   15
The fire started when a woman fell asleep in bed while smoking a cigarette and watching TV. Firefighters believe the lit cigarette fell from the woman's hand while she was sleeping. By the time the woman and her roommates escaped the house, the fire was burning out of control. Firefighters arrived at the scene within minutes. Two firefighters were injured while battling the flames. They are being treated at   20
Adderbrook Hospital and are expected to be released later tonight.

On the lighter side, a local man is the winner of this week's Lucky Pick lottery. Alberto Fiorentino bought the winning ticket at the Valu-Mart market in Glendale yesterday afternoon while he was doing his weekly shopping. Mr. Fiorentino was working at his job in the Bakerstown post office when he heard the news. He im-   25
mediately quit his job and went home to celebrate with his family. When our reporters contacted Mr. Fiorentino this afternoon, he was planning a trip around the world with his family.

Join us for more news after this commercial break.

Discussion Questions

1.   What happened at the Bartle Bank at 3:20?
2.   When did the police arrive?
3.   What happened in Clayton Corner?
4.   What was Mr. Fiorentino doing at the Valu-Mart market?

5. What are other "typical" news stories?

6. Do you watch the news? Why or why not?

A. The Past Continuous Tense

The past continuous tense describes activities happening or in progress at a specific time or during a period of time in the past.

Statements

	Examples	Notes
Affirmative	I **was watching** the news at 6:00. The anchorman was **telling** about a robbery.	Past continuous statements consist of a past form of *be* before the *-ing* form of a verb.
Negative	He **wasn't telling** about a murder. The bank tellers **weren't screaming.**	Negative statements include *not* after the *be* verb.

Note: For a review of the spelling rules for verbs with *-ing* endings, see page 38, Chapter 2.

Yes/No Questions

	Examples	Possible Answers	
		Affirmative	**Negative**
Affirmative	**Was** the manager **working?** **Were** the police **investigating** the robbery?	Yes, he was. Yes, they were.	No, he wasn't. No, they weren't.
Negative	**Wasn't** the policeman **running** after the suspect? **Weren't** the customers **screaming?**	Yes, he was. Yes, they were.	No, he wasn't. No, they weren't.

Information Questions

	Examples	Possible Answers
Affirmative	What **were** the suspects **wearing?** Who **was carrying** weapons?	They were wearing masks. Two of them were carrying weapons.
Negative	Why **weren't** the tellers **screaming?** Who **wasn't paying** attention?	They weren't scared. The guard wasn't paying attention.

1   Underline the past continuous verb phrases in the reading on page 174.

Example: According to eyewitnesses, all three <u>were wearing</u> masks, and two <u>were carrying</u> guns.

2 Fill in the blanks in the interviews below, using the verbs in parentheses to form past continuous verb phrases.

Interview 1

Reporter: What (do) _____*were*_____ you _____*doing*_____ when the robbery happened?

Manager: I (speak) ____*was speaking*____ to customers about opening an account.

Guard: I (sit) _*was sitting*_ by the safe.

Teller #1: I (cash) _*was cashing*_ a check for a customer.

Pair of Customers: We (fill out) _*were filling out*_ forms to open an account.

Interview 2

Reporter: What (do) _*were*_ you _*doing*_ when the fire began?

Person #1: I (sleep) _*was sleeping*_

Person #2: I (read) _*was reading*_ a book in bed.

Person #3: I (get) _*was getting*_ ready to go to bed.

Couple: We (eat) _*was eating*_ a late-night snack.

Interview 3

Reporter: What (do) _____were_____ you _____doing_____ when you found out
                                    1

that you won the lottery?

Father and Grandfather: We (watch) _____were watching_____ TV.
                                              2

Mother: I (work) _____was working_____ on the computer.
                            3

Mother: (*pointing to her children*) They (do) _____are doing_____ their homework.
                                                          4

Grandmother: I (knit) _____was knitting_____ a sweater.
                                5

3 Study the pictures in Activity 2. Then one partner closes his or her book and the other asks questions about one of the pictures, using the past continuous tense. The first partner tries to answer from memory. Change roles for each picture.

Example: A: Was the guard wearing a hat?

B: Yes, he was wearing a hat.

A: Was anyone screaming?

B: I think the teller was screaming.

B. The Simple Past Tense Versus the Past Continuous Tense

	Examples	Notes
Simple Past	I **read** the newspaper. She **didn't use** the computer last night. Did you **see** the movie?	Use the simple past tense to talk about events and activities that began and ended in the past.
Past Continuous	I **was reading** the newspaper when I fell asleep. She **wasn't using** the computer at 8:00 last night. **Were** you **watching** the movie when I called?	Use the past continuous tense to describe activities that were happening or in progress at a specific time or during a period of time in the past.

Note: Some verbs are not normally used in the continuous tense. These verbs, called nonaction verbs, include verbs that express feeling and thought, verbs that express possession, and verbs that express sensory perception. For more information on nonaction verbs, see chart B (*Nonaction Verbs*) on pages 42–43 in Chapter 2.

4   Choose between the simple past and the past continuous form of the verb in each set of parentheses.

A: What (did you do / were you doing) yesterday?
        1

B: Let's see. I (woke up / was waking up) at around 10:00 yesterday. It (rained / was
                  2   3

raining), so I (stayed / was staying) home and (read / was reading) the newspaper.
                        4   5

A: I called you at around 11:00. (Did you read / Were you reading) the newspaper then?
                                              6

B: Yes, I (did / was).
            7

A: We only spoke for a few minutes. What (did you do / were you doing) after we
                                                          8

hung up?

B: I (watched / was watching) TV for a while.
              9

A: (Didn't you go / Weren't you going) outside at all yesterday?
          10

B: Sure I did. I wasn't home between 5:00 and 6:00.

A: Why not? What (did you do / were you doing)?
                          11

B: I (returned / was returning) the video I (watched / was watching) last night.
    ‾‾‾‾12   ‾‾‾13

A: So, what (did you do / were you doing) last night?
                        ‾‾‾14

B: I (played / was playing) video games. I called to ask you to come over, but you
       ‾‾‾15

weren't home. What (did you do / were you doing)?
                        ‾‾‾16

A: What time (did you call / were you calling)?
            ‾‾‾17

B: About 8:00.

A: At 8:00 I (walked / was walking) my dog in the park. I (didn't want / wasn't want-
            ‾‾‾18   ‾‾‾19

ing) to stay home on such a beautiful night.

C. When *and* While *with the Simple Past and Past Continuous Tenses*

When and *while* are used to introduce time clauses. They can relate two events or activities that happened (simple past) or were happening (past continuous) at the same time in the past. *When* can also relate events that happened in a sequence.

	Examples	**Notes**
when	**When** the movie **ended,** we **went** home.	Clauses with *when* are most often in the simple past tense. If both verbs are in the simple past, the action in the *when* clause happened first.
while	She **was watching** TV **while** her husband **was using** the computer. **While** she **was watching** TV, her husband **was using** the computer.	Clauses with *while* are most often in the past continuous tense. If both verbs are in the past continuous, it means the two actions were going on at the same time. In these sentences, *while* can go at the beginning or in the middle of the sentence.
when or while	My mother **was listening** to the radio **when** she got the call. My mother **got** the call **while** she **was listening** to the radio.	The simple past and the past continuous can appear in the same sentence. In these cases, *while* begins clauses with the past continuous and *when* begins clauses with the simple past. One event began before the other one and was in progress when the second event interrupted it.

5 Circle the clauses beginning with *when* and *while* in the reading on page 174. Take note of the tense of the verbs used with *when* and *while*.

Example: The bank was closing for the day ⟨when the three robbers burst in.⟩

6 Fill in the blanks with either *when* or *while*.

1. I was reading a magazine ___*when*___ my friends arrived.

2. ___While___ it was time for the movie to start, we turned on the TV.

3. My roommate was listening to the stereo ___while___ we were watching the movie.

4. ___While___ a commercial came on, we ordered a pizza.

5. The pizza came ___when___ we were watching the movie.

6. The telephone rang ___while___ we were watching the last scene of the movie.

7. I tried to listen to the movie ___when___ I was speaking with my mother.

8. ___When___ I got off the phone, the movie was over.

7 Circle the correct choice in each set of parentheses in the following newspaper article. In a few cases, both choices may be possible. When this is the case, circle both choices.

The Hungry Burglar

The would-be victim (slept / was sleeping) last night
¹
(while / when) she (heard / was hearing) a noise. The
²   ³
strange noise (woke / was waking) her up. She qui-
⁴
etly (went / was going) downstairs and was
⁵
shocked at what she saw happening: a burglar
(robbed / was robbing) her house. But what she saw
⁶
next was even more surprising: the burglar

(opened / was opening) her refrigerator and (started / was starting) to make himself a
⁷   ⁸
snack. She called the police (while / when) he (ate / was eating) a big, chocolate
⁹   ¹⁰
cake. (While / When) he (heard / was hearing) her on the phone, he (ran / was running)
¹¹   ¹²   ¹³
out the back door without taking anything. The woman (put / was putting) her posses-
¹⁴
sions away (when / while) the police arrived. They (asked / were asking) her some
¹⁵   ¹⁶
questions, then (went / were going) to look for the suspect. Fifteen minutes later,
¹⁷

the woman (<u>fixed</u> / was fixing) the lock on her door (while / when) the police
<u>18</u>   19

(<u>called</u> / were calling). They (<u>told</u> / were telling) her that they found the burglar. When
20   21

she (asked / <u>was asking</u>) how they caught the burglar so fast, she (<u>got</u> / was getting) a
22   23

surprise. The policeman told her "It was easy ma'am. The suspect (<u>ate</u> / was eating)
24

while he (ran / <u>was running</u>) down the street. (While / <u>When</u>) we (<u>stopped</u> / were stop-
25   26   27

ping) him, he (<u>had</u> / was having) big, chocolate stains all over his shirt. We knew then
28

that we had our man."

Using What You've Learned

8 Play a video of a news segment or a commercial. Watch the video carefully and take
notes on what you see and hear. After watching the video, form small groups, then prepare 5–10 past continuous questions about the video. Use your questions to test how
much your group members remember about what they saw and heard.

Examples: 1.   *What color tie was the man wearing?*

2.   *Was he looking straight at the camera?*

3.   *What was he doing with his hands?*

9 An alibi is an explanation given by a suspect to prove that he or she was somewhere
else at the time of a crime. In this activity, half the class takes the role of detectives who
are trying to solve a crime, and the other half takes the role of suspects who must
provide alibis.

- ■ As a class, decide the details of the crime (such as the type of crime and the time
  and place of the crime).

- ■ Then the suspects pair up with a partner to create a detailed alibi to prove that they
  did not commit the crime. The suspects should use the past tense and the past continuous tense in their alibi.

- ■ Next, one suspect is interviewed by the detectives, while the suspect's partner
  waits outside. The detectives should ask questions using the past tense and the past
  continuous tense with *when* or *while*.

Example: *Detective #1:* What were you doing last night at 7:00 when the robbery
occured?

Suspect #1: I was at the Cineplex movie theater watching a movie.

Detective #2: What movie were you watching?

Suspect #1: I was watching "Gun Blast 2."

Detective #3: Who were you with?

Suspect #1: I was with John Simpson.

Detective #1: Did anyone see you and John while you were there?

- The detectives take notes on the first suspect's answers.
- When the second suspect is brought in for questioning, the detectives should take note of how well the second suspect's answers match the answers given by the first suspect.
- After all the pairs have been interviewed, the detectives decide which pair had the weakest alibi. That pair will be arrested for the crime.

PART 2 — Infinitives

Setting the Context

Are you ashamed to show your skinny body at the beach? Do the guys seem to laugh at you? Do the girls seem to ignore you? Well prepare for all of that to change. How would you like to impress   5
all the gang at the beach this summer with your incredible muscles? You would? Well then—you need to try Insta-muscle!

Insta-muscle is simple to use. Just   10
rub in a generous amount wherever you want muscles. Insta-muscle begins to work as soon as you put it on. It isn't unusual to see results in just one or two weeks. Continue to use Insta-muscle each day to build even bigger muscles. Remember to buy an extra jar or two to make sure you never run out.   15

In a few weeks, you won't be afraid to show your body anymore. You'll be able to take off your shirt with confidence. And when you do, the men are sure to respect you and the women are sure to notice you. (One warning: try not to break too many hearts!) So plan to be the most popular guy at the beach this summer. With Insta-muscle, you're guaranteed to make a splash.   20

It's easy to order Insta-muscle. Just dial the toll free number on your screen and say "I want to be an Insta-muscle man."

Discussion Questions

1. What kind of man is this commercial directed at?
2. What are the directions for using Insta-muscle?
3. Why does Mr. Muscle tell the viewer to buy an extra jar or two?
4. What does Mr. Muscle say will soon happen?
5. How do you feel about commercials like this? Why?

A. Infinitives After Verbs

An infinitive is *to* + the simple form of a verb. Infinitives can follow certain verbs. All the verbs in the following chart can take infinitives directly. The verbs with an asterisk (∗) can also take infinitives after objects.

Verbs		Examples	Notes
ask*	need*	Do you **want me to lower** the volume?	The verb before the infinitive can be in any tense.
begin	offer	Be quiet. I **am trying to listen** to the news.	
continue	plan		
decide	prefer	She **began to read** the book last night.	Depending on the intended meaning, in some negative sentences, *not* comes before the first verb; in other sentences, *not* comes between the first verb and the infinitive.
expect*	prepare*		
fail	pretend	I **don't know how to work** this remote control.	
forget	remember		
hope	seem	We'**re not planning to rent the** movie.	
know how	start		
learn	teach*	**Try not to watch** too much TV.	
like*	try		
manage	want*		
mean	would like*		

Note: Some verbs must be followed by an object before the infinitive (except when used in the passive voice). Such verbs include: *advise, allow, challenge, encourage, order, persuade, require, urge,* and *warn.*

1   Underline the verb + infinitive phrases in the reading on page 182.

Example: Do the guys <u>seem to laugh</u> at you?

2   Match each of the numbers on the left to the letters on the right to form complete sentences. Work in sequence from No. 1 to No. 10 to see a story develop. The matches should be grammatically correct and logical.

_d_ **1.** John asked

_h_ **2.** When I got home, I began

_e_ **3.** After trying on lots of outfits, I finally decided

_a_ **4.** My father started

_c_ **5.** He asked me what we planned

_b_ **6.** My father told me that he expected

_f_ **7.** John was surprised because he wasn't planning

_j_ **8.** My father didn't really try

_g_ **9.** I had fun on the date and I plan

_i_ **10.** But next time I'll offer

a. to ask me a lot of questions about John.

b. me to introduce him to John before the date.

c. to do on the date.

d. me to go to a movie with him.

e. to wear my new jeans and a black top.

f. to meet my father so soon.

g. to go out with John again.

h. to plan what I wanted to wear on the date.

i. to meet him at the theatre!

j. to be polite to John when they met.

3   Complete the sentences with the appropriate forms of the verbs in parentheses. Add *to* and an object, if necessary.

Host: And now it's time to play your favorite game show, "All or Nothing"! Let's welcome our current champion, John Martinez! John <u>started to play</u> our game just two
1 (start, play)

days ago, and he has already won $30,000 in prizes! John tells me that his wife, Gloria,

~~persuaded to come~~ on our show, So he ~~intends to win~~ some great
2 (persuade, come)   3 (intend, win)

prizes for her! And next, please welcome today's challenger, Nancy Johnson! Nancy is

a schoolteacher who ~~planed to get~~ married next month. Her fiancé
4 (plan, get)

~~encourage her play~~ "All or Nothing" to win some money for their honeymoon.
5 (encourage, play)

Now, you folks in the audience, please ~~remember not to shout~~ out the answers. All
6 (remember, not shout)

right, then, Nancy and John, do you both ~~know how to play~~ our game?
7 (know how, play)

Contestants: Yes, Bob!

Host: Great! Let me ~~urge you think~~ carefully before you
8 (urge, think)

~~trying to answer~~ any questions. Our game ~~requires you to think~~ fast. As al-
9 (try, answer)   10 (require, think)

ways, I ~~advised trust~~ your intuition. Your first answer is usually right on
11 (advise, trust)

the money on "All or Nothing"!

4   Complete the following sentences with your own ideas. When you are finished, share
your ideas with the class.

Example: The Internet allows people to *find information quickly.*

1.   The Internet allows people to ~~find information quickly.~~

2.   Television teaches children to ~~watch almost anything.~~

3.   Movies seem to ~~be good~~

4.   Commercials often try to _____

5.   I have begun to ~~prepared the food.~~

6.   I want to ~~go out tonight.~~

7. My teacher expects me to _do my homework._

8. I know how to _cook rice very well._

9. When I was a child, I liked to _play soccer around._

10. Now, I like to _watch it almost everyday._

11. I usually forget to _read my newspaper._

12. I am going to continue to _wr_

B. Infinitives After Adjectives

test

Some adjectives can be immediately followed by infinitives.

Adjectives		Examples	Notes
afraid	prepared	She's **happy to watch** almost anything.	These adjectives are often followed by infinitives in this pattern:
ashamed	proud	He was **proud to have** his letter printed in the newspaper.	Subject + *be* + adjective + infinitive.
fortunate	ready		Adjectives used in this pattern usually describe a person's feelings or attitudes.
glad	relieved	I wasn't **prepared to see** such a violent movie.	
happy	willing		
lucky	sad		
dangerous	irresponsible	It's **fun to read** the classified ads.	These adjectives are often followed by infinitives in this pattern:
difficult	necessary	It's **important to read** the newspaper every day.	It + *be* + adjective + infinitive.
easy	nice		
embarrassing	pleasant	It's **not possible to read** every article in the Sunday paper.	
expensive	possible		
fun	rude		
good	safe		
important	simple		
impossible	wrong		

5 Circle the adjective + infinitive phrases in the reading on page 182.

Example: Are you (ashamed to show) your skinny body at the beach?

6 Complete the following soap opera dialogue by unscrambling the words in each set of parentheses and writing them on the line provided.

Alexis: I must go. (be dangerous it's to) <u>It's dangerous to be</u> here with you. My

husband has a terrible temper.

Chase: No! Stay, my darling!

Alexis: But (to it impossible is go on) <u>it's impossible</u> <u>to go no</u> this way.

Chase: I know (love is it to wrong) <u>it's wrong to love</u> you. But I can't help myself!

Alexis: Oh, Chase! (difficult is say to it) <u>it's difficult to say</u> this, but . . . I . . . I love you!

Chase: (am I so be fortunate to) <u>I am fortunate to be</u> the man you love!

Alexis: But (live am ashamed I to) <u>I am ashamed to</u> this lie! I must leave

you forever!

Chase: (I not willing am give to) <u>I am not willing to give</u> you up! Will you leave

Monte Carlo and run away with me?

Alexis: Oh Chase! (it deny impossible to is) <u>it's impossible to deny</u> my feelings for you.

Chase: Do you mean . . . ?

Alexis: Yes! Yes! (am I to give up prepared) <u>I am prepared to give up</u> everything for you!

The mansion, the jewels, the yacht. . . . (glad am to I leave) <u>I am glad to leave</u>

all of it behind for you.

Chase: My love! (it so good is hear to) <u>it's so good to hear</u> you say that. Let us

leave immediately!

7 Complete the following sentences with your own ideas. If possible, all of your ideas
should relate to entertainment and/or the media. When you are finished, share your
ideas with the class.

Example: I am afraid to <u>watch horror movies by myself.</u>

1. I am afraid to <u>watch horror movies by myself</u>.
2. It is dangerous to _____.
3. I am prepared to <u>everything for myself</u>.
4. It is irresponsible to _____.
5. It is embarrassing to _____.

6.   It is wrong to _____.

7.   I am willing to _____.

8.   I am sad to _____.

9.   It is good to _____.

10.   It is important to _____.

11.   It is impossible to _____.

12.   It is pleasant to _____.

C. Infinitives of Purpose

Infinitives can be used to express the purpose or reason for an action.

Examples	Notes
Let's go outside **to get** some fresh air.	In a purpose phrase, *to* = *in order to*.
He turned on the TV **to watch** his favorite game show.	
The sign was removed **in order not to offend** the public.	A negative purpose is expressed with the phrase *in order not to* or *so as not to* + the simple form of a verb.

8   Put a box around infinitives of purpose in the reading on page 182.

Example: Continue to use Insta-muscle each day to build even bigger muscles.

9   Match each of the numbers on the left to the letters on the right to form complete and logical sentences.

e **1.** I read newspapers

g **2.** I have a laptop

a **3.** I bought a VCR

h **4.** I use the Internet

c **5.** I use a cell phone

b **6.** I signed up for cable TV

i **7.** I have a fax machine

j **8.** I have an answering machine

f **9.** I use a computerized appointment book

d **10.** I need a vacation

a. to record TV programs when I am out.

b. to get more TV channels.

c. to make calls from my car.

d. to get away from it all!

e. to know what is happening in the world.

f. to keep track of all of my appointments.

g. to do work when I am away from my office.

h. to send and receive e-mail.

i. to send and receive important paper documents.

j. in order to take messages when I'm not home.

Using What You've Learned

10 Interview your partner about your media interests and habits, using the words below to form questions with infinitives. Switch roles so that the person who was interviewed now becomes the interviewer.

Example: A: Do you like to read the newspaper?
            B: Yes, I do.
            A: Which one?
            B: I like to read the Daily Sun.
            A: Why?
            B: Because it has a good sports section.

1. like / read / the newspaper? (If so, which one(s)? Why?)
2. like / listen / music? (If so, what kind? Why?)
3. like / go / movies? (If so, what kind? Why?)
4. like / watch / sports? (If so, which one(s)? Why?)
5. prefer / watch TV or be outside?
6. need / watch TV every day?
7. willing / watch less TV?
8. happy / watch infomercials?
9. afraid / go to horror movies?
10. know how / create your own website?

Report to your class on what you learned about your partner.

11 In small groups, discuss one or more of the following statements.

■ It is irresponsible for the media to show graphic (strong) violence.
■ In some situations, it is necessary to censor (to remove parts of) books, movies, and records.
■ It is important for the media to provide role models (good examples for young people).
■ It is wrong for the media not to respect the privacy of famous people.

How many members of your group agree with the statement(s) you discussed? How many disagree? What did you learn from this discussion?

12 Brainstorm a list of reasons why people read newspapers. To help give you ideas, you may want to look through a newspaper while you do this activity.

Example: People read the newspaper to find out about local news.
            People read newspapers to look up movie schedules.
            People read newspapers to know what the weather will be like.

| PART 3 | # Summary of Modal Verbs; Summary of Pronouns, Indefinite Pronouns |

Setting the Context

Conversation

Yukio: This movie is so romantic. But why doesn't he kiss her?
Uma: He doesn't know that she loves him.
Yukio: I thought somebody told him.
Uma: No, nobody told him. Now watch the movie.
Yukio: This movie is confusing. Isn't that her child? Or is it his?
Uma: It's his. Now please, Yukio. You must be quiet.
Yukio: There's something else I don't understand . . .
Uma: Yukio, Nobody can hear the movie. Everybody is asking us to be quiet.
Yukio: Really? I didn't hear anybody say anything.
Uma: Will you please just be quiet?
Yukio: I don't like our seats. I can't believe that woman in front of us is wearing a hat. How can people be so rude? Somebody should tell her that she isn't the only person in this movie theatre!

Discussion Questions

1. Where are Yukio and Uma?
2. Why are the people around them annoyed?
3. What does Uma keep asking Yukio to do?
4. What does Yukio say about the woman in front of her?
5. What would you do in this situation if you were Uma?

A. Summary of Modal Verbs

Meaning	Modal	Examples
Ability	can/can't	I **can** write my own computer programs. I **can't** watch violent movies.
Future Possibility	may might	There **may** be a good movie playing tonight. We **might** be too late.
Future Plans, Predictions	will/won't	What **will** happen next? Will he die? No, he **won't**.
Requests	can/can't could/couldn't will/won't would	**Can** you help me? **Could** you change places with me? **Will** you please be quiet? **Would** you hand me the TV schedule?
Permission	may can/can't	**May** I have some popcorn? **Can** I watch another program?
Advice	should/shouldn't had better/had better not	You **should** get an e-mail address. We**'d better not** talk during the movie.
Obligation	have to must/mustn't	We **have to** show our ID cards to get into the campus movie theatre. You **mustn't** talk in the movie theater.

1   Fill in the missing modals in the following movie dialogues. In some cases, more than one answer is possible. After you have filled in the blanks, identify which dialogue is from a western movie, which is from a romance movie, and which is from a horror movie.

1. A: You _____'d better not_____ go in there. People say that old house is haunted. If you

do, you ___d' better___ not come out alive.

B: You _____ scare me with your silly ghost stories. I _____

go in that house, with you or without you.

A: OK. But you _____ take this knife with you, just in case you need it.

Type of movie _____

2. A: Don't go. Not yet.

B: Darling, I ___can___ go. The taxi's waiting.

A: How _____ you do this to me? You're my reason for living. I

_____ die without you.

B: We _____ be strong, my love. I _____ never forget you.
     4   5

A: I _____ believe we _____ never see each other again.
    6   7

Type of movie _____

3. A: _____ I help you, ma'am?
         1

B: Yes. I _____ find the sheriff immediately. _____ you
            2   3

tell me where he is?

A: Well now, Sheriff Jackson _____ be at the dry goods store, or he
                              4

_____ be over at the stables. Then again, at this time of night, you
     5

_____ find him in the saloon. I _____ help you
       6   7

find him if you'd like.

B: Thank you kindly. I'm sure I _____ find him myself.
                                 8

A: I think I _____ accompany you, ma'am. A young lady
                9

_____ be walking around by herself in this town at night.
       10

Type of movie _____

2   Complete the sentences with the missing modal verbs. In some cases, more than one answer is possible. Then, match each of the sentences to the appropriate speaker or thinker shown in the pictures. Write the letter of the speaker (found in the balloons) in the parentheses.

1. __*Would*__ you please turn down the volume? It's so loud, I __*can't*__ hear
       1   2 (not)

   myself think! (*b*)

2. Do you want sparkling teeth and minty fresh breath? Then you

   ____*May*____ use Glisten Toothpaste! (   )
        3

3. And now our reporter in the traffic helicopter _____ tell you free-
                                                   4

   way drivers about the present conditions. (   )

4. I __*Can't*__ stand all that noise! I _____ tell you one last
        5 (not)   6

   time—turn it down! (   )

5. The president _____ leave on a tour of Asia next month. His plans are
   <u>7</u>

   not yet certain, but there are reports that he _____ visit Tokyo. ( )
   <u>8</u>

6. Because of a major accident, there _____ be heavy traffic on
   <u>9</u>

   Highway 405. ( )

7. You _____ take another route if possible. ( )
   <u>10</u>

8. _____ you like some advice? If you want to be popular, you
   <u>11</u>

   _____ have a bright smile! ( )
   <u>12</u>

9. Tension is increasing on the border. It seems unlikely that negotiators

   _____ be able to come to an agreement. ( )
   <u>13</u>

10. You _____ watch so much TV, anyway! TV _____
    <u>14 (not)</u>   <u>15 (not)</u>

    help you improve your grades. ( )

B. Summary of Pronouns

Subject and object pronouns replace nouns. Possessive adjectives come before nouns;
possessive pronouns do not come before nouns. Reflexive pronouns refer to the subject of a sentence or sentence part.

Subject Pronouns	Object Pronouns	Possessive Adjectives	Possessive Pronouns	Reflexive Pronouns
I	me	my	mine	myself
you	you	your	yours	yourself
he	him	his	his	himself
she	her	her	hers	herself
it	it	its	—	itself
we	us	our	ours	ourselves
you	you	your	yours	yourselves
they	them	their	theirs	themselves

C. Indefinite Pronouns

Indefinite pronouns refer to people or things that the speaker or writer doesn't identify.
They begin with *some-, any-, no-,* or *every-* and end with *-body, -one,* or *-thing.*

Indefinite Pronouns	Examples	Notes
someone something somebody	**Someone** is making noise. I want to tell you **something.** Are you looking for **somebody?**	A pronoun with *some-* usually appears in an affirmative statement or in a question. A pronoun with *some-* refers to a specific unidentified person or thing.
no one nobody anything anybody/anyone	Who left early? **No one.** **Nobody** liked the movie. There isn't **anything** to watch on TV. There isn't **anybody** in the theatre.	A pronoun with *no-* usually appears as the subject. A pronoun with *no-* means "not a" or "not any." *Not + any-* is more common as the object. A pronoun with *any-* means "it doesn't matter which."
everybody/everyone everything	**Everybody** likes movies. Just pick one movie. We can't see **everything.**	A pronoun with *every-* means "all the people" or "all the things."

3   Circle the correct pronouns in the parentheses.

Look at these movies. (They / Them / Their) are all full of sex and violence! (I / me / myself) don't want (me / my / mine) children to see (they / them / theirs). (Anybody / Something / No one) should see garbage like this. When (I / me / myself) was a kid, I used to enjoy (me / mine / myself) at innocent romances and comedies. Kids today don't enjoy (their / them / themselves) at those kinds of movies. But (everyone / any / no one) knows that violence isn't only in the movies. Did (someone / anyone / no one) read the newspaper last night? A crazy man shot (he / him / his) wife and then (he / him / himself) killed (he / himself / herself)! (Us / Our / Ours) society is too violent. And the media doesn't do (anything / everything / something) to help. Actually, the media is part of the problem because it's always showing (us / our / ours) violence. I think the media should take responsibility for (it / its / itself) effect on society.

4   Fill in each blank with an appropriate pronoun.

__I__ 'm a football widow and __I__ hate TV! During the football season, __She__ don't have a husband because __her__ 's married to the TV set. When __I__ 'm in the room with __him__ , __ __ doesn't say a word to me; I often end up talking to __me__ .

For months _____ children forget that __*they*__ have a father. Dur-
9   10

ing football season, my husband can hardly remember __*my*__ names!
11

__*he*__ talked to __*his*__ neighbors about this situation and
12   13

__*we*__ all have the same problem with __*my*__ husbands. Does
14   15

_____ have a solution? _____ need advice! _____ please help me!
16   17   18

_____'m not sure _____ family can survive another football season.
19   20

Using What You've Learned

5 In most newspapers, there is a section called an "advice column" in which people write
to a person (called an advice columnist) about their problems, and ask the person for
advice. The advice columnist then publishes the letter in the newspaper, along with a
letter of advice. For this activity, you will take on the role of an advice columnist. Read
the letters below. Choose one, and respond to it with a letter of advice. Make sure you
use modal verbs and pronouns in your response.

Dear Doris,

My 5-year-old son is watching too
much TV. Every time I try to turn off
the TV, he screams and cries.

Help!

Panicky in Portugal

Dear Doris,

I am a "football widow." My husband
completely ignores me when football
season starts. It's impossible to get his
attention until football season ends.

What should I do?

Widowed in Washington

Dear Doris,

My 10-year-old daughter wants to be
just like her favorite rap star. Lately
she is dressing like this rap star (in
clothes that are much too old for her)
and she has started to use bad
language.

Can you give me some advice?

Agonizing in Amsterdam

6 Work in small groups. Choose a movie or an episode of a TV show that you have seen
recently, and explain the plot (the story) to the people in your group. The first time you
mention a character, you should use his or her name. After that, use only pronouns to
refer to the character.

Video Activities: Quiz Shows

Before You Watch.

1. Circle the kinds of TV shows you like to watch.

    a. comedies   b. dramas   c. quiz shows   d. soap operas

2. Do you like watching quiz shows on TV? Discuss with a partner.

3. Describe your favorite TV quiz show to your partner.

Watch.   Discuss the following questions with your classmates.

1. On all the game shows you saw in the video, what must contestants do in order to win money?

2. Why do television networks like to make game shows?

3. The contestants on today's game shows are _____.

         a. millionaires   b. ordinary people   c. scholars

Watch Again.   Write T if the statements below are true and F if they are false. Then correct all the false statements.

1. In the U.S., you can watch a game show on TV almost every night of the week.

2. Quiz shows are a new idea.

3. The first game show in America was called "Who Wants to be a Millionaire?"

4. If a television show is successful, other networks hurry to copy it.

5. Game shows are cheaper to make than sitcoms.

6. In the short term, American TV networks will stop making game shows.

7. The questions on the new "Twenty-One" show are called "relatable." This means they are about families.

After You Watch.   Complete the following sentences with the correct tense of the verb in parentheses. Then check the video to see if your answers are correct.

1. "Who Wants to be a Millionaire" _____ (start) the current quiz show craze last summer.

2. Other networks quickly _____ (jump) on the bandwagon.

3. Television networks always _____ (clone) shows that are popular, and now they _____ (do) it again.

4. Their motivation _____ (be) greed.

5. In the short term the networks _____ (make) more game shows, more quiz shows.

6. Game shows _____ (be) not a new idea.

7. In the late 1950s, the audience _____ (find out) the show Twenty-One was rigged, and quiz shows _____ (lose) popularity. Now NBC _____ (bring) back Twenty-One.

8. On the new quiz shows, you _____ (have to, not) be a scholar in order to be a millionaire.

9. The sixty-four thousand dollar question is, how long _____ the craze _____ (last)?

The Past Continuous Tense; the Simple Past Tense; Infinitives; Modal Verbs; Pronouns; Indefinite Pronouns

Standardized tests of English proficiency often have sections on the past continuous tense, the simple past tense, infinitives, modal verbs, and pronouns. Review what you studied in this chapter. Check your understanding of the grammar points by completing the sample items below.

Remember that . . .

■ The past continuous tense describes activities in progress during a period of time in the past.

■ The simple past tense is used to talk about events and activities that began and ended in the past.

■ *Can/Can't* are used to express present ability/inability.

■ Possessive adjectives come before nouns; possessive pronouns do not come before nouns.

Part 1.   Circle the correct completion for the following.

Example: I'm afraid she's very worried about _____ teenage son.

    a. she   b. herself   c. hers   **(d.)** her

1. Sorry I couldn't call you earlier. The phone _____ off the hook all morning.

    (a.) was ringing   b. rang   c. were ringing   d. rung

2. I _____ usually get through the first time I try calling my family overseas. The lines are all busy.

    a. had better not   b. can't   c. wasn't   **(d.)** haven't

3. She _____ the computer at 8:00 last night.

    a. was to use   **(b.)** didn't used   c. wasn't using   d. using

4. I wasn't prepared _____ such a violent movie.

    a. seeing   b. see   **(c.)** to see   d. to be seeing

Part 2.   Circle the letter below the underlined word(s) containing the error.

Example: The TV <u>seems</u> awfully loud; <u>do you</u> <u>want</u> me <u>lower</u> the volume?
                    A   B   C   **(D)**

1. <u>Usually</u> I <u>wake up</u> early, but yesterday I <u>was waking up</u> at <u>around</u> 10:30.
     A   B   **(C)**   D

2. Instead of <u>going out</u> for dinner, <u>while</u> the movie <u>ended</u> we went home.
           A   B   **(C)**   D

3. He said he <u>wanted</u> <u>to go</u> outside to <u>getting</u> some <u>fresh</u> air.
          A   B   **(C)**   D

4. I <u>can't</u> <u>cook</u> pastries very well, but I <u>can't</u> <u>bake</u> good bread.
  (A)   B   C   D

Chapter 9

Social Life

The Present Perfect Tense (2)

Setting the Context

Conversation

Rosa: What's wrong, Jess?

Jess: I'm bored. I've lived here for a year and I still don't really have a social life. I haven't gone to a party since the summer. I haven't even gone to a movie in weeks!

Rosa: The best way to meet people is to get involved in activities. I joined the soccer team last August, and I've made lots of new friends on the team since then.

Jess: I've meant to join a club all semester, but I haven't had any extra time since the semester started. Since September I've spent all my time studying and writing papers.

Rosa: I think you also feel bad because you haven't gotten any exercise for months. To feel good, you need to get some exercise every day.

Jess: You may be right. That may be why I haven't slept well since I stopped going to the gym.

Rosa: Is something else bothering you?

Jess: Now that you mention it, yes—my love life! I haven't met anyone since I broke up with Jack.

Rosa: Well that's no surprise. You've barely left the house for weeks. You need to make more of an effort to get out and meet people. Hey, I have a friend who might be perfect for you. Do you want me to introduce you?

Jess: Oh no. Not a blind date! I've always avoided them!

Rosa: Trust me. I think you'll really like John.

Jess: How long have you known him?

Rosa: I've known him since August. He's on the men's soccer team.

Jess: How long has he been on the team?

Rosa: I think he's been on the team for a year or two. His team has won a few trophies since he joined. He's really cute and really nice.

Jess: I guess he sounds OK.

Rosa: Great! He's been out sick since last week, so I haven't seen him for a few days. But I'll speak with him as soon as he comes back.

Jess: OK. But you'd better be right about this!

Discussion Questions

1. Why is Jess bored?
2. What has happened to Rosa since she joined the socc
3. Why hasn't Jess joined any clubs?
4. What does Jess ask about John?
5. Why can't Rosa contact John right away?
6. Are you happy with your social life? Why or why not?

A. The Present Perfect Tense (2)

The present perfect tense consists of *have/has* before the past participle form of a verb. The present perfect describes actions or situations that began in the past and continue to the present. This tense tells how long something has lasted up to this point.

Note that in other cases, the present perfect tense refers to actions or situations that occurred at an unspecified time in the past, or to repeated past actions. This use of the present perfect tense is covered in Chapter 6.

Statements

	Examples	**Notes**
Affirmative	We **have been** here since February. She **has played** tennis for a long time.	The present perfect can be contracted with subject pronouns: *I've, we've, you've, they've, he's, she's,* and *it's*.
Negative	I **have not seen** them since last week.	The negative contractions are *haven't* and *hasn't*.

Questions

	Examples	**Possible Answers**	
		Affirmative	**Negative**
Yes/No Questions	**Have** you **lived** here since January? **Have** you **been** married for a long time?	Yes, I have. Yes, I have.	No, I haven't. No, I haven't.
Information Questions	How long **have** you **known** him? How long **has** she **been** your girlfriend?	I've known him since January. She's been my girlfriend for a year.	

1   Underline the present perfect verb phrases in the conversation on page 198.

Example: I've lived here for a year and I still don't really have a social life.

2   Complete the following sentences with the correct present perfect verb phrases.

Example: His sister is married. She *has been* married since she was 22.

1. I know John. I _have known_ him for a few months.
2. He loves sports. He _have known_ sports since he was a little boy.
3. He works at the sports center. He _have been_ in the sports center since Christmas.
4. He lives alone. He _have lived_ alone for six months.
5. He has a beard. He _have been_ a beard for two years.
6. He is sick right now. He _have been_ sick for a week.
7. He and his best friend are in a band. They _have been_ in a band since 1999.
8. John plays the guitar. He _have known_ the guitar since he was a boy.
9. John doesn't eat meat. He _have known_ meat since he became a vegetarian.
10. He has a dog. He _____ a dog since October.

3 Form questions beginning with *How long* about each of the following statements.

Example: I'm a member of the chess club.

   How long have you been a member of the chess club?

1. Hisato lives with his best friend.

   How long have your been lives with his best friend?

2. I know the steps to this dance.

   How long have you been know the steps to this dance.

3. Mike is my soccer coach.

   How long have you been coaching soccer? ?

4. Thomas and Gina are married.

   How long have you been married? ?

5. My cousin owns a nightclub.

   How long have you been owns a nightclub? ?

6. Carlos and Daria are in love.

How long have you been in love? ?

7. Amile plays the guitar.

How long have you been plays the guitar? ?

8. My parents are on vacation.

How long have you been on vacation? ?

9. This club has a dance floor.

How long have been a dance floor ?

10. I like foreign movies.

How long have been like foreign movies ?

B. Time Expressions with the Present Perfect: For, Since, All, Always

This meaning of the present perfect usually appears with a time expression. A phrase with *since, for, all,* or *always* can answer the questions "*How long . . . ?*" or "*Since when . . . ?*"

	Examples	Notes
for	I have played soccer **for** five years.	Use *for* with the amount of time an activity or state has lasted. *Examples: for* an hour, *for* a week, *for* five years, *for* a long time
since	They have been married **since** January.	Use *since* with a time or point that shows when an activity or state started. *Examples: since* 7:00, *since* Monday, *since* May 15th, *since* my birthday
all	She has been at her friend's house **all** week.	Use *all* to express a time period. *Examples: all* day, *all* night, *all* week, *all* my life
always	We have **always** wanted to go skydiving.	Use *always* to show that an action or state began in the past and continues to the present. *Always* comes between the auxiliary verb and the main verb.

Note: It is also possible to use the time expression *in* for negative sentences. For example: I haven't been to a concert *in* years.

4 Fill in the blanks in the following sentences with *for, since, all,* or *always.*

Example: They have been at the beach _all_ day.

1. Sarah has _always_ been my best friend.
2. I have known her _since_ nursery school.
3. I have _always_ told her all of my secrets.
4. We have lived in this town _____ our lives.
5. We have _always_ wanted to travel.
6. We've talked about it _____ all _____ years.
7. She's been on summer vacation with her family _for_ three weeks.
8. She has been gone _since_ May.
9. I've been lonely and bored _since_ she's been gone.
10. The weather has been terrible _for_ week.
11. It has been grey and rainy _since_ last week.
12. I've tried to call my friend Sid _all_ afternoon.
13. His line has been busy _since_ 12:00.
14. I haven't spoken to him _since_ my birthday.
15. I haven't seen him _for_ a few weeks.
16. He's been too busy to get together _for_ the last week or two.
17. I've known Sid _since_ 1993.
18. He has _always_ made me laugh.
19. Maybe we can go out for dinner. I haven't eaten _all_ day.
20. I've been hungry _since_ this morning.
21. Maybe we can go dancing tonight. I haven't been to a dance club _since_ last summer.
22. I have to do something! I've done nothing but sit in the house _for_ weeks!

5 Combine each pair of sentences using the present perfect and *for* or *since*.

Example: She joined the soccer team last year. She is still a member of the soccer team.
She has been a member of the soccer team for a year.

1. Juanita liked Daniel three years ago. She still likes him.

   _____.

2. Adrian moved to Mexico last year. He still lives there.

   _____.

3. Angela was tired this morning. She's still tired.

   _____.

4. Jong got a cell phone in 1998. He still has a cell phone.

   _____.

5. They woke up at 8:00. They are still awake.

   _____.

6. She turned the stereo on an hour ago. The stereo is still on.

   _____.

7. She stopped talking to me five years ago. She still doesn't talk to me.

   _____.

8. I wasn't hungry last night. I'm still not hungry.

   _____.

9. My visitors arrived a week ago. They are still here.

   _____.

10. Dara got glasses when she was seven years old. She still wears glasses.

   _____.

C. Time Clauses with Since in the Present Perfect

Sentences in the present perfect (or present perfect continuous) tense often have a time clause with *since*.

Examples	Notes
They've been in love **since** the first time **they saw** each other. **Since I joined the gym, I've had** more energy.	The main clause must be in the present perfect (continuous) tense.
	The clause with *since* is usually in the simple past tense. A *since* clause can come at the beginning or at the end of a sentence.
	A comma is used after the clause when it comes at the beginning of the sentence.

6 Circle the time expressions (along with the periods or points in time that follow the time expressions) in the conversation on page 198. (Note: *always* is not followed by a time period.) Put a box around time clauses with *since*.

Examples: I haven't gone to a party (since the summer.)

That may be why I haven't slept well | since I stopped going to the gym. |

7 Combine each pair of sentences into one sentence using *since*. Combine the sentences in the order in which they appear. Use correct punctuation.

Example: Young went on a diet. He has lost a lot of weight.
Since Young went on a diet, he has lost a lot of weight.

1. Hanna has met a lot of new people. She joined the tennis club.
    Since Hanna has met a lot of new people, She joined

2. Alfonso went to the concert last night. He has had a headache.
    Since Alfonso went to the concert last night, he has

3. Taro went on vacation. He has been much more relaxed.
    Since Taro went on vacation, he has been much more

4. I haven't seen Reiko and Yoko. They moved to an apartment off campus.
    Since I haven't seen Reiko and Yoko, they moved

5. Patrick hasn't been in school. He broke his leg.
    Since Patrick hasn't been in school, he broke

6. He took an art history course. He has been interested in art.
    Since He took an art history course, he has been

7. We haven't gone to the movies very often. We had children.
    Since we haven't gone to the movies very often, we

8. I haven't heard from Juan. We went on a date last week.
    Since I haven't heard from Juan, we went on a

8 Fill in the blanks to form present perfect sentences about yourself.

Example: I've been extremely busy since the semester started.

1. I've been *extremely bu*since *the semester started*
2. I haven't been *busy* for *my classes.*
3. I've had *good time* since *school open*.
4. I haven't had *a good time* all *the time*.

5. I've known _my teacher_ for _long time_.
6. I've studied _for the test_ since _last week_.
7. I've always wanted _to go to the movies._
8. I've meant to _____ since _____.

Using What You've Learned

9 Interview a classmate about his or her life. Ask simple past tense questions and present perfect questions beginning with *How long.*

> **Example:** A: Where do you live?
> B: I live in Cobble Hill.
> A: How long have you lived there?
> B: About five years.
> A: Are you married?
> B: Yes, I am.
> A: How long have you been married?

Take notes on your classmate's answers. After the interview, write a list of present perfect statements about the person you interviewed. Do not put the person's name on the paper. Exchange your list with another student. Each student reads aloud the list he or she has been given. The class tries to guess the identity of the student based on the information in the list.

> **Example:** This student has lived in Cobble Hill for about five years.
> She has been married since she was 21.
> She has been a writer for the school newspaper for a year.

10 Each student writes five time expressions that can be used with the present perfect tense (such as *all week, for a minute, since last winter,* and *since I was a child*) on separate index cards or pieces of paper. The teacher collects these index cards. He or she then gives each pair of students ten of the cards, face down. With your partner, take turns turning over the index cards. As each index card is turned over, the student who has turned it over makes a true present perfect statement.

> **Example:** A. (*after turning over a card that says "all week"*) It has rained all week.
> B. (*after turning over a card that says "since last winter"*) I haven't gotten sick since last winter.
> A. (*after turning over a card that says "since I was a child"*) I haven't gone to the circus since I was a child.

The Present Perfect Continuous Tense; The Present Perfect Continuous Tense Versus the Present Perfect Tense

Setting the Context

Conversation

John: Jess?
Jess: John?
John: Hi! Sorry I'm late. Have you been waiting long?
Jess: No. I've only been waiting for five or ten minutes. You seem out of breath. Have you been running?
John: Yes, I have. I ran from my house in Chester Heights. The bus I take into town hasn't been running on time lately. So after waiting a few minutes, I decided to run here.
Jess: That's really far to run!
John: It's not that bad. And it's good exercise. I've been training for a ten kilometer race anyway.
Jess: Wow. You're on the soccer team and you're training for a race? You must be busy.
John: I am! Besides the race, I've also been learning karate, and lately I've also been doing volunteer work at a soup kitchen. But I'd rather talk about you! Rosa told me that you're from New York. How long have you been living here?
Jess: I've been living here for a year. I've been studying law at the university.
John: That sounds difficult. What do you do in your free time?
Jess: I usually read to relax. Though I've been so busy with school work that I've been reading the same book for a month! Also, to be honest, I've probably been watching too much TV. I've been meaning to get involved in some new activities. I'm thinking of taking a photography class.
John: Oh, you should! I've been taking a photography class for the last month or two. Since I started the class, my photos have gotten much better.
Jess: You're taking a photography class too? How do you find the time for everything?
John: Well, I've had some free time lately because I haven't been playing guitar with my band. We've been taking a break because everyone in the band is so busy right now. I've been needing more time to work on my book. Did I mention that I've been writing a book . . . ?

Discussion Questions

1. Why is John out of breath?
2. What has he been doing recently?
3. What has Jess been doing recently?
4. Why has John had some free time recently?
5. What have you been doing recently?

A. The Present Perfect Continuous Tense

The present perfect continuous tense consists of *have/has been* before the *-ing* form of a verb. When the present perfect continuous is used with time expressions, this tense stresses the duration or repetition of an action or situation that began in the past and continues to the present. It often implies that the action or situation will continue in the future. Time expressions often used with this tense include *for, since, all* (*day, week,* etc.), *today,* and *this* (*week, summer,* etc.). Questions with *How long* are frequently used with this tense. When the tense is used without mention of a specific time, it is used to talk about a general activity that has been in progress recently. This meaning of the present perfect can be used with inexact time expressions such as *recently, lately,* and *these days.*

Statements

Purpose	Examples	
	Affirmative	**Negative**
To Emphasize Duration of an Activity That Started in the Past and Continues to the Present	It**'s been raining** for an hour. She**'s been talking** on the phone all evening.	We **haven't been living** here for more than a month. I **haven't been playing** soccer this week.
To Express a General Activity That Has Been in Progress Recently	I**'ve been going** to a lot of parties recently. He**'s been reading** a good book.	He **hasn't been sleeping** well recently. I **haven't been doing** much.

Questions

	Examples	Possible Answers
Yes/No Questions	**Have** you **been seeing** a lot of movies? **Has** she **been living** here long?	Yes, I have. No, I haven't. Yes, she has. No, she hasn't.
Information Questions	Where **have** you **been living?** Who**'s been playing** music? What **have you been doing?**	I've been living in London. My neighbors have been playing music. I've been going to the beach a lot lately.

Notes: 1. See Appendix 4 for spelling rules for the *-ing* ending.
2. Some verbs are not normally used in the continuous tense. These verbs, called *nonaction verbs,* include verbs that express feeling and thought, verbs that express possession, and verbs that express sensory perception. For more information on nonaction verbs, see chart B (*Nonaction Verbs*) in Chapter 2, pages 42–43.

1   Underline the present perfect continuous verb phrases in the conversation on page 206.

Example: <u>Have</u> you <u>been waiting</u> long?

2   Form present perfect continuous sentences with the cue words that follow. Add a time expression (*since, for,* or *all*) to each.

Example: I / preparing for the party / 2:00 this afternoon

I have been preparing for the party since 2:00 this afternoon.

1. I / look forward to this party / weeks

    I have been look forward to this party since weeks

2. the music / play / night

    I have been play the music

3. everyone / dance / hours

    _____

4. that woman / flirt with that man / the party began

    _____

5. that couple / fight / the party began

    _____

6. the DJ / play disco music / long time

    _____

7. my head / hurt / about 10:00

    _____

8. we / wait for food / a long time

    _____

9. I / feel sick / I had a drink

    _____

10. I / want to go home / a few hours

    _____

3 Form present perfect continuous questions beginning with *How long* for each of the following sentences.

Example: A. He is saving money for a sports car.

B. *How long has he been saving money for a sports car?*

1. A: Oscar and Melina have been arguing a lot.

    B: _____?

2. A: She's been flirting with Felipe!

    B: _____?

3. A: She dyes her hair.

    B: _____?

4. A: He wears a hairpiece.

    B: _____?

5. A: He's dieting.

    B: _____?

6. A: Felipe lives downtown.

    B: _____?

7. A: His parents pay his rent.

    B: _____.

8. A: He's been stealing money from the cash register at work.

    B: _____?

9. A: Felipe and Alicia are dating.

    B: *How long has Felipe and Alicia been dating*

10. A: I've been planning a party.

    B: *How long has I been planning a party.*

4 Form sentences with the cue words below to answer the question "What have you been doing recently?" Fill in Nos. 9 to 12 with activities that you have been doing recently.

Example: read a good book *I've been reading a good book.*

1. go out with friends *I've been going out with friends*

2. play a lot of tennis *I've been playing a lot of tennis*

3. go to a lot of parties *I've been going to a lot of parties*

4. have friends over for dinner *I've been having friend over for*

5. rent videos *I've been renting videos.*

6. play soccer _____.
7. shop with friends _____.
8. spend time in cafes _____.
9. _____.
10. _____.
11. _____.
12. _____.

5 Fill in the blanks with the present perfect continuous form of the verbs in parentheses.

Jim: So, Diane. What have you been doing lately?

Diane: I *'ve been studying* a lot this semester. This week I ~~Ve been writing~~ a term
            1 (study)   2 (write)

paper. My roommate _____ me. But we _____ all the time. We
                         3 (help)   4 (not work)

_____ a good time, too. We _____ tennis and _____.
    5 (have)   6 (play)   7 (relax)

Jim: I'm glad to hear that you _____ yourselves. I _____
                                       8 (enjoy)   9 (not relax)

much. My wife _____ really hard these days, too. She _____
                   10 (work)   11 (not take)

any time off. She _____ for extra money and she _____ too.
                       12 (type)   13 (babysit)

We _____ about taking a vacation.
       14 (think)

Diane: Wow, it sounds like you both _____ much too hard. Stop thinking
                                            15 (work)

about taking a vacation. Just take one!

6 Study each of the pictures for clues that tell you what the person or people has/have
       been doing. Write a present perfect continuous statement for each picture.

1.   2.

She has been crying.   _____.

3.

_____.

4.

_____.

5.

_____.

6.

_____.

7.

_____.

8.

_____.

7 Fill in each of the blanks with the appropriate words to form the present perfect continuous form of the verbs in parentheses.

Sally: So what ___are___ you ___doing___ with yourself, Ann? _____ you
　　　　　　　　　　1　　　　2 (do)　　　　　　　　　　　　　　3

_____ much time in the library?
　4 (spend)

Ann: No. Actually, I _____ on my thesis very much this semester. I
                5 (not, work)

_____ out a lot.
   6 (go)

Sally: Really? Who _____ you _____ out with? I heard that you
              7   8 (go)

_____ the teaching assistant in our chemistry class. Is that true?
   8 (date)

Ann: Well, I . . .

Sally: _____ he _____ you to fancy restaurants? I bet he has!
       9   10 (take)

Where _____ you _____?
      11   12 (eat)

Ann: Well, we . . .

Sally: _____ he _____ you flowers?
      13   14 (send)

Ann: Well, uh . . .

Sally: Your life sounds so romantic. Married life is completely different. We

_____ out at all lately, have we Carlos?
   15 (not go)

Carlos: How can you say that? Why, just a month ago we went out for a pizza!

Sally: But what _____ we _____ since then?
           16   17 (do)

Carlos: We _____ lots of time alone. What could be more romantic than
         18 (spend)

that?

Sally: Oh, Carlos. Watching old horror movies on late night TV isn't exactly what I had
in mind.

B. The Present Perfect Continuous Tense Versus the Present Perfect Tense (2)

The present perfect continuous and present perfect tenses both describe actions or situations that began in the past and continue to the present.

	Examples	Notes
Present Perfect Continuous	We've **been talking** for hours. How long **has** it **been raining?**	The present perfect continuous emphasizes the duration or repetition of the activity or situation.
Present Perfect	She **has been** in London all summer. She**'s liked** him for years. I **have known** him for six years.	The present perfect emphasizes the length of time the activity or situation has lasted. The present perfect is used with verbs that are not usually used in the continuous tense (nonaction verbs). (NOT: ~~I have been knowing him for six years.~~)
Present Perfect Continuous OR Present Perfect	I **have lived** here since 1993. = I **have been living** here since 1993.	With certain verbs (such as *live*, *work*, and *teach*), there is little or no difference in meaning between the present perfect and the present perfect continuous when a time expression is used.

8 Circle the correct verb choice in each set of parentheses.

A. A: You look worried. Is anything wrong?

B: Well . . . I've (thought/been thinking) about asking out a girl in my English
1

class.

A: What's the problem?

B: I don't think she has (noticed/been noticing) me since the class began.
2

B. A: Rahim, wake up.

B: How long have I (slept/been sleeping)?
1

A: You've (snored/been snoring) almost since we started the video. I thought that
2

you liked horror movies.

B: I haven't (liked/been liking) them since I was a kid.
3

C. A: My boyfriend has (acted/been acting) strange lately.
1

B: What has he (done/been doing)?
2

A: Well, he hasn't (had/been having) much time for me for weeks now. He also
3

hasn't (been/been being) home for the last few nights. I have (called/been calling)
4   5

him, but nobody ever answers.

B: Hasn't he (studied/been studying) for final exams? Maybe he's been at the
6

library.

D. A: Hey, it's time to get ready for the party. We've got to clean up this apartment.

B: Can't you see that I've (cleaned up/been cleaning up) the apartment all
1

morning? Why haven't you two (helped/been helping) me?
2

C: I've (thought/been thinking) about the refreshments and the music for hours.
3

Someone has to make the plans.

E. A: Have you (heard/been hearing) the news about Helen and Laura?
1

B: No. What happened?

A: They haven't (gotten/been getting) along lately. They haven't (talked/been
2   3

talking) to each other for days and now Helen is moving out of the apartment.

Using What You've Learned

9 Interview your partner about a significant change that has taken place in his or her life recently, and how this change has affected his or her daily life. Possible changes to focus on include:

- starting high school/college
- getting married
- moving to a new town
- moving to a new apartment
- having children
- starting a new job

Take notes during the interview. Afterwards, tell the class what you learned about the changes in your partner's life, using the present perfect continuous.

Example: *Since moving to her new apartment, Anna is closer to school, so she has been walking to school every day. She has also been staying later at the language laboratory and meeting friends after school. However, because her new apartment is*

*more expensive than her last apartment, she has been going to the movies less often.
She has also been eating in restaurants less often.*

10 Choose a famous person whom you would like to pretend to be for this activity. You
can choose either a modern or a historical figure, as long as the person is someone your
classmates will know. Next, pretend that you are all at a party speaking with each other
as the famous people you have chosen. Ask the other people at the party about what
they have been doing recently, and discuss what you have been doing, but do not tell
anyone your identity. After the "party," you and your classmates try to guess the
identity of the people you spoke with at the party.

Student A: What have you been doing lately?
Student B: I have been inventing new computer programs. I've also been selling some
of the stock in my company.
Student A: That sounds interesting.
Student B: Yes, it is. I've been enjoying it because I've been making millions and mil-
lions of dollars. So, what have you been doing lately?
Student A: Oh, you know, just the usual. I've been ruling France, and invading
Russia . . .
Student B: That sounds tiring!

(Student A is Bill Gates. Student B is Napoleon Bonaparte.)

<table>
<tr><td>PART 3</td></tr>
</table>

Adverbs of Degree: *So, Such, Enough,* and *Too*

Setting the Context

Conversation

Rosa: Well, how was the date?
Jess: It was OK, I guess.
Rosa: Wasn't John handsome enough?
Jess: Are you kidding? He's handsome enough to be a
movie star.
Rosa: Wasn't he smart enough?
Jess: I don't think I've ever met such an intelligent
man. And he's so funny. I had such a great time.
Rosa: Then what's the problem?
Jess: He's so busy, I don't think he has enough time for me. He has too many hobbies
and interests.
Rosa: That's silly. If he likes you, he'll make time for you.
Jess: That's not the real problem, anyway.
Rosa: I'm so confused. What *is* the problem?
Jess: I'm sure he doesn't like me. He's so active and interesting. I'm just not exciting
enough. I think I'm too dull for him.

Rosa: John asked me not to tell you this but . . .

Jess: You've spoken with him since last night?

Rosa: Yes. He called me early this morning because he was so excited. He really liked you. He can't wait to see you again. But he's afraid you may not like him! He thinks he talked too much.

Jess: That's funny. I was so sure he wouldn't be interested in me.

Rosa: You're always so negative! You don't have enough confidence in yourself.

Jess: This is so exciting! Oh well, I'm sure he'll change his mind on the second date.

Rosa: Jess!

Discussion Questions

1. How does Jess describe John?
2. What does Jess say about John's hobbies and interests?
3. Why does Jess think that John doesn't like her?
4. Why does John think that Jess may not like him?
5. Do you think Jess and John are a good match? Why or why not?

A. So *and* Such

So and *such* make the meaning of an adjective or adverb stronger.

	Examples	**Notes**
so	The movie was **so** good.	*So* is used before an adjective or an adverb.
	The movie was **so** good **that** I would see it again.	*So . . . that* can be used to express results or consequences.
such	It was **such** a good movie.	*Such* is used before an adjective + noun. The indefinite article *a/an* appears between *such* and the adjective when the noun is countable.
	It was **such** a good movie **that** I would see it again.	*Such . . . . that* can be used to express results or consequences.

1 Underline each occurrence of phrases with *so* and *such* in the conversation on pages 215–216.

Example: I don't think I ever met <u>such an intelligent man.</u>

2 Fill in the blanks with *so* or *such,* then match the numbers to the letters to form complete sentences.

   h   1. I went to ___such___ a good party last night

      2. There was ___so___ delicious food

a. that everyone else in my family was sleeping.

b. that almost everyone was dancing.

c. that I made a bunch of new friends.

b   3. The music was _so_ good

c   4. The people were all _such_ friendly

j   5. I met a guy who was _so_ funny

a   6. I was having _such_ a good time

i   7. The hostess was _so_ kind

g   8. It was _so_ late when I got home

d   9. I was _so_ tired when I got home

e 10. My father was _so_ angry the next morning

d. that I fell asleep in just a few minutes.

e. that he told me I can't go to any more parties for a month!

f. that it was all eaten really quickly.

g. that I didn't realize how late it was getting.

h. that nobody wanted it to end.

i. that she called a taxi for me.

j. that I couldn't stop laughing.

3   Fill in the blanks to make true statements about your own life and experiences. If you wish, you can add a *that* clause to the sentence.

Example: My social life is so _busy (that I'm almost never at home)_

1. My social life is so _____ (_that I'm alway be/hap_

2. The last movie I saw was so _funny_ (_that was very interested_

3. The last party I went to was so _good_ (_that was great_).

4. The last restaurant I went to was so _expensive_ (_that_ _____).

5. I have such _____ friends (_____).

6. I have such a _____ house/apartment (_____).

7. I have such _____ weekends (_____).

8. I have such _____ clothes (_____).

test
final escam

B. Enough *and* Too

possive
questing
Negative
subordin
coordinating
Relative
Passive
Tenses

	Examples	Notes
enough	She is old **enough**. (She can date.)	*Enough* means "as much or as many as needed." It implies a positive result. *Enough* comes after adjectives and adverbs.
	There are **enough** chairs here. (We can all sit down.)	*Enough* usually comes before nouns.
	There are**n't enough** chairs here. (Some of us have to stand.) *always*	*Not enough* implies a negative result.
	She is old **enough to** have a boyfriend.	. . . *enough* . . . *to* . . . can be used to express positive results.
too	She is **too** young. (She can't date.)	*Too* indicates a problem. It implies a negative result. *Too* comes before an adjective or adverb. It is the opposite of adjective/adverb + *enough*.
	There are **too many** chairs here. (They are in the way.)	*Too much/too many* comes before a noun. *Too many* is used with countable nouns; *too much* is used with noncount nouns. They express the opposite of *enough* + noun.
	He eats **too much**.	*Too much* can also be used as an adverb.
	She is **too** young **to** have a boyfriend.	. . . *too* . . . *to* . . . can be used to express negative results.

Note: It is possible to drop the noun after *enough* or *too much/many* if the meaning is clear. Example: *I've eaten too much (food).*

4 Put a circle around each occurrence of *enough* and *too* in the conversation on pages 215–216.

Example: Wasn't John (handsome enough)?

5 Fill in the blanks with *enough* or *too*.

Example: Why don't we go swimming? It's warm *enough.*

1. Makoto is _____ *too* _____ young to start dating.

2. The music is _____ *too* _____ loud. I can't hear what you're saying.

3. The movie theatre is close _____ *enough* _____ to walk to.

4. She is thin _____ *enough* _____ to be a model.

5. Can I call you back later? I'm _____ *too* _____ busy to talk now.

6. You aren't walking fast _____ *enough* _____. We're going to be late.

7. You're speaking _____ *too* _____ quietly. I can't hear what you're saying.

8. I'm tired _____ *enough* _____ to fall asleep right here!

9. This food isn't hot _____ *enough* _____. I'm going to send it back.

10. This dress is _____ *too* _____ expensive. I can't afford it.

6 Fill in the blanks with *enough, too, too many,* or *too much.*

Rikki: How did you like that restaurant?

Tamu: It was good, but the food was a little ___*too*___ spicy. Also, there wasn't ___*enough*___ food. I'm still hungry.

Rikki: Really? I'm stuffed. I thought there was ___*too much*___ food!

Tamu: I hope this movie is good. I've seen ___*too many*___ stupid movies lately.

Rikki: Wow. Look at that price. That's ___*too much*___ money for a ticket.

Tamu: Do you have ___*enough*___ money? If you don't, I can lend you some.

Rikki: No, I've got ___*enough*___.

Tamu: The line is ___*too*___ long. Let's get a cup of coffee and come back.

Rikki: Do we have ___*enough*___ time? The movie starts in ten minutes.

Tamu: There's a café right next door. It won't take ___*too much*___ time. Let's go.

7 Write a sentence about each of the following pictures, using either *. . . too . . . to* or *. . . enough . . . too.*

Example: *The women don't have enough money to pay the bill.*

1.   2.

_____.   _____.

3.

4.

_____. _____.

5.

_____.

8   Finish the following sentences with true statements about yourself.

Example: I am old enough to _have a driver's license._

1. I am old enough to ___have a boyfriend___.
2. I am too old to ___play with children___.
3. I am young enough to ___start dating___.
4. I am too young to ___talk about boyfriends___.
5. I have enough money to ___spend at the mall___.
6. I don't have enough money to ___buy a gift___.
7. I have enough time to ___do my homework___.
8. I don't have enough time to ___study for my exam___.

Using What You've Learned

9   Describe a movie or a restaurant that you went to recently, using the adverbs of intensity: *so, such, too,* and *enough.*

Example: *Last week I went to see "Last Exit." It was such a silly movie. There were too many explosions and car crashes. There weren't enough interesting characters. The movie was so long that I fell asleep while I was watching it.*

10   Find out about an athletic or academic club at your school. You may want to visit the club or speak to a member to learn more about the club. Find out what the requirements for new members are. Do you have to pass any tests? Are there any membership fees? What kind of time committment does the club require? Write an evaluation, explaining whether or not you can and would be interested in joining the club. Use *so, such, too,* and *enough* in your evaluation.

Video Activities: Online Love Story

Before You Watch.   Discuss these questions in a group.

1. What is a "chat room"? Have you ever visited one?
2. Do you think the Internet is a useful way to meet new people?
3. How do you usually meet people?
4. Do you believe that there is only one man or woman in the world who is exactly "right" for each person?

Watch.   Number the following events in the order that they happened.

_____ Patrick and Vesna chatted online.

_____ They got married.

_____ Patrick came home from work late and couldn't sleep.

_____ Patrick and Vesna got engaged.

_____ Vesna came to Patrick's house.

Watch Again.   Discuss these questions in a group.

1. Patrick asked Vesna, "What do you look like?" Her answer was "You won't run from me." What did she mean?
2. Why was it easy for Patrick and Vesna to meet?
3. How soon after they met did Patrick and Vesna get engaged?
4. How soon after that did they get married?
5. What did Patrick and Vesna's friends predict about their relationship?
6. What do Patrick and Vesna say about one another?
7. What is the "Romance Network"?

After You Watch.   Discuss one of the following topics in small groups.

1. Do you think Patrick and Vesna are attractive people? If they were single, would you like to go out with them? Tell why or why not. Use *so, such, enough,* and *too* in your sentences. For example: "I like Patrick because he's so tall." / "I think Vesna is too loud."
2. Describe your "dream" person. It can be your real husband / wife, boyfriend / girlfriend, or perhaps a movie star or a singer. Use *so, such, enough,* and *too* to explain why this person is perfect for you. For example: "My dream person is Ricky Martin. He has so much energy and such a great smile!"

Focus on Testing

The Present Perfect Tense; The Present Perfect Continuous Tense; Adverbs of Degree: So, Such, Enough, and Too

Standardized tests of English proficiency often have sections on the present perfect tense, the present perfect continuous tense, and adverbs of degree such as *so, such, enough,* and *too.* Review what you studied in this chapter. Check your understanding of the grammar points by completing the sample items below.

Remember that . . .

- The present perfect describes actions or situations that began in the past and continue to the present.

- A sentence in the present perfect or present perfect continuous tense often has a clause with *since.*

- *For* usually refers to a specific amount of time; *since* means from a past time period until now.

Part 1.   Circle the correct completion for the following sentences.

Example: You've been sick a lot this semester, _____ you?

    a. have   (b.) haven't   c. were   d. weren't

1.   Who _____ my soda? It's only half full now and I've only had one sip!

    a. drank   b. has been drinking   c. has drunk   d. drunk

2.   How long have you _____ here?

    a. worked   b. been working   c. working   d. a and b

3.   I have always _____ to be a famous movie star.

    a. want   b. been wanted   c. been wanting   d. wanted

4.   _____ I joined the gym, I've had more energy.

    a. For   b. After   c. When   d. Since

Part 2.   Circle the letter below the underlined word(s) containing the error.

Example: My cousin has been living in New York since three months.
               A   B   C   (D)

1.   I have been going to Disneyland four times since I came to the United
    A   B   C   D
    States.

2.   He has been going to graduate school since over ten years.
      A   B   C   D

3.   Since Hanna joined the tennis club, she has been met a lot of new people.
      A   B   C   D

4.   We have been lived in Tokyo for almost three months now.
        A   B   C   D

Chapter 10

Customs, Celebrations, and Holidays

| **PART 1** | # Gerunds and Infinitives as Subjects |

Setting the Context

Conversation   *(A family is celebrating two birthdays at the same time. The grandfather is 70 years old and Jenny is five years old today.)*

Mother: Isn't this fun, Dad? It's so nice to celebrate your birthdays together.

Grandfather: Well, maybe it's fun to celebrate Jenny's birthday, but I'm too old to like birthdays. Besides, it's silly to have a birthday party for such an old man.

Jenny: But Grandpa, having a birthday is very special. You *have* to enjoy yourself.

Jimmy: Come on everybody. It's time for Grandpa and Jenny to make a wish and blow out the candles.

Jenny: Remember, Grandpa, it's important to make a wish when you blow out the candles.

Grandfather: Blowing out 70 candles is too hard.

Father: Doing it alone is hard. But you have Jenny to help.

Mother: After you blow out the candles, it's your job to cut the cake, Dad.

Grandfather: Eating cake and ice cream is bad for an old man.

Jenny: But you have to have some cake! And after we eat cake, we get to open our presents! Opening the presents is so much fun. It's hard to wait.

Grandfather: Giving presents on birthdays isn't necessary.

Jimmy: Grandpa, shhh . . .

(The family sings "Happy Birthday." Then Jenny and the grandfather blow out the candles.)

Jenny: Hooray! Now all our wishes will come true! *(She hugs her grandfather.)*

Grandfather: (*smiles*) Well, maybe having a birthday isn't so bad after all.

Discussion Questions

1. What does Jenny think about birthdays? What does the grandfather think? Why?
2. What birthday customs are mentioned in the reading?

3. What are some birthday customs in your family?
4. Do you like celebrating birthdays? Why or why not?

A. Gerunds and Infinitives as Subjects

Gerunds and infinitives can appear as subjects of sentences. Their meaning is identical.

Examples		Notes
Infinitive	**Gerund**	**Notes**
It's fun **to get** presents.	**Getting** presents is fun.	A sentence with an infinitive subject begins with the impersonal *it;* the infinitive follows the adjective or noun.
Is it universal **to celebrate** birthdays?	Is **celebrating** birthdays universal?	A gerund is formed by putting an *-ing* ending on a verb. A gerund or a gerund phrase can be used as the subject of a sentence.

Note: Not is placed in front of a gerund to make the gerund negative.

1 Underline the gerund subjects and circle the infinitive subjects in the conversation on page 224.

Examples: It's so nice ⟨to celebrate⟩ your birthdays together.

But Grandpa, <u>having</u> a birthday is very special.

2 In two different ways, tell the opinions of these people about celebrating birthdays. Use each of the words or phrases in the balloons to form one sentence with a gerund as the subject, and one sentence with an infinitive as the subject.

1.

a. wonderful

b. great

2.

a. important

b. a tradition

a. *Celebrating birthdays is wonderful.*

= *It's wonderful to celebrate birthdays.*

b. _____

= _____

a. _____

= _____

b. _____

= _____

3.

a. silly

b. depressing

4.

a. a lot of work

b. a big mess

a. _____

= _____

b. _____

= _____

a. _____

= _____

b. _____

= _____

3 Make an equivalent sentence, with a gerund or an infinitive, for each of the following sentences.

Example: Guessing what's in the box is hard.
It's hard to guess what's in the box.

1. It's hard to blow up balloons.

_____

2. It's fun to make a birthday cake.

_____

3. Decorating the house with balloons and colored streamers takes time.

_____

4. Singing "Happy Birthday to You" is traditional.

_____

5. It's not easy to blow out all the candles.

_____

6. Making a wish before you blow out the candles is very important.

_____

7. Opening the presents is exciting.

_____

8. It's great to be with all of your friends.

_____

9. It's sad to say goodbye to your guests.

_____

10. Washing the dishes after the party isn't fun.

_____

Using What You've Learned

4 Choose a holiday or a celebration. One student tells a tradition that is a part of the holiday or celebration, using a gerund as the subject. Then the second student tells another tradition that is part of the holiday or celebration, again using a gerund as the subject. Keep taking turns until you cannot think of any more traditions. The last person to tell a tradition wins the game. Play the game again with a new holiday or celebration. This time tell the traditions using infinitives as subjects.

Example: _Student_ A: Eating cake is a birthday tradition.
  Student B: Blowing out candles is a birthday tradition.
  Student A: Making a wish as you blow out the candles is a birthday tradition.
  Student B: Getting presents is a birthday tradition.
  Student A: Getting cards is a birthday tradition.
  Student B: Singing "Happy Birthday" is a birthday tradition.
  Student A: I can't think of another birthday tradition!

PART 2 # Gerunds and Prepositions

Setting the Context

Reading

China

United States

Brazil

New Year's Day Around the World

"New Year's Day is the most important festival of the year in my country. Because it is so important, most Chinese people insist on doing everything right to prepare for the celebration. People aren't satisfied with just cleaning their houses well before the New Year. They clean them perfectly! Good luck wishes are written in Chinese on red paper and hung all over the walls and doors of the house. The   5 living room is decorated with flowers. Plates of oranges and tangerines are put all around the house because oranges are symbols of happiness. After preparing for many days, finally on New Year's Eve and New Year's Day families get together and eat feasts of delicious, traditional foods. Firecrackers are set off, and brand new clothes are worn. At midnight on New Year's Eve, we believe in letting the old   10 year out by leaving every door and window in the house open."

—Yian Chen, China

"In my country, people usually get excited about going to New Year's Eve parties. Other people are content with staying home. At most New Year's Eve parties, people celebrate by dancing, singing, and drinking a toast to the New Year. At   15 midnight, fireworks explode, horns are blown, and people hug and kiss. These parties can go on for hours after midnight. I've heard of New Year's parties lasting until four or five o'clock in the morning! On New Year's Day some people have to recover from staying out all night. After celebrating the New Year, many people make New Year's resolutions. These are promises people make to themselves   20 when they want to change something about their lives. For example, someone could decide 'I am tired of being overweight. I am going to go on a diet' or 'I'm going to work at quitting smoking.' Of course these are difficult promises and many people don't succeed in keeping them!"

—Justin Korfine, USA   25

"Everyone looks forward to celebrating New Year's in Brazil. In all the cities, we have a big party on New Year's Eve. Many Brazilians look forward to being with large groups of friends for New Year's. We have a special tradition for New Year's clothes: we believe in wearing white clothes on New Year's Eve because we think this brings good luck and peace for the coming year. After midnight, many people   30 go to the beach and jump into the waves. Many people also light candles in the sand and throw flowers in the sea while making a wish for the New Year. Fireworks start at midnight and usually last for about half an hour. During this time, everybody makes wishes for the new year. We dream of having love, health, and fortune in the New Year. It's a wonderful evening. I never get tired of celebrating New Year's."   35

—Carlos Huaman, Brazil

Discussion Questions

1. How is New Year's celebrated in China?
2. How is New Year's celebrated in the United States?
3. How is New Year's celebrated in Brazil?
4. How is New Year's celebrated in other countries you know?
5. What similarities and differences are there in the way that New Year's is celebrated in these countries?

A. Gerunds as Objects of Prepositions

Examples	Notes
Thanks **for coming** to my party.	Gerunds can be used as the objects of prepositions.
She wrapped the present **before giving** it to me.	A gerund can have an object.

1   Fill in each blank with a gerund. Choose from the following verbs.

add	dry	serve
bake	eat	sit
buy	look	stand
carve	put	start
clear	save	stuff

(Thanksgiving is a holiday celebrated in November in the United States and in October in Canada. People celebrate this holiday by getting together with family or friends to give thanks for their good fortune and to eat a large turkey dinner.)

Making Thanksgiving dinner is not an easy job. Only by _starting_ very early can the cook finish everything. Some cooks save time by _buying_ [1] the rolls and pies instead of _baking_ [2] them themselves.

Before _putting_ [3] the turkey into the oven, the cook usually fills it with a bread mixture. By _stuffing_ [4] the turkey, he or she prevents it from _drying_ [5] out. Three to six hours later, the turkey is ready. After _carving_ [6] it with a sharp knife and _serving_ [7] it to family and guests, the cook can finally sit down and enjoy the meal. [8]

It seems that only a short time after _sitting_ [9] down at the table, everyone finishes. After _eating_ [10] all that food, no one feels much like getting up. Especially because they know, without even _looking_ [11], that the kitchen is a complete mess. Finally, one brave family member starts by _standing_ [12] up and beginning to clear off the plates. After _clearing_ [13] everything off the table, the family has to put away the leftover food. Many cooks plan for turkey soup or turkey sandwiches by _saving_ [14] all the leftover turkey. Some cooks even save the carcass. By _adding_ [15] the bones to soup, cooks make a rich, flavorful broth their families will enjoy for days.

B. Gerunds After Adjectives with Prepositions

A gerund can follow an adjective-preposition combination.

Examples	Expressions	
I'm **pleased about spending** the holidays with you. I'm **responsible for cooking** the holiday dinner.	afraid of	nervous about
	capable of	pleased about
	content with	responsible for
	dedicated to	sad about
	excited about	satisfied with
	famous for	scared of
	happy about	tired of
	interested in	worried about

2 Look back at the reading on pages 228–229. Then answer the questions below with full sentences. Base your answers on the reading or on your own experiences, as appropriate.

Example: What aren't many Chinese people satisfied with doing before the New Year?

Many Chinese people aren't satisfied with just cleaning their houses well before the New Year.

1. What do many Americans get excited about doing on New Year's Eve?

   _____

2. What are other Americans content with doing on New Year's Eve?

   _____

3. What do many Brazilians look forward to on New Year's Eve?

   _____

4. Are you satisfied with celebrating New Year's Eve the way you usually do?

   _____

5. Are you interested in doing anything different next New Year's Eve?

   _____

3 Underline the gerunds after the prepositions in your answers to Activity 2.

Example: *Many Chinese people aren't satisfied with just cleaning their houses well before the New Year.*

4 Complete the sentences with the missing prepositions and gerunds. Use *with, or, to, of,* or *about* with the verbs in parentheses.

to of about

or   with

El Dia de los Muertos (The Day of the Dead) is one of the most popular holidays in Mexico. It is a holiday to remember ancestors, family members, and friends who have died. It is believed that the spirits of the dead return to visit with the living on this day. The people are not scared _of visiting_ with the spirits of the dead. Instead,
_{1 (visit)}
they are happy _about honoring_ the dead and they are excited _about participating in the_
_{2 (honor)}   _{3 (participate)}
many activities that are a part of the holiday.

During the Day of the Dead, families visit cemeteries and gather around the graves of relatives who have died. People are not sad _about going_ to the graveyards. In-
_{4 (go)}
stead, they are happy _about been_ with each other and with the spirit of their
_{5 (be)}
loved ones. Part of this day is dedicated _to cleaning_ and decorating the graves of
_{6 (clean)}
the dead. Local musicians are often hired to come to the cemeteries as well. They are responsible _for playing_ the favorite songs of the people who have died. People
_{7 (play)}
stay at the graves together until late at night. They are not nervous _about been_
_{8 (be)}
there. They are pleased _about spending_ this time together. During the night, hundreds
_{9 (spend)}
of candles are lit and gifts of food and flowers are left for the dead.

Many activities take place in the home during this holiday as well. In homes across the country, tables full of food and drink are laid out for the dead. People are not satisfied _with preparing_ small offerings. Instead, these tables are filled with flowers, candles,
_{10 (prepare)}
fruits, vegetables, and the favorite foods of individual spirits. Paths of flower petals and burning incense lead spirits to the houses of their living relatives. After the spirits have

had a chance to enjoy the food and drink prepared for them, the living people are excited

about eating the food that is "left over." Of course, since the spirits of the dead
11 (eat)

aren't capable *of eating* very much, this leaves a lot of food for the living!
12 (eat)

5 Finish each of the following sentences with true statements about yourself. Use gerunds.

Example: I'm afraid of *walking alone at night.*

1. I'm afraid of *watching scary movies* .
2. I'm capable of *eating very much.* .
3. I'm excited about *going to the beach.* .
4. I'm good at *drawing superman.* .
5. I'm interested in *playing soccer.* .
6. I'm nervous about *giving a speech.* .
7. I'm responsible for *playing soccer.* .
8. I'm tired of *cleaning bathroom.* .

6 Take turns sharing your true statements from Activity 5 with a partner. Practice finding similarities and differences.

Examples: A: I'm afraid of walking alone at night.
                 B: I am too. I always ask someone to go with me.
                 B: I'm excited about going to the Valentine's Day Dance.
                 A: You are? Not me. I'm not a very good dancer.

C. Gerunds and Phrasal Verbs

A gerund can follow a phrasal verb or verb-preposition combination. The preposition can have an object in addition to the gerund.

Examples	Expressions	
I **plan on going** home for Christmas. He **apologized for forgetting** my birthday.	admit to believe in choose between count on plan on dream of apologize for	give up heard of look forward to object to thank (someone) for think of recover from

7 Look back at the reading on pages 228–229. Then answer the questions below with full sentences.

1. What do many Chinese people believe in doing at midnight on New Year's Eve?

_____.

2. What do some Americans have to <u>recover from</u> doing on New Year's Day?

_____

3. What don't many Americans <u>succeed in</u> keeping?

_____

4. What do many Brazilians <u>believe in</u> wearing on New Year's Eve?

_____

5. What do many Brazilians <u>dream of</u> having in the New Year?

_____

8 Underline the gerunds after the phrasal verbs in your answers to Activity 7.

Example: *Many Chinese people believe in <u>leaving</u> all doors and windows open at midnight on New Year's Eve.*

9 Fill in each of the blanks with the missing preposition and gerund. Use *of, for, on,* or *between* and the verb in parentheses.

(Valentine's Day is a holiday that celebrates love. It is celebrated in many parts of the world. It is common to send cards, flowers, or gifts to express affection on Valentine's Day. In the following conversation, Michael has just received flowers on Valentine's Day. The cards that came with the flowers says only "From a Secret Admirer.")

Michael: (to himself) Red roses! They're beautiful! I bet they're from Janet. It's so nice

of her to think <u>of sending</u> me flowers on Valentine's Day. I'll call her.
        1 (send)

(He dials Janet's number. The phone rings.)

Janet: Hello?

Michael: Hi, Janet. It's Mike. I just wanted to thank you <u>for been</u> so roman-
                                              2 (be)

tic. I've often dreamed <u>of getting</u> roses from a woman.
                        3 (get)

Janet: Roses? I . . . uh . . . didn't send you roses. Anyway, haven't you heard? Phil and

I are dating.

Michael: Sorry, Janet! I didn't know! I apologize <u>for calling</u>.
                                                   4 (call)

Janet: Why don't you try calling Sarah?

Michael: Sarah?

Janet: She told me that she was thinking <u>of sending</u> you flowers. The last time
                                           5 (send)

I spoke with her, she was trying to choose <u>between sending</u> you a card or flowers.
                                            6 (send)

Michael: Really? I didn't even know that she liked me.

Janet: She's been planning _on telling_ you, but she's so shy!

<u>7 (tell)</u>

Michael: Wow. Thanks _for letting_ me know. I've always had a crush on her

<u>8 (let)</u>

too! I'm going to call her right now.

Using What You've Learned

10 As a group, use the Internet or resource books in the library to find out about a holiday from another culture. Prepare a description of the holiday for the class, using as many gerunds as you can.

Example: *Germans look forward to celebrating Fasching (Carnival) every spring. Dancing and participating in parades are common activities, and it's traditional to wear costumes. People look forward to having a great time at Fasching all during the long, cold winter.*

11 With a partner, write a role play that takes place during a holiday. Perform your role play for the class. You may want to include some of these phrasal verbs:

approve of	feel like	put off
believe in	forget about	rule out
care about	get out of	succeed in
count on	hear of	talk about
decide against	look forward to	work at
dream of	plan on	worry about

12 Take turns reading out loud an example of an adjective-preposition and verb-preposition combination from the lists below. Your partner must use the adjective-preposition or verb-preposition combination to make up a sentence that includes a logical gerund.

Example: A. good at
 B. Hmmm. My roommate is very good at avoiding his turn to do the dishes. Ok, it's your turn: dream about
 A. I dream about speaking perfect English.

Common Adjective-Preposition Combinations

good at	successful in	guilty of
adequate for	content with	innocent of
enough for	careful about	jealous of
famous for	happy about	proud of
good for	afraid of	tired of
necessary for	aware of	preferable to
sorry for	capable of	similar to

Common Verb-Adjective Combinations

believe in	dream about	object to
succeed in	forget about	look forward to
approve of	talk about	decide against
dream of	worry about	put off
hear of	count on	feel like
get out of	plan on	rule out

PART 3   # Verbs and Gerunds; Verbs Before Objects and Simple Forms of Verbs

Setting the Context

Reading

Body Language

Many body movements and gestures, sometimes called body language, are specific to a given culture. For example, in some cultures, when two friends greet each other, they kiss on the cheek or hug. In other cultures, women may hug or kiss each other, while men may shake hands. In some cultures, people may prefer standing very close while speaking to each other, while in others, people may avoid standing closer than arms length. In some cultures, people commonly use   5

their hands to gesture while speaking. However, in others people are taught to
speak quietly while keeping their hands still. Before visiting another country, a
person should consider learning about the body language used in that country.
Otherwise the visitor could risk insulting others by accidentally using inappropri-   10
ate body language.

Discussion Questions

1.   How do each pair of people outside the restaurant prefer greeting each other?
2.   What kinds of body language do you notice inside the restaurant?
3.   According to the reading, what are some examples of the ways body language can
     be different in different cultures?
4.   What countries or cultures could each of the examples in the reading refer to?
5.   Which forms of body language are common in your country?

A. Verbs Often Followed by Gerunds

If a verb comes after these verbs, it must be the gerund form.

Examples	Verbs		
He **avoids going** to parties.	avoid	discuss	quit
My parents **enjoy cooking** holiday meals.	celebrate	dislike	risk
	consider	enjoy	suggest
	deny	keep	understand

B. Verbs Often Followed by Gerunds or Infinitives

Either a gerund or an infinitive can follow these verbs with little or no difference in
meaning.

Examples	Verbs		
I **hate celebrating** my birthday.	begin	hate	love
I **start shopping** for Christmas in October.	can't stand	intend	prefer
	continue	like	start

1   Fill in each of the blanks with one of the verbs below.

avoid	keep
can't stand	like
consider	quit
continue	risk

1.   Why do you ___*keep*___ interrupting me? In my culture we never interrupt a speaker!
2.   Some people ___*consider*___ making eye contact with strangers to be rude.
3.   Many people ___*can't stand*___ sitting next to smokers in restaurants.
4.   In many countries people ___*like*___ standing very close to one another.

5. In Mexico City guests _____risk_____ being considered rude if they come on time for dinner.

6. _____quit_____ pointing! Don't you know that it's rude to point?

7. In Asian cultures, people often _____Continue_____ smiling, even when they are angry or upset.

8. Wine is a very popular drink in France. In fact, some French children even _____avoid_____ drinking a little wine with their dinner.

2 Circle the letter of the correct answer to fill in each blank. If both the gerund and the infinitive are possible, circle both letters.

1. In some Latin cultures, children avoid _____ directly into the eyes of their elders while the elder is speaking to them.
    a. looking
    b. to look

2. In many Asian cultures, people dislike _____ touched by someone they do not know well during a conversation.
    a. being
    b. to be

3. In Russia, people risk_____ a cook if they do not have a second helping of food.
    a. insulting
    b. to insult

4. In Spain, many people prefer _____ dinner after 8:00.
    a. having
    b. to have

5. In Bulgaria, people understand _____ the head from side to side means "yes." In most European cultures, it means "no."
    a. shaking
    b. to shake

6. In the United States, many people don't mind _____ interrupted while they are speaking. In many other countries, this is considered very rude.
    a. being
    b. to be

7. In many Arab and Asian cultures, people avoid _____ physical affection in public.
    a. showing
    b. to show

3 Fill in each blank with a gerund verb phrase in the appropriate tense. Use the two verbs in parentheses.

The Dinner Party (Part 1)

Martin was pleased when his American friend, Keith, invited him to a dinner party

on Friday night. Martin immediately _____began planning_____ for the party. He

1 (begin/plan)

_____likes bring_____ gifts to people, so he asked his roommate, Kevin, for sugges-

2 (like/bring)

tions. Kevin _____suggested taking_____ a bottle of wine. But Martin didn't drink wine, so

3 (suggest/take)

he bought Keith a new CD player for his car. Kevin also _advised wearing_ casual

4 (advise/wear)

clothes to the party, but Martin _prefer wearing_ his best suit and tie.

5 (prefer/wear)

C. Verbs Before Objects and Gerunds

Certain verbs that take objects can come before gerunds. The object of the main verb performs the action of the *-ing* verb.

Examples	Verbs		
The waiter **heard the man hissing.**	feel	hear	see
Didn't you **notice them waving?**	find	notice	watch

Note: Certain verbs that are often followed directly by gerunds can also be followed by objects and gerunds. These verbs include: *appreciate, can't stand, (don't) mind, hate,* and *like.*

4   Fill in each blank with a gerund verb phrase in the appropriate tense. Use the two verbs (and the object, if there is one) in parentheses.

The Dinner Party (Part 2)

When Friday night arrived, Martin _started getting_ ready several hours

1 (start/get)

in advance. The invitation said that the party was going to begin at 7:30. Mar-

tin always _avoided been_ late, so he arrived at Keith's house at 7:00.

2 (avoid/be)

He _finded Keith girlfriend cooking_ in the kitchen, and he _hear Keith taking_ a

3 (find/Keith's girlfriend/cook)   4 (hear/Keith/take)

shower. After Keith got dressed, he came out to the kitchen to talk to Martin.

"Martin, I didn't know that you were coming early! Would you _mind helping_ me

5 (mind/help)

with some cooking?"

Martin didn't want to _risk making_ mistakes in Keith's kitchen so he

6 (risk/make)

didn't help. Instead, he _continue talking_ to Keith while Keith worked. Martin

7 (continue/talk)

also gave him the present.

"Martin, I really _appreciate giving_ me this lovely gift, but I can't accept it.

8 (appreciate/your/give)

It's too much," said Keith.

Martin felt embarrassed. "Please take it. I _hate returning_ gifts."

9 (hate/return)

Then Keith had an idea. "I _suggest keeping_ it for yourself, Martin."

10 (suggest/keep)

5   Combine each pair of ideas into one sentence with a gerund.

1.   Keith heard + Martin was talking to his girlfriend in the kitchen.
     Keith heard Martin talking to his girlfriend in the kitchen.

2.   Martin saw + Keith's sister was sitting in front of the TV.
     Martin saw Keith's sitting in front of the TV.

3.   He enjoyed + He was watching the show with her.
     He enjoyed, He watching the show with her.

4.   Finally Martin heard + Other guests were arriving.
     Finally Martin heard other guest were arriving.

5.   He noticed + They were wearing casual clothes.
     He noticed them wearing casual clothes.

6.   Martin continued + He was watching TV.
     Martin continued he watching TV.

7.   Keith saw + Martin was watching TV.
     Keith saw Marting watching TV.

8.   Keith noticed + Martin was ignoring the other guests.
     Keith noticed Martin ignoring the other guests.

6   Complete each sentence with your own ideas. Use gerunds in each sentence. Then, compare sentences with one or two classmates.

Example: *I can't stand people talking very loudly in restaurants.*

1.   I can't stand people _____.
2.   I sometimes hear people Saying things about me _____.
3.   I sometimes notice other students _____.
4.   My teacher doesn't mind me _____.
5.   Have you seen anyone _____?
6.   I really appreciate friends _____.

D. Verbs Before Objects and Simple Forms of Verbs

Examples	Notes
Let me introduce myself.	The verbs *have*, *let*, and *make* can all appear as the first verb in the pattern verb + object + verb.
I **watched them cook.**	In general, verbs of perception that can take the pattern verb + object + verb-*ing* (such as *see*, *watch*, *notice*, and *hear*) can also appear in the pattern verb + object + verb. The *-ing* form of the verb emphasizes the continuation of the action.
I **watched them cooking.**	

7 Fill in each blank with the appropriate tense and form of the two verbs and the object in parentheses.

The Dinner Party (Part 3)

From his chair in front of the TV set, Martin _____*watched the guests socialize*_____.

1 (watch/the guests/socialize)

He waited for Keith to introduce him to his friends, but Keith was busy. Finally a

woman who _____ there spoke to him.

2 (see/Martin/sit)

   "Hi. _____ myself. I'm Susan. I'm Keith's cousin.

3 (Let/me/introduce)

Don't you have anything to drink? I'll _____ you something."

4 (have/Keith/fix)

   Martin was thirsty, but he wanted to be polite. "No, Susan. I don't want to

_____ me," he answered.

5 (make/Keith/serve)

   "Okay," said Susan. "Anyway, it's time for dinner. Come on. I'll

_____ next to me."

6 (have/you/sit)

   "Thank you," said Martin. " _____ you with your chair."

7 (let/me/help)

   "Oh, Martin. That's not necessary. You're so old fashioned!"

   As Martin _____ out her own chair, he

8 (watch/Susan/pull)

thought to himself "I have a lot to learn about this culture."

Using What You've Learned

8 The goal of this activity is to try to retell all three parts of "The Dinner Party" without looking back at the story. Form a circle with a small group. Going around the circle, each person contributes one sentence to the story, using a gerund, if possible. Continue going around the circle as many times as necessary until the story is complete.

Example: *Student A:*   *Ok.* I think the story began when Keith invited Martin to a dinner party.

                Student B: Right. Then Martin began planning for the party.

                Student C: Then Martin discussed buying a present with his roommate.

9   In small groups, discuss the story "The Dinner Party." Answer these questions, using gerunds when possible.

1.   What social mistakes did Martin make?
2.   What mistakes might he make next?
3.   What social rules are there for dinner parties in your culture?

Example: Martin insisted on wearing a suit. When he noticed the other guests wearing casual clothes, he felt uncomfortable.

Summarize your discussion for the class.

Video Activities: Puerto Rican Day Parade

Before You Watch.   Discuss these questions in a group.

1.   What is a parade?
2.   What kinds of things and people can you see in a parade?
3.   What do you know about Puerto Rico?

Watch.   Discuss these questions in a group.

1.   What does the Puerto Rican Day Parade commemorate?
2.   Which of the following things or people were part of the parade?

spectators	a marching band	floats
a fire truck	clowns	police
a queen	flag wavers	the mayor of New York

Watch Again.   Fill in the missing information.

1.   Columbus discovered Puerto Rico _____ years ago.
2.   The queen says she feels _____ of her people.
3.   The kind of music that Tito Puente plays is called _____.
4.   _____ people traveled from Puerto Rico to New York for the parade.

After You Watch.   Fill in the blanks with the gerund (verb + *-ing*) or infinitive (*to* + verb) form of the verb in parentheses. If no verb is given, write the missing preposition.

Last weekend I traveled to New York City to participate _____ the Puerto Rican Day Parade. Normally I don't like _____ (go) to parades. I avoid _____ (stand) in crowds, and I can't stand _____ (listen) to speeches. But this year I decided _____ (attend) the parade because my brother and his wife invited me _____ (stay) with them in their apartment.

On Saturday morning we got up very early and went down to 46th St. We found a good place and waited for the parade _____ (begin). The atmosphere was very festive. I saw people _____ (dance) in the street and heard them _____ (sing) in Spanish. It was exciting for me _____ (be) with so many happy Puerto Rican people. I felt proud _____ my country and my people.

The parade was fantastic. There were horses, dancers, clowns, musical groups, and of course floats. The beautiful young queen of the parade sat on one of them. I watched her _____ (smile) and _____ (wave) to the crowd, and I dreamed _____ (meet) her someday.

At the end of the day we were tired _____ (stand), so we went back to my brother's apartment. I felt very happy. Next year I plan _____ (return) to New York for the Puerto Rican Day Parade. I am really looking forward _____ it.

Focus on Testing

Gerunds and Infinitives as Subjects; Gerunds and Prepositions; Verbs and Gerunds; Verbs Before Objects; Simple Verb Forms

Standardized tests of English proficiency often have sections on gerunds, verbs before objects, and simple verb forms. Review what you studied in this chapter. Check your understanding of the grammar points by completing the sample items below.

Remember that . . .

- Sometimes the *-ing* form of a verb is a gerund.
- A gerund functions as a noun and can be the object of a preposition.
- A gerund can follow a phrasal verb, or an adjective-preposition, or verb-preposition combination.

Part 1.   Circle the correct completion for the following sentences.

Example: People rarely get tired of _____ the congratulations and good wishes of their friends and relatives on their wedding day.

   (a.) hearing   b.   hear   c.   to hear   d.   heard

1.   I believe in all people _____ equal pay for equal work.
   a.   earned   b.   have been earning   c.   earning   d.   earn

2.   Although the children are very young, their parents let them _____ up as late as they want.
   a.   staying   b.   stay   c.   stayed   d.   to stay

3.   They enjoy _____ holiday meals
   a.   to cook   b.   cook   c.   cooking   d.   cooked

4.   Please let me _____ myself.
   a.   to introduce   b.   introduce   c.   introducing   d.   to be introduced

Part 2.   Circle the letter below the underlined word(s) containing the error.

Example: Many children are afraid of to sleep in the dark
                     A   B   (C)   D

1.   Get married can be one of the biggest events of a person's life.
     A   B   C   D

2.   A: I have never liked the taste of alcohol.
            A   B

     B: Neither do I.
            C   D

3.   I try to start shop for the holidays in October.
        A   B   C   D

4.   The waiter heard the man to call, but he was too busy to answer.
                   A   B   C   D

Chapter 11

Science and Technology

PART 1

The Passive Voice with the Simple Present and Simple Past Tenses

Setting the Context

Reading

Communication Technology

Technology is changing what, where, when, how, and with whom we communicate. In the past, people could only communicate quickly and easily with people who were near them. Communication was changed forever when the   5 first electronic message was sent by telegraph in 1837. For the first time, people could send messages over long distances very quickly. Communication technology has developed quickly since then. Today, billions of people around the world are connected by telephones, cellular phones, fax machines, and the Internet. It is   10 possible to make instant contact with almost anyone, anywhere, at anytime. For businesses, this means that work is done more quickly. For students, this means that information is found and shared more easily.

There are many advantages to communication technology. But are there disadvantages too? Many people think that a price is paid for all of the advantages   15 of communication technology. They worry that fewer letters are written because of e-mail. They also worry that less in-person contact is made between people because of telephones, cellular phones, and the Internet.

Discussion Questions

1. How is communication technology changing the way we communicate?
2. How are communication technologies used in offices? How are they used in schools?
3. What are the advantages of communication technology? What are the disadvantages?
4. What kinds of communication technology do you use each day?
5. Which do you like better: traditional forms of communication (like talking face to face and writing letters), or newer forms of communication (like communicating with cellular phones and e-mail)? Why?

A. Introduction to the Passive Voice

Most verbs that take an object can be used in both the active voice and the passive voice. The passive and active forms have similar meanings, but different focuses. The active voice focuses on the person or thing that does the action. The passive voice focuses on the person or thing the action is done to. In the passive voice, the object of an active verb becomes the subject of the passive verb.

	Examples	Notes
Active **Passive**	*subject* *verb* *object* Alexander Graham Bell invented the telephone. The telephone was invented by Alexander Graham Bell. *subject* *verb* *agent*	focus of active sentence: Alexander Graham Bell focus of passive sentence: the telephone
Active **Passive**	*subject* *verb* *object* My brother sent the message. The message was sent by my brother. *subject* *verb* *agent*	focus of active sentence: my brother focus of passive sentence: the message

Note: The agent can often be left out of a passive voice sentence, as in the following example: *The message was sent.* For more information, see chart C, Uses of *By* + Agent, page 249.

1 Write an *A* next to the sentences that are in the active voice, and a *P* next to the sentences that are in the passive voice.

1. __A__ Technology is changing our lives.
   __P__ Our lives are being changed by technology.

2. __A__ Many people own cellular phones.
   __P__ Cellular phones are owned by many people.

3. __P__ Millions of documents are sent by fax machines every day.
   __A__ Fax machines send millions of documents every day.

4. __P__ Phone messages are taken by answering machines.
   __A__ Answering machines take phone messages.

5. __A__ The Internet connects people around the world.
   __P__ People around the world are connected by the Internet.

6. __A__ People write fewer letters these days.
   __P__ Fewer letters are written these days.

7. __P__ Messages are often sent using e-mail.
   __A__ People often send messages using e-mail.

8. __P__ Friendships are formed over the Internet.
   __A__ People form friendships over the Internet.

9. __A__ People start romances over the Internet.
   __P__ Romances are started over the Internet.

10. __P__ Almost everyone and everything is affected by communication technology.
    __A__ Communication technology affects almost everyone and everything.

B. Passive Voice: Uses

The passive voice is usually used in the following situations.

Uses	Examples
When the Doer of the Action Isn't Known	New technology **is developed** every day. (Passive) *Instead of:* People **develop** new technology **everyday.** (Active)
When It Isn't Necessary to Mention the Doer Because the Doer Is Obvious	He **was arrested.** (Passive) *Instead of:* A policeman **arrested** him. (Active)
When We Are More Interested in the Action Than the Doer	A computer room **was added** to the community center. (Passive) *Instead of:* The town council **added** a computer room to the community center. (Active)
When We Want to Avoid Placing Direct "Blame" on A Doer	Too many long-distance calls **were made** this month. (Passive) *Instead of:* You **made** too many long-distance calls this month. (Active)

2   All of the following *A* sentences are in the active voice. All of the *B* sentences are in the passive voice. For each pair of sentences, circle the best choice.

Example: A.   A person stole my laptop.
　　　　　　(B.)   My laptop was stolen.

1.   A.   Salespeople sell cellular phones in the mall.
　　(B.) Cellular phones are sold in the mall.

2.   (A.) This telephone was made in Taiwan.
　　 B.   People made this telephone in Taiwan.

3.   (A.) My mother called me this morning.
　　 B.   I was called by my mother this morning.

4.   A.   Computer programmers write new computer programs each day.
　　(B.) New computer programs are written each day.

5.   (A.) Gerard bought a fax machine.
　　 B.   A fax machine was bought by Gerard.

6.   A.   I don't blame anyone, but you made mistakes on this project.
　　(B.) I don't blame anyone, but mistakes were made on this project.

7.   (A.) Our teacher asked us to do research on the Internet.
　　 B.   We were asked to do research on the Internet by our teacher.

8.   A.   I turned on the computer.
　　(B.) The computer was turned on by me.

C. Uses of By + Agent

In most passive sentences, it is not necessary to mention the doer of the action. In cases where it is necessary, *by* + a noun or pronoun (also called an *agent*) is used at the end of a passive voice statement to tell the doer of the action. Do not include a *by* + agent phrase in a passive voice sentence when the information is obvious or unimportant. *By* + agent phrases should only be used in the following situations.

Uses	Examples
When the Phrase Is Necessary to the Meaning of the Sentence	TV signals are carried to homes **by radio waves**.
When the Phrase Includes a Name or Idea That Is Important in the Context	The first radio was developed **by Marconi**.
When the Phrase Introduces New or Unusual Information	Many sales calls are made **by computers**.

Note: Some verbs can be followed with either *by* and/or other prepositions in the passive voice. These verbs include: *be based (on), be connected (by, to), be contacted (by, with, for) be cured (by, with), be filled (by, with), be involved (in, with), be known (by, for, as),* and *be replaced (by, with).*

3 All of the following sentences are in the passive voice. The *A* sentences do not include a *by* + agent phrase. The *B* sentences do include a *by* + agent phrase. For each pair of sentences, circle the best choice.

Example: (A.) Millions of phone calls are made each day.
        B.   Millions of phone calls are made each day by people.

1. A. The phonograph was invented.
   (B.) The phonograph was invented by Thomas Edison.

2. (A.) Telephone bills are sent out each month.
    B. Telephone bills are sent out each month by telephone companies.

3. A. People all around the world are connected.
   (B.) People all around the world are connected by the Internet.

4. A. Microsoft was created.
   (B.) Microsoft was created by Bill Gates and Paul Allen.

5. (A.) The first pay phone was installed in Hartford, Connecticut in 1900.
    B. The first pay phone was installed in Hartford, Connecticut in 1900 by a telephone company worker.

6. (A.) Many important inventions were developed in Europe.
    B. Many important inventions were developed in Europe by European inventors.

7. A. A world chess champion was beaten in a game of chess.
   (B.) A world chess champion was beaten in a game of chess by a computer.

8. (A.) One hundred thousand new computers are linked to the Internet each day.
    B. One hundred thousand new computers are linked to the Internet each day by companies that link computers to the Internet.

D. The Passive Voice with the Simple Present and Simple Past Tenses

	Examples	Notes
Simple Present Tense	Active: The repairman **checks** the phones every week. Passive: The phones **are checked** every week (by the repairman).	The passive voice of verbs in the simple present tense is formed with *am/is/are* + the past participle. The negative is formed by adding *not* after *am/is/are*.
Simple Past Tense	Active: The repairman **checked** the phones yesterday. Passive: The phones **were checked** (by the repairman) yesterday.	The passive voice of verbs in the simple past tense is formed with *was/were* + the past participle. The negative is formed by adding *not* after *was/were*.

4   Underline the simple present tense verb phrases in the passive voice and circle the simple past tense verb phrases in the passive voice in the reading on page 246.

Examples: Communication (was changed) forever when the first electronic message

(was sent) by telegraph in 1837.

Today, billions of people around the world are connected by telephones, cellular phones, fax machines, and the Internet.

5   Fill in the blanks with either the simple present tense or the simple past tense of the verbs in parentheses. Use the passive voice.

Example: The walls of caves _were painted_ by cavemen more than 20,000 years ago.

1.   The first writing inks (develop)_are developed_ in ancient Egypt and China in about 1500 B.C.

2.   The first inks (make) _were made_ from plants and animals.

3.   In ancient China, the hairs of rats and camels (glue) _was glued_ together at the end of a stick to make brushes for writing.

4.   Paper (create)_was created_ in China sometime around 90 A.D.

5.   Before printing (invent)_was invented_ each copy of every book was written out by hand.

6.   The first books (print)_were printed_ by the Chinese and Japanese in the sixth century A.D.

7.   A sheet of paper (press) _was pressed_ against a carved and inked block of wood.

8.   The printing press (develop) _was developed_ by the German printer Johannes Gutenberg around 1447.

9.   Books (produce)_were produced_ much more quickly and easily after the Industrial Revolution.

10.   Now, millions of books (print) _are_ each year.

11.   Some books (record) _are_ on audio tape.

12.   Electronic books (sold) _are sold_ over the Internet.

6 Fill in the blanks with either the active or the passive form of the verbs in parentheses. Be sure to use the correct tense (simple present or simple past).

The history of modern communication technology began when the electric telegraph _was invented_ by the American Samuel Morse in the 1830s.
1 (invent)

The telegraph _linked_ two places by electric wire. By switching the
2 (link)

electricity on and off, messages _were_ down the wire by a code.
3 (send)

For the first time, people could send long distance messages almost instantly.

By the 1860s, all the big cities in the United States _were linked_ by the tele-
4 (link)

graph. In 1866, a telegraph cable _was laid_ under the Atlantic. This made it
5 (lay)

possible to send messages across the Atlantic as well.

In 1876, Alexander Graham Bell invented the telephone when he _discovered_
6 (discover)

a way to send human speech down an electrical wire. Eventually, telephones became

so common in many parts of the world, that they _are taken_ for granted by many
7 (take)

people. Only international calls _remained_ expensive and difficult to make.
8 (remain)

This began to change when the first communications satellite _was launched_ into
9 (launch)

space in 1962. Satellites made it possible to bounce telephone signals around the world

quickly and easily. It quickly _became_ much easier and cheaper to make interna-
10 (become)

tional calls. Today, more than 150 communication satellites _orbit_ the earth.
11 (orbit)

Another important step in communication technology was the invention of

the cellular phone. These phones _were developed_ in the early 1980s and
12 (develop)

quickly became a very popular and common technology. This _was followed_
13 (follow)

by the most important invention of the 1990s: the Internet. The Internet _linked_
14 (link)

computers around the world. It _is used_ to send millions of messages each day.
15 (use)

Communication technology never stops developing. Improvements

_____ and new technologies _____ all of the time. What new
16 (make)   17 (research)

kinds of communication technology do you think we will have in the future?

7 The following active voice sentences explain how a fax machine works. Change each sentence to a passive voice sentence. (The subjects of the passive voice sentences are given.) Include *by* + agent only when the information is necessary.

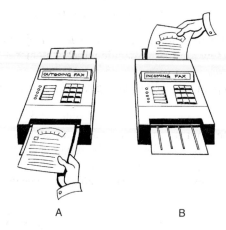

A   B

1. Someone lays the pages on the feeder tray of fax machine A.
   The pages *are laid on the feeder tray of fax machine A.*

2. Someone enters the phone number of fax machine B on the keypad of fax machine A.
   The phone number of fax machine B _____.

3. Fax machine B answers the call.
   The call *is answered* _____.

4. A roller in fax machine A pulls each page through.
   Each page _____.

5. The roller passes each page over a scanner.
   Each page _____.

6. Fax machine A sends electrical signals to fax machine B.
   Electrical signals _____.

7. Fax machine B prints out a copy.
   A copy _____.

8. Fax machine B cuts the document into pages.
   The documents _____.

Using What You've Learned

8 Work with a small group to create four passive voice sentences that tell facts about different technologies or inventions. You may want to use reference books or the Internet to find ideas for your sentences. Use four of the following verbs in your sentences.

develop	discover	improve	build
use	invent	create	research
start	make	study	find

Write down your four sentences. Then, change information in two of the sentences to make those sentences false.

Example: *The radio was invented by Marconi. (true)*

The first automobile was designed in 1805. (false)

The camera was invented by John Kodak. (false)

The Internet was developed by the United States army. (true)

When all of the groups are ready, one group reads their sentences. The other groups take a few minutes to decide which statements they think are true and which they think are false. Repeat this process until all the groups have read their sentences. Each group gets a point for each correct guess. The team with the most points at the end wins the game.

 **9** Technology is all around us. Toasters, coffee makers, dishwashers, microwaves, and answering machines are a part of our everyday lives. Work with a partner to write an explanation of how an everyday piece of technology works, using the passive voice. You may want to draw a picture for each step of your explanation.

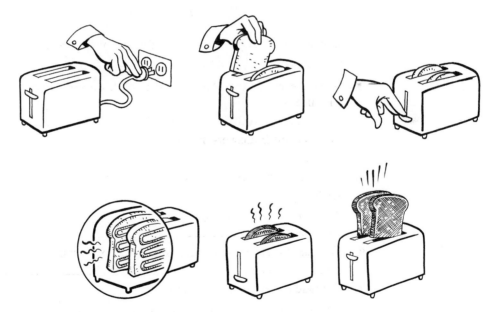

Example: How a Toaster Works

1. The toaster is plugged in.
2. Two pieces of bread are put into the slots of the toaster.
3. The bar is pushed down.
4. The wires in the toaster are heated up by electricity.
5. The bread is toasted by the electrical wires.
6. The toast is pushed out of the toaster when it is ready.

Share your explanations (and your pictures, if you made any) with the class.

10 With a partner, choose a technology that you are interested in learning about. Then use the Internet or resources in the library to find information to answer one of the following questions:

■ When, where, and how was the technology invented/developed?

■ How is it made?

■ How is it used?

Give a short presentation about what you learned.

PART 2 # The Passive Voice with the Present Perfect Tense

Setting the Context

Reading

Space Technology

People have always dreamed about traveling in space. But until recently, space travel seemed impossible. Then, in the 1920s, the first rocket was invented. Space technology developed quickly after that. On April 12, 1961, the Russian astronaut Yuri Gagarin became the first person to travel in space. Many important space technologies have been developed since then. Reusable rockets have   5 been introduced, satellites have been launched, space stations have been built, and the moon has been visited.

The dream of space travel has been achieved, but scientists haven't stopped working on space technology. Now the goal is to go farther and stay longer in space. Many predictions have been made about the future of space technology.   10 Some scientists even think that someday we will have the technology to live on the moon!

Discussion Questions

1. Who was the first person in space? When was this person sent into space?
2. What space technologies have been developed since then?
3. When was the first rocket invented?
4. What is the goal of space technology now?
5. Do you think people will live on the moon someday? Why or why not?

A. The Passive Voice with the Present Perfect Tense

	Examples	**Notes**
Present Perfect Tense	Active: Researchers **have developed** a new spacesuit. Passive: A new spacesuit **has been developed** (by researchers).	The passive voice of verbs in the present perfect tense is formed with *has/have* + *been* + the past participle. The negative is formed by adding *not* after *have/has*.

1 Underline the present perfect verb phrases in the passive voice in the reading on page 254.

Example: Since then, many important space technologies <u>have been developed</u>.

2 Fill in the blanks with the present perfect passive form of the verbs in parentheses.

1. Many important things (do) *have been done* by astronauts in space.
2. Outer space (explore) _has been explored by me_
3. The moon (walk on) _has been walk on_ .
4. Moon rocks and dust (collect) _has been collected_
5. A lunar car (drive) _has been driven_ .
6. The effects of space travel on the body (study) _has been study_
7. New products (test) _has been testing_ .
8. Experiments (perform) _has been perform_ .
9. Space stations (build) _has been builded_ .
10. Satellites (repair) _has been repair_ .

3 Change the following sentences from the active voice to the passive voice. Leave out the agent (scientists).

1. Scientists have improved space technology.
    Space technology has been improved.

2.   Scientists have built lighter rockets.

Lighter rockets has been built.

3.   Scientists have developed better equipment.

Better equipment has been developed.

4.   Scientists have invented better computer programs.

Better computer programs has been invented.

5.   Scientists have created reusable rockets.

Reusable rockets has been created.

6.   Scientists have designed better spacesuits.

Better spacesuits has been designed.

7.   Scientists have made space stations safer.

Space stations safer has been made.

8.   Scientists have improved space food.

Space food has been improved.

9.   Scientists have launched important satellites.

Important satellites has been launched.

10.   Scientists have planned new technologies.

New technologies has been planned.

4   Astronauts are very busy in space, but they also have some free time. What kinds of things have been done by astronauts in their free time? Some of the things may sound surprisingly familiar. Make sentences by filling in each of the blanks with the passive present perfect form of one of the verbs in the box.

use	~~take~~	play	write
~~drink~~	eat	~~sleep in~~	~~wear~~

1.   Regular clothes *have been worn* inside spaceships.

2.   Soda *have been drunk.*

3.   Chocolate *have been eaten.*

4.   Sleeping bags *have been sleep in.*

5.   Toilets *have been used.*

6.   Photographs *have been taken.*

7.   Postcards *have been written.*

8.   Card games *have been played.*

5   Imagine that a spaceship is about to be launched. A colonel is reading a final checklist to an astronaut in the spaceship. In pairs, take turns asking and answering questions with the following cue words. Give short answers using only the past participle.

Example: (the electrical systems / test)?
        A: Have the electrical systems been tested?
        B: Tested!

1.   (fuel tank / fill)?
2.   (the computers / program)?
3.   (launch pad / clear)?
4.   (the radio / check)?
5.   (control panel / set)?
6.   (radar / adjust)?
7.   (doors / locked)?
8.   (the engines / start)?

6   Circle the correct verb choice in each set of parentheses. In a few cases, both choices may be possible. When this is the case, circle both choices.

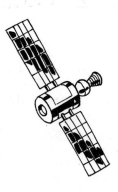

A satellite is an object that goes around another object. The first man-made satellite ((was launched)/has been launched) into space in 1957. Since then, hundreds more (are launched/have been launched) into space. These satellites (are designed/have been designed) to collect important information and send it back to earth. Different kinds of satellites (are sent/have been sent) into space to do different things.

Communications satellites (are used/have been used) to bounce messages from one part of the world to another in seconds. These messages can be telephone calls, TV pictures, or Internet connections. More than 150 communications satellites (are launched/have been launched) into space since the 1960s.

Weather satellites (give/have been given) us information about the weather on earth. Information from these satellites (has predicted/has been predicted) many

dangerous storms and volcanoes. Many lives (saved /(have been saved)) by these
⁹
satellites.

Navigation satellites ((give)/ have been given) information about where something
¹⁰
or somebody is in the world. These satellites (have used /(have been used)) by millions
¹¹
of airplanes, boats, and cars to figure out their position on earth.

Other satellites are used for scientific research. Some satellites ((take)/ have been
¹²
taken) pictures of the earth from space. These satellites ((send)/ have been sent) scien-
¹³
tists important information about the earth's environment. Other satellites ((collect)/ have
¹⁴
been collected) and ((send)/ have been sent) back important information about space.
¹⁵

Because satellites give such valuable information, many countries ((have spent)/
¹⁶
have been spent) a lot of money developing and launching satellites. Occasionally

satellites ((have broken)/ have been broken) or (have lost /(have been lost)) in space.
¹⁷   ¹⁸
Sometimes astronauts ((have fixed)/ have been fixed) or rescued these satellites in
¹⁹
space. A few satellites (have brought /(have been brought)) back to earth for repairs
²⁰
and then re-launched into space.

Using What You've Learned

7   Work with a small group to learn more about one kind of space travel technology, such as space suits, rockets, space shuttles, or satellites. Use resource books from the library or the Internet to find out how the technology you chose has been developed, improved, or changed in the past few years.

When you are finished, give a short presentation to your class about what you have learned.

8   Imagine you live in the year 3000 and have used a time machine to come back to the present. You want to tell people about the advances that have been made in space travel technology in the last 1,000 years. Discuss and decide with your group:

- What changes and improvements have been made.
- What new technology has been invented.
- What has stayed the same.

When you are ready, tell the class about space technology in the year 3000.

PART 3

The Passive Voice with the Present Continuous Tense

Setting the Context

Reading

Technology in the Home

Technology is a big part of our everyday lives. Our homes are being filled with more and more technology all the time. Most of us use basic household technology constantly and can't imagine life without it. For example, in homes all over the world right now, food is being kept cold in refrigerators, floors are being cleaned by vacuum cleaners, and hair is being dried by hair dryers. Most of us take these   5
items for granted. But none of these household inventions even existed 100 years ago!

These days more and more hi-tech technology is being added to many homes. These items are changing the way we live. For example, technology is making it possible to do more and more everyday chores from home. Instead of   10
going to the bank and the supermarket, many people are now paying bills and buying groceries over the Internet. Hi-tech technology in the home is even making it possible for many people to work from home.

Amazing new technologies are being developed every day. Many of these technologies will eventually become a part of our lives and a part of our homes.   15

Discussion Questions

1. What kind of basic technology is being used in homes around the world right now?

2. How is new hi-tech technology changing our everyday lives at home?

3. What will happen to many of the new technologies that are being developed now?

4. Do you think hi-tech home technologies improve life for most people? Why or why not?

A. The Passive Voice with the Present Continuous Tense

	Examples	**Notes**
Present Continuous Tense	Active: Scientists **are developing** new technology every day. Passive: New technology **is being developed** every day (by scientists).	The passive voice of verbs in the present continuous tense is formed with *is/are/am* + *being* + the past participle. The negative is formed by adding *not* after *is/are/am*.

1 Underline the present continuous verb phrases in the passive voice in the reading on page 259.

Example: Our homes <u>are being filled</u> with more and more technology all the time.

2 Fill in the blanks with the passive form of the present continuous verbs in parentheses.

1. A lot of money (spend) _is being spent_ on home technology.
2. TV technology (improve) _is being improved_.
3. Faster computers (design) _are being design_.
4. Smaller laptop computers (sell) _are being sold_.
5. More and more digital cameras (buy) _are being bought_.
6. Videophones (develop) _is being developed_.
7. Computer controlled robots (research) _are being researched_.
8. Energy efficient houses (build) _is being builded_.
9. New websites are (create) _are being created_.
10. New uses for the Internet (find) _are being found_.

3 Use the cue words under the pictures to write sentences that describe what is being done in each picture. Use the passive form of the present continuous tense.

1. the carpet / vacuum
The carpet is being vacuumed.

2. the TV / turn on
The TV is being turn

3. the clothes / dry

The clothes are being dry.

4. the computer / shut down

The computer is being shut down

5. the microwave / plug in

The microwave is being plug in

6. the clothes / iron

The clothes are being iron.

7. the eggs and butter / mix

The eggs and better are being mixe.

8. a call / make

A call is being make.

4 Circle the correct verb choice in each set of parentheses. In a few cases, both choices may be possible. When this is the case, circle both choices.

Computers ((are changing)/are being changed) the way we live. Many of the things

people could only do outside the home in the past (are now doing/are now being

done) at home with a computer. For example, many things that could only be bought

in stores in the past (are buying/are being bought) over the Internet now. Books, CDs,

clothing, and airline tickets are just some of the things that (are sold/are being sold)

over the Internet.

Computers (use/are being used) for educational purposes too. Educational com-

puter programs (are used/are being used) by many children at home to help them

with their schoolwork. Also, some colleges (are offering/are being offered) classes

over the Internet now. These courses (are usually taken/are usually being taken) by

people who don't have time to go to school.

Computers even make it possible for some people to do their jobs at home. These

people (use/are being used) fax machines, the Internet, and e-mail to communicate

with their offices.

Technology ((is making)/is being made) our lives more and more convenient. The

only problem is that soon people won't have any reason to leave their homes!

Using What You've Learned

5 Find out how technology is being used in another kind of setting (place) such as schools, offices, supermarkets, banks, or post offices. First, write a list of predictions about how you think technology is being used in the setting you chose. Then, find out more by interviewing a person who works in this setting. For example, if you want to learn more about how computers are being used in schools, you may want to interview a teacher. If you want to know how computers are being used in banks, you may want to interview a bank employee. After the interview, check your list of predictions. What things were you right about? What things surprised you? Tell other students about what you learned.

PART 4

The Passive Voice with Modal Auxiliaries

Setting the Context

Reading

Medical Technology

Medical technology has developed very quickly over the past few years. New technologies have made it possible to do many things that couldn't be imagined in the past. Many new tests can be given, diseases can be discovered, and operations can be done because of breakthroughs in medical technology. Doctors and scientists predict that in the next few years, many important drugs will be   5
developed, many diseases will be cured, and many operations will be improved. Some amazing choices could also be offered by medical technology in the future. Soon it could be possible to pick the sex, IQ, and eye color of children before they are born. It is even possible that human beings could be cloned (copied exactly) in the future!   10

But as these amazing technologies develop, some important questions are being asked: Should nature be controlled by technology? Could new technologies make our world less "human"? These questions should be considered carefully as medical technology continues to develop.

Discussion Questions

1. What kinds of things can be done because of breakthroughs in medical technology?
2. What do doctors predict will be done in the next few years?
3. What amazing choices could be offered?
4. What important questions are being asked?
5. What are some examples of modern medical technology?

A. The Passive Voice with Modal Auxiliaries

To form the passive voice of modal auxiliaries, use modal + *be* + past participle.

	Examples	**Notes**
can	Active: Scientists **can see** germs with microscopes. Passive: Germs **can be seen** (with microscopes).	Use *can* with the passive to express present ability. Use *can't* with the passive voice to express impossibility.
could	Active: Scientists **could find** a cure for cancer soon. Passive: A cure for cancer **could be found** (by scientists) soon.	Use *could* with the passive to express past ability and future possibility.
should	Active: A doctor **should test** your eyes every year. Passive: Your eyes **should be tested** (by a doctor) every year.	Use *should* with the passive to express advisability.
will	Active: In the future, robots **will perform** operations. Passive: In the future, operations **will be performed** (by robots).	Use *will* with the passive to talk about the future.

Note: Negative passive modals are formed by adding *not* after the modal.

1 Underline the modal verb phrases in the passive voice in the reading on page 263.

Example: Many new tests <u>can be given</u> . . .

2 Fill in the blanks with the passive form of the words in parentheses.

A. *Doctor:* If you look over there, your baby's arms <u>*can be seen.*</u>

    1 (can/see)

   Patient: I can't wait to find out whether it's a boy or a girl.

   Doctor: That question <u>Can be ans</u> right now.

    2 (can/answer)

   Patient: Really? Tell me!

Doctor: You are going to have a girl.

Patient: That's great news! I can't believe that the baby's sex _can be dis_ so

easily.

<u>3 (can/discover)</u>

Doctor: Technology _can be used_ in many amazing ways.

<u>4 (can/use)</u>

Patient: Finally, "her" room _can be decorated_!

<u>5 (can/decorate)</u>

B.   *Patient:* How long will the test take?

Doctor: It _will be fi_ in about twenty minutes.

<u>1 (will/finish)</u>

Patient: How does it work?

Doctor: Your brain _will be scan_ by the machine.

<u>2 (will/scan)</u>

Patient: That sounds scary!

Doctor: Don't worry, you _won't be hurt_ by the machine.

<u>3 (won't/hurt)</u>

Patient: Then what will happen?

Doctor: The information _will be sent_ to our laboratory. It doesn't take long

<u>4 (will/sent)</u>

to get the results. You _could be_ with the results in just two or three days.

<u>5 (could/call)</u>

C.   *Patient:* Well, doctor. Do you think the laser surgery _could be done_

<u>1 (could/do)</u>

on my eyes?

Doctor: Yes. We can schedule the surgery for next week if you want.

Patient: That's great! Where _the surgery will be done_?

<u>2 (will/the surgery/do)</u>

Doctor: It _can be done_ either in this clinic or at the hospital. It's easier if we

<u>3 (can/do)</u>

do it in the clinic.

Patient: OK. Will the laser hurt?

Doctor: No. It _can barely be felt._

<u>4 (can/barely/feel)</u>

Patient: This is so exciting. I can't see anything without my glasses and I hate

wearing them.

Doctor: In a few days, that problem _will be solved._

<u>5 (will/solve)</u>

Patient: An appointment can be schedule for next Wednesday?
            6 (can/an appointment/schedule)

Doctor: The clinic _will be close_ on Wednesday. How about Thursday?
                          7 (will/close)

Patient: That sounds good!

3   Circle the correct choice in each set of parentheses.

A. Modern medical technology offers many ways to see inside the human body. X rays

(can use/(can be used)) to take pictures of bones through skin and muscle. Before
        1

the X ray was invented, bones (can not be seen/(could not be seen)) through the body.
                                                            2

CAT scans are another important technology that lets us see inside the body. Doctors

((can examine)/can be examined) soft tissue inside the body, for example, muscle, as
              3

well as the brain with CAT scans. Another technology that helps us see inside the body

is ultrasound. With ultrasound, a developing baby (can see/(can be seen)) inside a
                                                                4

pregnant woman. X rays, CAT scans, and ultrasounds are all very important technolo-

gies that (will probably use/(will probably be used)) for many years to come.
                                     5

B. Many organs (can transplant/(can be transplanted)) from one person to another.
                                            1

One hundred years ago this kind of operation (shouldn't be imagined/(couldn't be
                                                                              2

imagined)). Most transplanted organs are from people who have died recently. But

living people ((can donate)/can be donated) some organs and tissues, such as blood,
                          3

kidneys, and livers. Because donors (can find/(can't be found)) for all of the people who
                                                      4

need transplants, scientists are developing artificial organs. In the future, organs

made of plastic and metal (will use/(will be used)). Organs from certain animals
                                              5

(could use/(could be used)) someday as well. But until these technologies are devel-
              6

oped, many people (will die/(will be die)) while waiting for an organ donation. In many
                                  7

countries, people who are interested in becoming organ donors ((can sign)/can be
                                                                            8

signed) organ donor cards.

4   Find the mistakes in the underlined portion of the following sentences, then rewrite the sentence correctly. Not all sentences contain mistakes. If there are no mistakes in a sentence, write *correct*. All of the sentences should contain a passive modal.

Example: Lasers <u>can been used</u> to give nearsighted people perfect vision.
  Lasers can be used to give nearsighted people perfect vision.

1. In just a few years, artificial arms and legs <u>will been controlled</u> electronically.
    I just a few years, artificial arms and legs will be controlled

2. These days, surgery <u>can performed</u> on babies even before they are born.
    These days, Surgery can be performed on babies even

3. People in comas <u>can be keep</u> alive with life-support machines.
    People in comas can be kept alive with

4. A kidney <u>can transplanted</u> from one person to another.
    A kidney can be transplanted from one person.

5. Before the X ray was invented, the bones inside our bodies <u>shouldn't be seen.</u> *couldn't*
    Before the X ray was invented, the bones inside our bodies couldn't be

6. All new medical technology <u>should be tested</u> thoroughly.
    All new medical technology should be tested thoroughly.

7. Most medications <u>will been taken</u> with water.
    Most medication will be taken with water.

8. Computers <u>will use</u> to help perform many surgeries in the future.
    Computers will be used to help perform many surgeries in the future.

9. In the future, we <u>could be give</u> checkups in our homes by computers.
    In the future, we could be given checkups in our homes

10. Answers to many medical questions <u>will found</u> soon.
    Answers to many medical question will be found soon.

Using What You've Learned

5   With a small group, make a list of things that couldn't be done three hundred years ago that can be done today. Use passive modals in your sentences. You may use your own ideas or ideas from this chapter. Share your lists with another group.

Example: *Three hundred years ago, telephone calls couldn't be made.*

6   With a small group, make predictions about the future of medical technology. What technology will be invented? What diseases will be cured? What operations will be performed? Discuss your ideas.

Example: *Student A:* I think that in the future, surgery will be performed by robots.
        Student B: I don't think that will ever happen. Maybe doctors will be helped by robots, but the surgery won't be done by them.

7 Modern medical technology makes many amazing things possible. But not everyone agrees that all of these things *should* be possible. Some people feel that technology has gone too far. In small groups, discuss one of the following questions. One person in the group takes notes on the discussion. After the discussion, this person gives a summary of the discussion to the class.

■ Should people be cloned?

■ Should people in comas be kept alive on life support machines?

■ Should the sex of babies be chosen by their parents?

■ Should animal organs be transplanted into people?

Video Activities: Sight for the Blind

Before You Watch.   Discuss the following questions with your class or in a small group.

1.   How can technology help physically challenged people? Give examples.
2.   As a child, did you ever try to "pretend" you were blind (unable to see)? How did it feel?

Watch.   Write answers to these questions.

1.   Who is Jerry, and who is Craig? _____
2.   How does the new technology help Jerry? _____
3.   Jerry is _____ years old. He became blind _____ years ago.
4.   Craig has been blind for _____ year(s).

Watch Again.   Circle the correct answers.

1.   Craig became blind

　　a.   at birth　　　　　b.   in an accident　　　　c.   because of a disease

2.   According to Craig, when people pretend to be blind, they always cheat. He means:

　　　　a.   They ask someone to help them.
　　　　b.   They never really close their eyes.
　　　　c.   They open their eyes just a little.

3.   The new device that helps Jerry to see uses a

　　a.   camera　　　　　b.   computer　　　　　c.   transistor

4.   Craig's biggest dream is to _____ again.

　　a.   work　　　　　b.   drive　　　　　c.   see

5.   How does Craig feel about the future?

　　a.   sad　　　　　b.   hopeful　　　　　c.   worried

After You Watch.   Fill in the blanks with the active or passive form of the verb in parentheses. Be careful to use the proper verb tense or modal.

Eyeglasses _____ (invent) in Italy around 1284 by the inventor Salvino D'Armate. These early glasses _____ (can, use) only for reading. Glasses for seeing far away _____ (invent) later. A portrait of Pope Leo X, which _____ (paint) by Raphel in 1517, shows the Pope wearing them.

In 1794 the American inventor Benjamin Franklin _____ (invent) bifocals. Such glasses _____ (divide) into two parts, one part for seeing far and the other for seeing near. For hundreds of years eyeglasses _____ (make) of glass. In recent years, however, plastic lenses _____ (become) more popular.

The first contact lenses _____ (develop) by Adolf Fick in 1887. These lenses _____ (make) of glass. They were uncomfortable and _____ (could, not, wear) for long. Hard-plastic contact lenses _____ (became) popular in the U.S. in the 1960s, and soft contact lenses _____ (introduce) in the 1970s. Nowadays soft lenses _____ (wear) by millions of people all over the world.

Focus on Testing

The Passive Voice with the Simple Present and Simple Past Tenses; The Passive Voice with the Present Perfect Tense; The Passive Voice with the Present Continuous Tense; The Passive Voice with Modal Auxiliaries

Standardized tests of English proficiency often have sections on the passive voice. Review what you studied in this chapter. Check your understanding of the grammar points by completing the sample items below.

Remember that . . .

■ The passive voice focuses on the person or thing the action is done to.

■ In the passive voice, the object of an active verb becomes the subject of the passive verb.

■ In cases where it is necessary, *by* + a noun or pronoun (also called an *agent*) is used at the end of a passive voice statement to tell the doer of the action.

Part 1.   Circle the correct completion for the following sentences.
Example: The telephone _____ by Alexander Graham Bell.

    a.   invented   b.   was invent   (c.) was invented   d.   invent

1.   Our lives _____ changed by technology.
    a.   being   b.   be   (c.) are being   d.   been

2.   Researchers _____ new cures for diseases.
    a.   developing   b.   has developed
    c.   have developed   (d.) have been developed by

3.   New technology _____ every day.
    a.   has developed   (b.) is being developed
    c.   developed   d.   developing

4.   With continued research, a cure for cancer _____ soon.
    (a.) could be found   b.   could find
    c.   could be find   d.   could found

Part 2.   Circle the letter below the underlined word(s) containing the error.
Example: Today's technology can be to use in many amazing ways.
                    A   B (C)   D

1.   Before printing invented, each copy of every book was written out by hand.
                          A   B   C   D

2.   The first man-made satellite has been launched into space in 1957.
                                A   B   C   D

3.   Many of the things people could only do outside the home in the past are now
    A   B   C
doing at home with a computer.
    D

4.   Doctors can be examined soft tissue inside the body like muscle as well as the
          A   B   C   D
brain with CAT scans.

Chapter 12

The Global Consumer

| PART 1 | # Review of Tenses |

Setting the Context

Predictions

Work with your partner to make up some predictions about the picture above.

1.   What is the problem?
2.   Who has the man called?
3.   What is he saying?
4.   Why is the man holding a guarantee?
5.   What will he do when he gets off the phone?
6.   How does the man feel?
7.   Has something like this ever happened to you? If so, tell your partner about your experience.

Group Discussion   Join another pair of students. Share and compare your predictions. Report the most interesting similarities and differences to the class.

Example: *We all thought that the man's refrigerator broke down. But the two of us thought that the man was calling the store where the man bought the refrigerator, and the pair we spoke to thought that he was calling the manufacturer of the refrigerator.*

A. Simple Forms

Most verb phrases appear in the time frame of the past, the present, the present perfect, or the future. Here are the simple forms of each tense.

	Examples	**Notes**
Past	I **bought** a refrigerator a few months ago. **Did** you **do** anything to it?	The simple past tense expresses actions or situations that began and ended in the past.
Imperative	**Come** quickly! **Don't wait** any longer.	Imperatives express orders or directions. Imperatives use the simple form of verbs.
Present	I **have** a problem. Repairs **are** expensive, **aren't** they? The fridge **smells** terrible. We often **get** calls like this, **don't** we?	The simple present tense expresses facts, habits, repeated actions, perceptions, and existing conditions.
Present Perfect	I**'ve called** them twice. The fridge **has broken down.** It **has been** out of order for a week. You **haven't had** any food all this time, **have** you?	The present perfect tense can express actions or situations completed at unspecified past times. It can also express actions or situations that began in the past and continue to the present.
Future going to will	What **are** they **going to do?** What **will** they **do?** The food **is going to spoil, isn't** it? The food **will spoil, won't** it?	*Going to* expresses predictions, plans, and intentions. *Will* expresses offers, promises, requests and spontaneous plans and intentions.
Modal Verbs	They **couldn't go** yesterday. We **can't come** out now, can we? I**'ll tell** the manager right away. He **may come** next week.	A simple modal verb phrase (modal + verb) may refer to past, present, or future actions or situations.

1   Identify the form of the underlined verb or verb phrase in each of the following sentences. Next to each sentence, write *Past, Imperative, Present, Present Perfect, Future,* or *Modal.*

Example: I <u>go</u> to the mall at least once a week. _Present_

1.   I <u>love</u> to shop at the mall. _future_

2.   My husband rarely <u>comes</u> to the mall with me. _imperative_

3.   The last time we <u>went</u> together, we had a fight. _past_

4.   I <u>wanted</u> to look in all of the stores. _present perfect_

5.   He <u>got</u> impatient. _past_

6.   He <u>has</u> never <u>liked</u> to shop. _present perfect_

7.   I <u>hate</u> when he rushes me. _present_

8.   He said, "<u>Hurry</u> up!" _comperative_

9.   I said, "<u>Relax</u>!" _present_

10.   I said, "Why <u>should</u> I <u>hurry</u>?" _Modal verbs_

11. I said, "I <u>haven't been</u> to the mall in almost a week!" *presen perfect*

12. I said, "I'm going to take my time." *future*

13. He yelled, "Fine! I'll wait in the car!" *fut*

14. The next time I go to the mall, I'm going to leave my husband at home.
    _____

2   Fill in the blanks with the correct form of the verbs in parentheses. Fill in the blanks that have no verbs with the appropriate auxiliary verb. In some cases, more than one answer may be possible.

Carlotta: Ugh! Something ___*smells*___
1 (smell)

terrible in here. What ___*happening*___?
2 (happen)

Luis: The refrigerator ___*breaks*___ down
3 (break)

last night, and all the food ___*spils*___.
4 (spoil)

Carlotta: You ___*are not having*___ that fridge very
5 (not have)

long, _____ you? _____
6   7 (be)

it still covered under the warranty?

Luis: It _____ right now, but the guarantee _____ next
8 (be)   9 (expire)

Wednesday, and the repairman won't _____ until Thursday.
10 (come)

Carlotta: But the trouble _____ last night and you _____ him
11 (start)   12 (call)

this morning, _____ you?
13

Luis: Yes, I _____.
14

Carlotta: Then the warranty _____ still good _____, it?
15   16 (be)

Luis: Yes, it _____—I _____!
17   18 (hope)

Carlotta: Well, what _____ you _____ next? I can _____
19   20 (do)   21 (tell)

that you _____ the food out of the refrigerator yet, _____ you?
22 (not take)   23

Luis: No, I _____. _____ home all day. And since I
24   25 (not be)

_____ home, I _____ the energy to move.
26 (get)   27 (not have)

Carlotta: Why? What _____ you _____ doing?
28   29 (be)

Luis: Well, first I _____ to the supermarket, then I _____ a de-
30 (go)   31 (try)

partment store, then . . .

Carlotta: You _____ when the refrigerator _____, you _____
32 (mean)   33 (break)   34 (go)

shopping? That's strange. What _____ you _____?
35   36 (buy)

Luis: Nothing! I _____ to buy a cooler to keep the food cold, but I couldn't
37 (want)

_____ one in the middle of January!
38 (find)

B. Continuous Forms

Continuous verb forms are used to indicate progressive, continuous action. Only action verbs can appear in the continuous form.

	Examples	**Notes**
Present Continuous	The ice **is melting.** What **are** you **doing** now? It **isn't working,** is it? He**'s coming** next week.	The present continuous expresses action that is happening at the present time. It can also be used to express future plans.
Past Continuous	It **was working** fine yesterday. What **were** you **doing** when it broke?	The past continuous expresses an action that was in progress at a specific time in the past.
Present Perfect Continuous	I**'ve been having** problems with it for a long time. How long **have** you **been using** it?	The present perfect continuous stresses the duration or repetition of an action that began in the past and continues to the present.

3   Fill in the blanks with the correct continuous form (past, present, or present perfect) of the verbs in parentheses. Fill in the blanks that have no verbs with the appropriate auxiliary verb. In some cases, more than one answer may be possible.
(Luis's mother calls him on the phone.)

Mother: Hi, honey. How __*is*__ everything __*going*__?
1   2 (go)

Luis: Well . . . things _are not going_ so well
3 (not go)

right now . . .

Mother: Why?! What's the matter? _with you_
4

you _are not feeling_ well? You _taking_
5 (not feel)   6 (take)

your vitamins lately, _____ you?
7

Luis: Yes, of course I _____ , Mother. And I _____ enough
                                 8   9 (get)

rest, and I _____ well.
                10 (eat)

Mother: Well then, what _____ ? You _____ trouble
                                11 (happen)   12 (not have)

in school, _____ you?
              13

Luis: No, I _____ . It's my refrigerator. It _____ .
                14   15 (not work)

Mother: Your refrigerator? But it _____ fine a few days ago,
                                          16 (run)

_____ it?
      17

Luis: Yes, it _____ . But when I came into the kitchen this morning, the
                  18

food _____ and everything _____ all over the floor. I
          19 (melt)   20 (drip)

_____ out _____ for a cooler all day, and Carlotta and I
      21   22 (look)

_____ up all evening. Right now she _____ the floor.
      23 (clean)   24 (mop)

Mother: Carlotta? _____ you still _____ out with her? You
                      25   26 (go)

two _____ serious, _____ you? _____ you
      27 (not get)   28   29

_____ anyone else?
      30 (date)

Luis: Mother, I thought we _____ about the refrigerator!
                            31 (talk)

Mother: So, you _____ serious?
                  32 (get)

C. Time Expressions

The following are examples of time expressions used with specific tenses.

	Examples
Past	yesterday, the day before yesterday, an hour ago, last week, in 1967
Present	(right) now, at this moment, at present, this week, these days
Future	tomorrow, the day after tomorrow, next week, in a few days, a year from now
Past to Present (Present Perfect)	up until now, so far, this week, since Wednesday, since I got up
General (Unspecified)	every day, once a week, now and then, often, sometimes, never, for a long time

4   Fill in the blanks with the correct tense form (simple, past, present, present perfect, or future tense, simple or continuous) of the verbs in parentheses. Fill in the blanks that have no verbs with the appropriate auxiliary verb. In some cases, more than one answer may be possible.

On Saturday, Luis _*threw*_ out the spoiled food from the
1 (throw)

refrigerator. All week long, he _____ meals
2 (eat)

in restaurants. Finally, when Luis _____
3 (arrive)

home from school on Thursday, Bruno, the refrigerator

repairman, _____ for him.
4 (wait)

"Where ___*are*___ you ___*been*___?" ___*ask*___ Bruno. "I
5   6 (be)   7 (ask)

_____ for you for ten minutes!"
8 (wait)

"Well, I _____ for you for six days!" _____ Luis.
9 (wait)   10 (answer)

"_____ on. I'll _____ you up to the apartment. I can't
11 (come)   12 (take)

_____ it any longer."
13 (stand)

Luis _____ Bruno upstairs. While Bruno _____ on the re-
14 (lead)   15 (work)

frigerator, Luis _____.
16 (watch)

"That should _____ it," Bruno finally _____. "You
17 (do)   18 (say)

_____ any more problems with this refrigerator." He _____ out
19 (not have)   20 (hold)

his hand. "I _____ $79.88 for the repairs."
21 (need)

"I _____ a guarantee." Luis _____ him the warranty, and
22 (have)   23 (hand)

Bruno _____ at it quickly.
24 (look)

"Sorry, buddy," he _____ after he _____ Luis back the form.
25 (reply)   26 (give)

"This warranty _____ yesterday."
27 (expire)

"But the refrigerator _____ since last Friday. And I _____
28 (not run)   29 (call)

you last Friday."

"That _____. I _____ just _____ the the repair,
30 (not matter)   31   32 (finish)

and that guarantee _____ valid since midnight last night."
33 (not be)

Luis _____ to get angry. "I _____ a refrigerator for the last
34 (begin)
35 (not have)

six days. I _____ out all week because I couldn't _____ any food
36 (eat)
37 (keep)

in the house. And now you _____ me that the guarantee _____
38 (tell)
39 (not be)

good any more. I _____ a guarantee, and I _____!"
40 (have)
41 (not pay)

   "Well, then, I _____ to the store manager. We _____ about
42 (talk)
43 (see)

this . . ." _____ Bruno as he _____ the apartment.
44 (shout)
45 (leave)

   "You _____ darn right we _____ about this!", Luis
46 (be)
47 (see)

_____. "And if you think that I _____ for this repair, then I
48 (reply)
49 (pay)

_____ you in court!"
50 (see)

Using What You've Learned

5 Take turns reading out loud the time expressions from the chart on page 276. After one
person chooses and says one of the time expressions out loud, the other makes up a
sentence with that time expression. Make sure the form of the verb used matches the
time expression given.

Example: A: for a long time
       B: Hmmm. I have been studying English grammar *for a long time.*
       A: Good. Now you pick one for me.

6 First read the dialogue in Activity 4 out loud. Then imagine a conversation between
Bruno and the store manager, and then a telephone conversation between Luis and the
manager. Role play these conversations. Use as many different verb tenses as possible
in your role plays. Summarize any possible solutions that came out of these role plays
for the class.

7 Work in small groups. Discuss these questions, using as many verb tenses as possible.

1. Have you had any problems with products that broke down?
2. How did the product break?
3. What did you do about the situation?
4. Were you satisfied with the results? Why or why not?
5. Are you having any consumer trouble now? What are you going to do?

8 Use your answer to item No. 5 of Activity 7 to write a letter of complaint to a store or
a manufacturer about a product you bought that broke. Include the following information in your letter:

- when and where you bought the item
- what happened to the item
- what you want the store/manufacturer to do (replace, return, or repair the item)

Exchange your letters with a partner. Edit each other's letters. Rewrite your letter, incorporating your partner's changes and suggestions. If you wish, mail the letter.

PART 2   Review of Infinitives and Gerunds; Verb Complements

Setting the Context

Class Discussion   Discuss the following ideas.

1. What does it mean to buy something on credit?
2. What are the advantages and disadvantages of buying things on credit?
3. What are the advantages and disadvantages of buying things with cash?
4. Ho do you prefer to pay for things? Why?
5. What kind of stores do you like to shop in?
6. Do you look for items that are on sale? Why or why not?

Discussion Questions   Answer these questions about the picture above.

1. What kind of store is this?
2. Name and describe the items in the store.
3. What do the signs mean?
4. Describe the people. How do they look, and how are they probably feeling?
5. Would you like to shop in this store? Why or why not?

A. Infinitives and Gerunds

Infinitives (*to* + verb) and gerunds (verb-*ing*) can be used in sentences in various ways.

Examples		
Infinitives	**Gerunds**	**Notes**
We agreed **to buy** a dining room set. The salesclerks advised us **to buy** on credit.	I suggest **buying** on credit. They saw the children **jumping** on the mattresses.	Both infinitives and gerunds can appear after verbs; sometimes the main verb takes an object.
It's not difficult **to qualify** for credit.	**Qualifying** for credit isn't difficult.	Both infinitives and gerunds can be subjects; a sentence with an infinitive subject usually includes the impersonal *it*.
The salesclerks are eager **to sell** furniture. Which is the best couch **to buy?**		Infinitives can appear after adjectives or nouns.
	You can save money by **paying** cash. Wer're interested in **choosing** a mattress. I don't believe in **buying** on credit.	Gerunds can appear after prepositions. They can be the object of a preposition, they can come after an adjective + a preposition, or they can come after a phrasal verb.
You can use your credit card **to make** a purchase.		An infinitive phrase can be used to express purpose.

Note: For lists of verbs commonly used with gerunds and with infinitives, see Chart A and Chart B on page 237 of Chapter 10.

1 Fill in the blanks with either the infinitive or gerund form of each verb in parentheses. In some cases, both forms may be possible.
(Leo, Marie, and their son Scott are on their way home after a dinner party at the home of Dan and Ruth.)

Leo: Well, I certainly enjoyed ___seeing___ Dan and Ruth again. The food was delicious, and they were really excited about ___getting___ that new dining room set.

1 (see)   2 (get)

Marie: Well, at least Ruth was. I think that Dan only agreed ___to buy___ the set because he was tired of ___shopping___.

3 (buy)   4 (shop)

Leo: Maybe. But Ruth said the deal was too good ___at resisting___. The salesclerk suggested ___to sign___ a credit agreement, so they need ___to pay___ only $35 a month.

5 (resist)   6 (sign)   7 (pay)

Marie: I know that Ruth was eager ___to take___ his advice, but I'm afraid that Dan wasn't.

8 (take)

Scott: Why? _____ on credit is a good idea, isn't it? You can get more things by ___making___ monthly payments, can't you?

9 (buy)   10 (make)

Marie: Yes, but ___using___ finance plans costs a lot more than ___paying___ cash.

11 (use)   12 (pay)

Leo: Right. Stores like customers ___agreeing___ on finance plans because it's easy

13 (agree)

for them ___to make___ more money that way. The store charges the customer a

14 (make)

monthly finance charge.

Scott: Oh. But you like ___using___ credit cards, don't you? Isn't it more conve-

15 (use)

nient and safer _____ credit cards than it is to carry cash?

16 (carry)

Leo: Yes, it is. But if you don't pay the credit card bill on time, the bank will keep

___charging___ you interest each month.

17 (charge)

Marie: Exactly. It's dangerous ___to put___ too many purchases on a credit card

18 (put)

if you can't afford ___paying___ for everything right away. I don't like to see

19 (pay)

people ___getting___ into debt that way.

20 (get)

Leo: Me neither. I'm glad that we save our money ___purchasing___ expensive things

21 (purchase)

with cash instead of ___buying___ on credit.

22 (buy)

B. Verb Complements

Certain verbs can appear in various patterns with complements.

Verb Complements	Examples	Notes
Verb + *to* + Verb	What have you **decided to buy?**	
Verb + Object + *to* + Verb	The clerk **advised us to charge** our purchases.	Most verbs used in this pattern are verbs indicating speech (*tell*, *warn*, etc.).
Verb + Verb-*ing*	I **suggest paying** cash as often as possible.	
Verb + Object + Verb-*ing*	We **appreciated her giving** us advice. She **saw us discussing** our decisions.	A possessive form often comes before a gerund. Many verbs used in this pattern are verbs of perception (*hear*, *see*, *smell*, etc.).
Verb + Object + Verb	I won't **let you get** into debt. What did you **hear them say?**	The verbs *have*, *let*, and *make* can follow this pattern. Other verbs used in this pattern refer to perception.

Here are examples of common verbs for patterns with complements.

verb + *to* + verb			
begin	hate	like	remember
continue	have	need	try
decide	hope	plan	want

verb + object + *to* + verb			
advise	force	order	teach
allow	like	persuade	tell
ask	need	promise	want

verb + verb-*ing*			
advise	continue	like	stop
avoid	hate	prefer	suggest
begin	enjoy	remember	try

verb + object + verb-*ing*			
appreciate	hate	notice	remember
can't stand	hear	(don't) mind	see
find	like	observe	watch

verb + object + verb			
have	let	notice	see
hear	make	observe	watch

2   Complete these sentences with verb complements, adding objects when necessary. Use your own experiences and opinions on making purchases and managing money.

Example: I've always tried *to save at least part of my weekly paycheck.*

1. I've always tried _____.

2. I usually advise my _____.

3. I often promise _____,
    but then I can't stop _____.

4. I don't let my _____.

5. I've decided _____.

6. I've often suggested _____.

7.   I don't like to see _____.

8.   My _____ sometimes tell(s) me _____

_____.

9.   I plan to continue _____.

10. My _____ likes _____

but I prefer _____.

11. He/She hates _____.

12. When I have children, I'll teach them _____.

13. Many people hope _____.

14. My parents (never) forced me _____.

15. Most people prefer _____.

16. Some people can't stand _____.

17. More people need _____.

18. Too many parents let _____.

19. I don't mind _____.

20. I must begin _____.

Using What You've Learned

3 Read out loud and discuss the sentences you wrote for Activity 2, Nos. 1 to 5. Take turns: the first student reads his or her sentence for No. 1, and the second asks questions about it. Then the second student reads his or her sentence for No. 1, and the first asks questions about it. Continue doing this for Nos. 2 through 5.

Example: *Student A:* I've always tried to buy things on sale.
Student B: What kinds of things have you bought on sale?
Student A: Well, I bought this shirt on sale. It's an expensive designer shirt, but I got it for half price! I also bought my bicycle on sale for a really good price.

When you are finished with your discussion, summarize some of the most interesting parts of your discussion for the class.

4 With your partner, write a 30-second radio or TV commercial, using as many verb complements as possible. Underline each verb complement you use. Perform your commercial for the class.

Example: A: Do you <u>notice</u> other people <u>getting</u> promoted while you stay in a dead-end job? Don't you <u>want to be</u> a success, too? Of course you do!

B: Well, folks, today is your lucky day. Our new videotape training session is all you <u>need to buy</u> to change your life for the better forever!

<table>
<tr><td>**PART 3**</td><td></td></tr>
</table>

Review of Comparisons with Adjectives and Adverbs

Setting the Context

Pair Interviews   Take turns interviewing each other. Take notes on the information you learn.

1. Do you like to go shopping for food? Why or why not?
2. Do you make a shopping list before you go food shopping? Why or why not?
3. Do you ever use coupons from newspapers or magazines? What are the advantages and disadvantages of using coupons?
4. Do you compare prices when you are food shopping? Why or why not?
5. Do you prefer shopping at a large supermarket or a small neighborhood market? Explain the reasons for your preference.
6. Does your town or city have any markets geared towards specific cultures, such as Italian, Asian, or Mexican markets? Have you ever been to one? Describe your experience.

1   With your partner from the interview activity above, join another pair of students. Take turns sharing information you learned about your partner's shopping habits. Take note of similarities and differences. Share the most interesting similarities and differences with the class.

A. Comparisons with Adjectives and Adverbs

Comparisons	Examples
Simple Form	Generic products aren't **expensive.** We have to decide **quickly.**
Comparative Form: *as* + adjective/ adverb + *(as)*	Store brands aren't **as attractive as** name brands, but they may be just **as good.**
Comparative Form: adjective/adverb + *-er (than)*	Prices are **higher** this year **than** last year, and they're going up **faster.**
Comparative Form: *more/less* + adjective/ adverb (+*than*)	Generic brands are **more economical than** name brands. Processed food is usually **less nutritious.**
Superlative Form: *the* + *most/least* + adjective/adverb	The largest package may not be **the most economical** choice for your family. This brand is **the least** expensive.
Superlative Form: *the* + adjective/ adverb + *-est*	People sometimes buy the product with **the nicest package.**

Note: Irregular forms include: *good/better/best, well/better/best, bad/worse/worst, badly/worse/worst, far/farther/farthest, little/less/least, many/more/most,* and *much/more/most.*

2 Rewrite the following sentences, correcting any mistakes in the underlined words. If there are no mistakes in a sentence, write *correct* under it.

Example: My supermarket is open <u>late</u> yours.

My supermarket is open later than yours.

1. The Regency supermarket is <u>close</u> supermarket to my house.

_____

2. But it's <u>expensiver</u> than the Value-Save supermarket.

_____

3. Actually, I think it's the <u>expensivest</u> supermarket I've ever shopped at.

_____

4. I think the quality of the food at Value-Save is <u>as good</u> the quality of the food at Regency.

_____

5. The foods just come in <u>fancier</u> packages at Regency.

_____

6. In fact, the fruit I buy at the Regency seems to spoil <u>fastest</u> than the fruit I buy at Value-Save.

_____

7. Of course that could be because the fruit at Regency is grown with <u>less</u> chemicals.

_____

8. The lines at Value-Save are <u>long than</u> the lines at the Regency.

_____

9. It's also much more <u>crowdeder</u>.

_____

10. I guess one supermarket isn't really any <u>more good</u> than the other.

_____

3 Fill in the blanks with the correct form of the words in parentheses.

Prices are _____*higher*_____ this year than they were last year. Every year things
 　　　　　　1 (high)

get _____. To save money, you need to pay the _____
 　　2 (expensive)　　　　　　　　　　　　　　　　　　　　　　　3 (low)

possible prices for the items that you need. Here are some suggestions:

Compare prices of _____ products. Some brands of products are
 　　　　　　　　　4 (similar)

_____ than other brands, and the quality may not be much
5 (expensive)

_____. The quality of _____ brands, which come in
6 (good)　　　　　　　　　　　　　7 (generic)

_____ packages than the _____ "brand names," may be
8 (plain)　　　　　　　　　　　9 (famous)

just as _____ as the quality of the _____ items.
 　　　　10 (good)　　　　　　　　　　　　　　　11 (high-priced)

When you buy an item on sale, check that the "bargain" price is really

_____ than the _____ price. If possible, compare the sale
12 (low)　　　　　　　　13 (regular)

price of the item in _____ stores to make sure you are getting the
 　　　　　　　　14 (different)

_____ price.
15 (good)

Before you go shopping, make a list of the items that are the _____

16 (important)

for you to have, and buy only those things. Don't buy things that you don't need just

because they are _____ than usual.

17 (cheap)

It's not a _____ idea to go food shopping when you are hungry: You

18 (good)

will probably be _____ than usual and make the _____

19 (careful)

20 (bad)

choices about what you really *need* to buy.

Using What You've Learned

4 Tell your partner about an unwise purchase or deal you made sometime in the past. When you have both finished, choose the most interesting story to share with the class.

Example: Once I got a letter in the mail saying that I had won either a brand new car, a new color TV, a diamond ring, or a remote control phone. All I had to do to collect my prize was visit a housing development and listen to a sales pitch for an hour. It sounded like a super deal to me so I went. It turned out that the place was over an hour's drive from my house, the sales pitch was a lot longer than one hour, and they really pressured me to buy a house. The final insult was the cheap phones they gave us as our "prizes" as we left. That was the day I learned there's no free lunch. Now when I get those "You have won . . ." letters in the mail, I throw them right in the trash.

5 Choose a type of store that you enjoy shopping in (such as a shoe store, an athletic equipment store, or a furniture store). Go to two or three different stores of this type. Compare the merchandise, prices, styles, sales, store design, and sales assistants. Report on your experience to the class, using as many comparisons as possible.

6 In small groups, discuss the meanings of the expressions below. Decide if you agree or disagree with them and explain why. Try to think of other similar sayings.

1. There's no free lunch.
2. If it seems too good to be true, it probably is.
3. Money talks.
4. You get what you pay for.
5. A bird in the hand is worth two in the bush.

7 With a partner, choose one of the situations below and prepare a dialogue. Then perform your conversation for the class.

1. You want to buy a used car from a dealer, but you don't know a lot about cars. You want to pay the lowest price possible; the dealer wants you to pay the highest.
2. You are sitting in a park in a big city. You have heard that there are many shopping bargains in the city, and you want to take advantage of them. Get advice from the person on the bench next to you about where to shop.
3. Choose a consumer situation of your own to write a dialogue about.

Video Activities: Spoiled Kids

Before You Watch.   Discuss these questions in a group.

When you were a child:

1.   How often did you receive gifts from your parents and relatives?
2.   Was it hard for your parents to say "no" to you?
3.   Did you have to work in the house?
4.   Did you receive money from your parents?

Watch.   Write answers to these questions.

1.   What are some of the toys and things that Bret (the boy) and Jessica (the girl) have in their rooms? _____
2.   How did Bret and Jessica get their things? _____
3.   What is Jane Annunziata's profession? _____
4.   Why do some parents give their children so much? _____

Watch Again.   Match the opinions on the left with the speakers on the right.

Opinion	Speaker
_____ 1. It's OK to have a lot of things if you appreciate what you have.	a. Psychologist
_____ 2. People have a lot of money and they love their children, so they buy them toys.	b. Jessica's mother
_____ 3. It's easier to say yes to children than to say no.	c. Bret
_____ 4. What children really want is time with their parents, not just a lot of stuff.	d. Toy store owner

After You Watch.   Look at the items below and write sentences using *as much . . . as, as many . . . as, more/less.*

Example: Young children / have stuff / older children
            Young children don't have <u>as much stuff as</u> older children.

1.   Children in the past / have toys / children nowadays.
2.   Parents nowadays / spend money on their kids / parents in the past.
3.   Parents nowadays / spend time with their kids / parents in the past.
4.   Kids in the past / spoiled / kids nowadays.
5.   Kids in the past / do work around the house / kids nowadays.
6.   Teenagers in the past / respectful / teenagers nowadays.

Focus on Testing

Review of Tenses; Review of Infinitives and Gerunds; Verb Complements; Review of Comparisons with Adjectives and Adverbs

Standardized tests of English proficiency often have sections on various verb tenses, as well as complements, adjectives, and adverbs. Review what you studied in this chapter. Check your understanding of the grammar points by completing the sample items below.

Remember that . . .

■ The simple past tense expresses actions or situations that began and ended in the past.

■ The simple present tense expresses facts, habits, repeated actions, perceptions, and existing conditions.

■ The present perfect tense can express actions or situations completed at unspecified past times. It can also express actions or situations that began in the past and continue to the present.

■ *Going* to expresses predictions, plans, and intentions. *Will* expresses offers, promises, requests, and spontaneous plans and intentions.

■ Continuous verb forms are used to indicate progressive, continuous action.

Part 1. Circle the correct completion for the following sentences.
Example: I _____ a television a few months ago.
    a. buy   b.   did buy   (c.) bought   d.   will buy

1.   The refrigerator _____ since Monday.
     a.   has been broken   b.   broke   c.   has been broked   d.   braked

2.   It _____ fine last weekend.
     a.   will work   b.   did work   c.   was working   d.   works

3.   _____ on credit can be more expensive.
     a.   to buy   b.   buy   c.   bought   d.   buying

4.   What have you _____?
     a.   buying   b.   decide to buy   c.   to buy   d.   decided to buy

Part 2. Circle the letter below the underlined word(s) containing the error.
Example:

1.   The next time I go to the mall, I go to leave my credit cards at home.
         A   (B)   C   D

2.   I have been have problems with my homework all month.
          A   B   C   D

3.   Buy on credit can cost the customer more in monthly services charges.
      A   B   C   D

4.   Prices are high this year than last year, and they're going up faster.
             A   B   C   D